The Mutuality of Care

Roy Herndon SteinhoffSmith

Biblical quotations, unless otherwise noted, are from the *New Revised Standard Version Bible*, copyright 1989, Division of Christian Education of the National Council of Churches of Christ in the USA. Used by permission.

Scripture quotations marked (NEB) are from the *New English Bible*, copyright Oxford University Press and Cambridge University Press 1961, 1970. Reprinted by permission.

Cover: Ross Sherman
Interior design: Elizabeth Wright

This book is printed on acid-free, recycled paper.

Visit Chalice Press on the World Wide Web at
www.chalicepress.com

10 9 8 7 6 5 4 3 2 1   99 00 01 02 03

Library of Congress Cataloging–in–Publication Data

SteinhoffSmith, Roy Herndon, 1948–
    The mutuality of care / by Roy Herndon SteinhoffSmith
        p.   cm.
    Includes bibliographical references.
    ISBN 0–8272–2324–2
    1. Pastoral counseling. 2. Pastoral theology.   I. Title.
    BV4012.2.S724   1999   99–12978
    253.5—dc21   CIP

Printed in the United States of America

To my mother,
Jane Herndon Smith (1912–1997),
and my friend,
Terry Fleming (1960–1998).

Table of Contents

List of Illustrations

Preface

In this book, I introduce you, the reader, to a way of thinking about care. Behind this book lie twelve years of teaching courses about care in a seminary, ten years of friendships with very poor people, a lifetime of listening to and reading stories from the Bible, and over twenty years of work as a psychotherapist, pastoral counselor, and minister. Fifteen years ago, I thought of care as condescension (though I would not have used this word then), a relation between someone who has power, knowledge, and what is good and someone who lacks power, knowledge, and what is good. In condescension, the one who has gives something to or does something for or to the one who lacks. I now think of care as mutuality, a relation in which all who are involved participate, need, desire, do for, give to, and receive from each other. In this book, I chart this movement from condescension to mutuality.

I do so by describing and analyzing cases. In most books about pastoral care, pastoral theology, and practical theology, "cases" usually illustrate a particular theory or technique. I think of and call such "cases" "examples." While I use examples, and will sometimes draw examples from case studies, my main focus in this book is on learning how to practice care by beginning with a particular situation and the events in it, developing and using theories to understand this "case," and then constructing more compassionate responses to the specific situation and events. In this book, the movement of thought in a "case study," from descriptions of events or situations to theories and techniques, is the opposite of the movement of thought in an "example."

In one sense, this book is an extended case study of a conversion, for the change in my understanding of care was part of a transformation in my way of conceiving and constructing the world and myself. In 1986, I took the position of Assistant Professor of Pastoral Care and Psychology of Religion at what was then The Graduate Seminary of Phillips University (now Phillips Theological Seminary). I had never taken a course in the practice of pastoral care, but those who offered me the position assumed that I could teach the subject because I had both a Ph.D. in Religion and Psychological Studies, which included a great deal of work in theology and ethics, and extensive training and experience as a psychotherapist and pastoral counselor.

As I reviewed the literature in pastoral care in preparation for teaching Introduction to Pastoral Care for the first time, I became increasingly uncomfortable. I had learned in my clinical psychology training that good therapeutic practice requires extensive experience doing psychotherapy and ongoing, disciplined thought about this practice. Beginning therapists learn how to think about therapy not primarily from books, but from hundreds of hours in supervision, during which an experienced therapist models ways of finding out what is happening in the lives and minds of particular clients and of examining therapeutic interactions in minute detail. Very few psychological or psychotherapeutic texts are about this discipline of therapeutic thinking. Rather, they assume it. They articulate theories that suggest what might be going on in the lives and minds of clients with common characteristics and therapeutic interventions that have been effective with such clients. In other words, theory does not rule effective therapy. Rather, the function of theory is heuristic, to suggest possible ways of thinking about one's practice in particular situations.

In contrast, in most pastoral care and pastoral counseling texts, theory rules. The texts mimic those in psychotherapy, in that they provide ways of diagnosing what is happening to certain parishioners or churches and techniques for pastors to respond to such people or situations. But, unlike psychotherapeutic texts, which articulate truths discovered through disciplined thinking about the practice of psychotherapy, texts in pastoral care usually do not articulate truths discovered through disciplined thinking about the practice of pastoral care. With very few exceptions, the writers assume that pastoral care involves applying truths discovered in theology, church history, or psychology. This understanding of good care as application determines how the authors use "cases," or what I call "examples," to demonstrate the correctness of their favored theological, traditional, or psychological theories.

When I began teaching courses in pastoral care, I decided to use what I had learned in my psychotherapeutic training. Because discussions of cases, in which student therapists talked about their meetings with clients, had been so central in my training, I had students present and discuss cases, situations, and events in which they felt called to care. And I ferreted out the pastoral care and counseling texts that actually focused on what pastors do, or should do, in caring for others.

But here I encountered a second difficulty. Neither my psychotherapeutic training nor the few more truly practical texts in pastoral care and counseling prepared me for the cases students presented. One student, serving a rural parish, described her attempts to help her congregation deal with the suicides of, first, a farmer and, then, his son. Another, serving another rural church that, along with the small town in which it was located, was dying, described his despair, which mirrored the lack of hope in his church. Another, serving an isolated congregation in a small town thirty miles away from any professional counseling services, wondered how she could help a psychotic man with no family, no car, and no means of getting professional help. An African American student, serving as an associate minister, primarily for evangelism, in a medium-sized urban congregation, was caught up in the conflict between older members of his church who didn't like "loud" services and a few younger members who told him that only if church services were "loud" would they attract other young black people in the neighborhood, who needed a supportive and affirming community. A minister with training and excellent skills in counseling was burning out because of the demands on her time, even though there were other ministers on the staff of her church and it had an active Stephen Ministers program. Another student, who had been a professional psychotherapist, faced possible expulsion from his church because parishioners wrongly thought he was having an affair with a woman he was counseling. A number of students were dealing with intense and vicious conflicts, often expressed in attacks on them as ministers, in churches in which, we often discovered only after extensive research, previous pastors had sexually abused or exploited members of the congregation. As students presented these and other cases and we discussed them, we discovered that the pastoral care texts rarely addressed such situations.

As we thought together about these cases, my students and I learned a crucial truth: theories and techniques, even those developed through close reflection on practices, are specific to the practices in which and for which they are constructed; they may be, but are not necessarily, useful in other practices. The practice of care by a pastor in a church is very different from the practice of psychotherapy or even pastoral counseling (which, today, is more like psychotherapy than pastoral care). Practicing care requires paying attention to the particular situations and events in which one and one's community cares. This realization led me to construct, with the students, the method or way of attending to the practice care presented in this book.

The change in my thinking would not have happened, and so I would not have written this book, were it not for the students who questioned my ways of teaching and understanding care, who risked discussing difficult situations with me and each other, and whose insights sparked my thinking. I have never ceased to be amazed by their wisdom and compassion, which, I hope, are reflected here.

The Mamre community (which I discuss in chapter 2) remains for me the model for a caring community. The people of Mamre cared for me at a time when I thought I had to care for everyone else. They taught me that care is mutual and that it is as natural as breathing. In so doing, they liberated me. With them I knew joy.

My partner, Carolyn, is a visionary poet. I have followed her lead as she befriended poor and homeless people. Her poetry, in which language impacts the body and senses, has decisively shaped my understanding of language as action.

She and my daughters, Phoebe and Chloe, love me and I love them. They are remarkably skilled at identifying and deflating condescension and so at freeing me from the burden of believing that, if I am not perfect, I am a failure as a human being. With them, I know that heaven means living fully here in this world. Without them, I would not have been the person who wrote this book.

A small circle of friends sustains me. I hope I sustain them. Conversations with them are a primary form of worship for me. A number of them helped me, directly and indirectly, with this book. I'll only name one here, Jon Berquist, my editor.

Introduction

After participating in numerous case studies, including the ones discussed in this book, I came to recognize certain movements of thought and how they wove together, a way of thinking about or doing research on care. I was initially hesitant to call this way a "research method" because of the popular connotation of "research" as an esoteric practice that only experts can do. Such a notion contradicts a major theme in the understanding of care that has emerged through this research, which is that care is not what experts do, but what all of us do.

In other words, the way of thinking or doing research that I am presenting in this book assumes an understanding of care as mutuality rather than condescension. Care is our responsiveness to each other, the way we live together in communities by attending to each other. I decided to go ahead and use the label "research method" because it is accurate and because one of the purposes of this book is to show that we all do what experts do, we all engage in the movements of thinking that constitute this research method, just as we all care for each other.

A second popular connotation of "research" also does not hold true for this method. Traditionally, social scientific researchers, even as participant observers, are not centrally involved with the people they are studying; they primarily observe social reality. In contrast, the purpose of this research method is, to paraphrase Karl Marx, not just to understand reality, but to change it, to strengthen the practice of care. The researcher in this method is a cultural worker, a central participant in the situation that he or she is studying; his or her practices and their effects in the situation are the primary focus of the study.

Throughout the book, I discuss case studies that I and other *individuals* have done. I assume that most of you who read this book will be using it to think about your particular, individual situations, ones in which the other people involved are not reading the book or using the method. However, I encourage readers in the same community or situation to use this method to do shared research about their own and their community's practices of care. See appendix A for suggestions about how a group can use the method.

The method initially may seem complex and difficult. You may feel clumsy using it. I assure you that such responses are natural for anyone who tries out a new practice. But they are not the only responses I and others have had to using this method. My attempt in the method is simply

1

to name, so that we can intentionally practice what any of us does when faced with a situation that requires intentional care. As I and others have utilized this method, we have come to value what we and others are doing; we have found just how caring we have been and are. As with any method, we've also discovered that, as we practice it more, we get better at it and it becomes easier and less time consuming. Given a bit of familiarity with the movements, tasks, and contexts of the method, we've found that we don't have to go through all of them when facing a new situation; the method becomes a resource of questions and ways of thinking about a situation or event that we can access when needed. Most importantly, most of us have found that, when we use the method, we can significantly improve our individual and communal care. Finally, for many of us, utilizing the method opens us up to the richness of our own and others' day-to-day lives.

In the book, I construct a certain rhythm, first case studies, then discussions of method and theory, then back into case studies. In the more theoretical chapters and parts, I compose the book itself as a demonstration of the method, a movement from description through analysis and into imagination. In the fifth chapter, I *describe* the method of thinking about care. In Part Three, using everything that I have written thus far as description, I move into an *analysis* of care, more specifically, into the presentation of theories. In Part Five, I *imagine* an ethic of care. But even within these more abstract chapters and parts, the rhythm continues, as I repeatedly begin a discussion of theory by returning to the case studies.

By emphasizing this movement from immersion in descriptions of situations and events to theory building, I do not mean to suggest that description or, indeed, any thought or human practice is free of theorizing. I am proposing neither a "value-neutral" phenomenology nor an "objective" science of care—I don't believe either is possible. I do mean to say that, when we abstract theories from our day-to-day thinking about care, we should remember the origins of these conceptual models and our reasons for developing them. Methodological and theoretical models are bric-a-brac we construct and use to help us understand and live as well as we can in mundane reality. Just as the world continually changes, so do we continually adjust and change the theories we use to find our ways in it. In other words, the more abstract discussions in this book are instances of ongoing thinking about how to practice care in specific situations and events.

Using this method over the years has raised radical questions about current individual, communal, institutional, social, religious, and even global practices of care. By "radical," I mean that these questions expose the root assumptions of these practices. In Part One, I discuss three case studies that changed my understanding of care from condescension to mutuality. I close this part with an introduction to the method, which is both a result of, and partially contributed to, this conversion. In Part Two, I present a semi-fictional case study, which focuses on care as a communal activity, which, in a church, is or is not practiced in worship. This study reveals how domination causes suffering and suggests some ways of resisting domination. In Part Three, I explore the psychological, social, economic, political, and religious dimensions of domination. I discover condescension to be an ideologically determined practice of "care" in which care givers dominate care receivers and others. At the end of Part Three, I point out how people resist domination and condescension by practicing mutual care.

In Part Four, I present three case studies, in which pastors enter into caring relations with others. I chose these studies because they are of the kinds of situations—visiting the sick, crisis counseling, and pastoral counseling—in which pastors typically, in America at this time, exercise their professional skills. I also chose these studies because, in each one, the "pastor" called into question the appropriateness and morality of the pastoral position, as she or he understood it, and, by the end of the case study, opted for an understanding and practice of care as mutuality. In Part Five, I take these practitioners' insights, along with the other insights emergent out of the previous case studies and analyses, and imagine how care should be practiced in our situation—an ethic of care.

PART ONE

From Condescension
to Mutuality

CHAPTER 1

Teaching and Learning Care

Before the first class of an Introduction to Pastoral Care course, a student approached me in the hall outside the classroom and said, with some force, but also a bit of hesitation, "I really need this class to learn how to counsel and care for people."

I was surprised and was silent for a moment. This recently widowed woman had, for thirty years, helped her husband, who was a pastor, by doing most of the visiting and counseling in the churches they served. I thought, "This woman has at least twice the number of years of experience in care and counseling that I have, and hers have all been in the church. What does she mean she doesn't know how to counsel and care for people?"

Then, in my mind and with my eyes, I turned toward the woman and said, with hesitation mirroring hers, feeling as if I were letting her down, but also wanting to respond to her question and to let her know that I valued her thirty years of practicing care, "I hope you can learn about what you already know from your experience. And I hope we can all learn from you."

She jerked her eyes toward mine and quickly came back with, "No, you don't understand. I really need to learn counseling skills."

By the time the student approached me in the hall, I was not teaching "counseling skills" in the Introduction to Pastoral Care course. Rather I was working on how to help students learn from their own and each other's practices of care. While the contents of the student's comments were not new to me (at the beginning of the course, students generally were not aware of what they knew about care from their own experiences and they tended to equate "care" with "counseling skills"), I thought of these obstacles to practicing care as relatively minor effects of the widespread tendency to devalue the practice of parish ministry.

The incongruity between the student's thirty years of practicing care in a congregation, her dismissal of my response about learning from this experience, and the intensity of her expressed need for "counseling skills" suggested a more radical question: Why did she so strongly repudiate her wisdom? The difference between this question and my earlier insights about care lies in the distance between neglect and active denial. The student's comments pushed me to take the obstacles I had identified more seriously and, specifically, to wonder if these obstacles rooted themselves in presuppositions about theological education.

In most denominations, theological education marks the movement from lay to ordained status. Currently, theological education is primarily theoretical, not practical. The "higher" theological disciplines, biblical studies, church history, and theology, are also the more "academic" ones in which students study texts, scholarly methods, and theories. In the currently dominant theological traditions, the "practical" disciplines are where students learn to "apply" the truths learned in the "academic" ones. Thus homiletics is the practice of preaching these truths, religious education the practice to teaching these truths, worship the practice of constructing services in accord with these truths, and pastoral care the practice of evoking these truths in the lives of parishioners.

The primary emphasis in these practical disciplines is usually on "theological reflection," the capacity to articulate and justify the theological presuppositions of one's practice. For instance, a colleague who teaches an introductory course in worship patiently explained to me that the primary purpose of the course was to teach students how to evaluate worship services theologically, not to teach the "techniques" of worship leadership. This example reveals the implicit identification of what is true or valuable with theology as theory and not with practice. Practice is mere "technique." This reduction of practice to techniques and applied truths helps to explain why the student did not value her own practice. She had not yet been "theologically" educated and so, presumably, did not know how to evaluate the "techniques" of care she had been practicing.[1]

When the student said that she needed to learn "counseling skills," she exposed two other effects of this theological devaluation of practice: the narrow definition of care as a specific set of counseling techniques, and the reliance on psychotherapy for knowledge about these techniques. The connection between the theological devaluation of practice and these effects lies in what this devaluation obscures. As students and I discovered, attempting to reduce the practice of care in a parish or other community to applied truths or techniques just doesn't work. When I asked students to present cases in which they felt called to care, they presented a variety of overwhelming situations, from individual difficulties to conflicts in

---

[1] For further discussion of this understanding of the relation between theory and practice, see the discussion of "Figure 22: Tradition, Human Sciences, Practice" in appendix B, 219.

committees and boards, to issues of community survival. Derived theological truths and applied psychotherapeutic techniques were simply not very helpful in guiding their practices in this wide range of situations. They did not alert the students or me to the changing contexts. They thus did not lead to what H. Richard Niebuhr called "fitting" responses, or what is known as "wisdom" in the biblical tradition, practice responsive to the particularities of what is happening in a specific event.[2]

Derived truths can only be helpful if one narrows one's definition of care to include only situations to which the truths apply. For example, I recently received a telephone call from a minister who was planning a funeral service for an alcoholic gay man who was a friend of mine. The minister opened the conversation by asking me if I had any knowledge about whether this man had known "Christ as his personal savior" or had any "spiritual discernment." I explained that churches had seriously hurt this man and his partner and so he did not talk in those terms with me, but that he had carefully nursed his partner for months when his partner was recovering from a near-fatal shooting and that he had realized just how important it was to express his love for his partner every day. The minister responded by saying that, well, he couldn't do anything for the man who had died, the service was really for the surviving family (which did not include the partner), and that he would try to bring some good out of a "bad situation." While I cannot be sure about what was going on in this minister's mind, I think that he had difficulty discerning any value or truth in my friend's love for his partner because that love did not conform to his narrow understanding of christian[3] living as the result of applying particular truths derived from the study of the scriptures. My friend and his partner did not fit into a category of people for whom pastoral care was appropriate, and so the pastor did not see how he could respond in a way that valued or cared for them. They were a "bad situation" to be dismissed.

To their credit, most current writers about pastoral care would assert that this minister's understanding of care was too narrow. Still, most also tacitly agree with him that pastoral care is limited to responding to the "spiritual" troubles or "ultimate concerns" of individuals.[4] This understanding narrows pastoral care to "counseling" situations. Thus, most pastoral care texts do not include discussions of care in relation to, for instance, board meetings or the survival of threatened communities.

[2] H. R. Niebuhr, *The Responsible Self: An Essay in Christian Moral Philosophy* (San Francisco: Harper & Row, 1978), 60–61.

[3] I agree with Carter Heyward and follow her usage, as explained in *Staying Power: Reflections on Gender, Justice, and Compassion* (Cleveland: Pilgrim,1995), 151, n. 3: "Using the lowercase 'c' with reference to 'christian' is a spiritual, intellectual, and political discipline for me as a member of a religious tradition so arrogant and abusive historically in relation to women, children, and nonruling class men; lesbian/gay/bisexual/transgendered/sexual nonconformists; Jews, Muslims, wicca, and practitioners of other religious traditions; persons whose cultural/racial/ethnic origins are other than European; and all other-than-human members of creation."

[4] William A. Clebsch and Charles Jaekle, *Pastoral Care in Historical Perspective* (New York: Jason Aronson, 1983), 6.

In the last century, psychotherapists have displaced pastors as the experts in counseling, even about "spiritual" or "ultimate" matters. For instance, many, if not most, of the most popular writers about "spirituality" during the past forty years have been psychotherapists or followers of psychotherapists—for example, Rollo May, Carl Rogers, Victor Frankl, James Hillman, Morton Kelsey, John Sandford, M. Scott Peck, and Gerald May. Without their own tradition of looking to their practices and experiences for truths about how to practice "care," pastoral care experts have naturally looked to psychotherapy, a tradition which (whatever other difficulties it has, which I will explore later) generates theory out of reflection on practice, as the source for effective techniques.

While these experts recognize that pastors should not do psychotherapy with parishioners, still they assume that good care is something like psychotherapy and requires the use of skills derived from psychotherapy— for instance, setting up a contract with a troubled parishioner, diagnosing his or her difficulties, using reflective listening techniques with him or her, handling transference, reframing issues, and referring him or her. Because the student had not received training in these and other therapeutic skills, she assumed that she did not know how to counsel or care.

To summarize this case, before I met the student, I had moved away from the tradition that narrowed pastoral care to counseling situations and that relied on truths derived from theology or techniques derived from psychotherapy. My students and I had begun to develop a way of describing a wide range of situations, of analyzing what was happening in them, and of imagining how to respond in more caring ways to what was specifically happening in these situations. The meeting with the student led me to think much more carefully about the obstacles to practicing this way of thinking about care. I began to identify these obstacles as rooted in the theological devaluation of practice as application.

CHAPTER 2

Illumination

Soon after I met the student, I had an experience that identified another obstacle, one much more deeply rooted in my own soul. At the time, my family and I lived in Enid, Oklahoma. With another white, middle-class, mainline church member and three black, working-class members of poor black churches, my wife and I had begun a weekly communion service and meal—the liturgy was incorporated into the meal—for very poor and disabled members of the community. We met in the Fellowship Hall, a twelve-by-twenty-foot room, in the tiny rundown (the building literally leaned) Tabernacle Baptist Church in Southern Heights, the small, poor, black neighborhood of town. Vietnam veterans called this part of town "the Ville," tacitly comparing the poor blacks, Indians, and whites who lived there to the Vietnamese who lived near U.S. bases in Vietnam. At that time, "Mamre," as we called it, met on Friday evenings every week. We in the "mission group" chose its name to remind ourselves that God or the angels or Christ dwelt among and in the poor guests who came to this meal.[1] Each week we in the mission group would bring food, set up the meal, and I would pick up people who needed a ride and, after the meal, take them home.

At this time, I was doing a lot of reading in liberation theology. I was intellectually convinced that the preferential option for the poor was central to christian practice. I assumed, based on my reading of the judgment scene in Matthew 25:31–46 and passages like it, that we were to find Christ by serving the least.

During the first months of the meal, however, I faced a contradiction between beliefs and my experience. I picked people up and drove them home in an old VW bug. Each week, a number of unwashed, sometimes

---

[1] Genesis 18:1–15 (NEB).

drunk people—"the least of these"—would crowd into the car. It was winter, the windows were closed, the heat on, the stink unavoidable. At the meal and in conversations with the guests afterward, I heard disturbing stories. One of our guests had been accused of child molestation. Another had run down the street naked one night in the middle of winter. Another, living on a small Social Security check, had run up large gambling debts. A number were sometimes violent alcoholics. They seemed to be members of a different species. I could only understand the notion that Christ dwelt in *these* people as a morally justifiable rhetorical trick, a way of making me and other middle-class people like me feel obligated to help those whom we would otherwise naturally avoid.

About three months after we began the meal, and after a conflict over whether one should question the literal meaning of biblical passages, the original mission group fell apart. The black members left. My wife, Carolyn, the other white member, and I were left with responsibility for Mamre. The black congregation had moved out of the dilapidated building but had not invited us to do the meal in the new building, so we continued to meet in the old one. I was close to despair. I did not see how we three middle-class white people could continue to shoulder the increasing burden of supporting and serving a community of, by now, about twenty-five mainly poor, black, and disabled people. I felt responsible for alienating the black members, now ex-members, of the mission group. Each Friday I would pick people up, lead the liturgy of the communion service, and drive people home, but I did so in a depressed stupor.

About two months after the breakup of the mission group, on a cold night, I was standing alone in the fellowship hall after the meal. I had taken people home and returned to the church to lock up. I remember the smallness of the space; I am not a tall man, but, even so, the ceiling felt close. The room looked abandoned—peeling paper on the walls, a yellowed hand-drawn Sunday school poster, stained and worn cheap green carpeting. I had just turned off the gas furnace, a big old unit in one corner.

Standing there, I experienced an illumination. I realized that, while I had been going through the motions of "serving" the least, the people I had been "serving" were coming religiously to the meal. Each week, although many of them regularly did not have enough money and food stamps to get through the month, they brought most of the food we needed. They prayed for each other. And, with a start, I became aware that they prayed for me; they asked me how my family and I were doing, expressed concern, and gave me good and needed advice. For instance, one man, who was suffering with schizophrenia, noticed that I was rubbing my chest, asked me if I was having chest pains, and, when I admitted that I was, ordered me to see a doctor, "Don't mess around with that, Roy; take care of yourself." And they were helping each other in specific, appropriate, and effective ways. Here I had been thinking that the meal depended solely on me and the other members of the mission group. I had carefully maintained the boundary between "them," "the least of these," who were lacking, and myself, who had resources. My task was to serve them, their job was to receive what I had to give. Now I saw the other side of the truth. I was in need, and they had recognized and met my need. Each of them was as necessary to the continuing success of the community as I was.

This illumination, strengthened, deepened, and extended by ten years of intentional friendships with the very poor, has awakened, liberated, and converted me. Before, I dreamed of reality as divided between the haves and the have-nots; and I wondered why this dreamed reality was so unclear, slightly out of focus, distant—I couldn't quite connect with it. Now, I know that my dream of myself and the poor as fundamentally different was false. My sense of being out of touch was due to the division between the privileged self I knew and the needy self I denied; hence the false difference between myself as only having and the poor as only lacking. We both have lacks and abilities; we need each other. With this awakening came a liberation. I was free of the crushing burden of always having to take care of others, of being responsible for whatever happened to others, of having therefore to control others, and of feeling that my need for others was a sign of dysfunctional dependency, shameful selfishness, worthless laziness, or just plain childishness. And with this liberation came a conversion to a faith in this reality of relation, of the interdependence of and co-creation by all humans and all beings.

This awakening, liberation, and conversion threw a different light on the obstacles I encountered with my students and on my meeting with the widowed student. I had tended to think of the students primarily as ministers or professionals. Most of them were already in professional positions, as pastors of churches or as chaplains. I identified with them in their vocations. We shared a call to utilize the power, knowledge, skills, and gifts that we possessed to care for each other, parishioners or clients. I tended not to recognize the implication of this way of thinking, that parishioners and clients are unable to care for each other and so are dependent upon us, the pastors and professionals, for care. I also did not realize the degree to which the relation between students and myself mirrored the relation between parishioners or clients and pastors or professionals. For students, the theological devaluation of practice reinforced what they assumed, that I, as a theological professional, possessed the power, knowledge, skills, and gifts that they, as students, lacked. They felt they desperately needed to get these abilities from me precisely because, as new pastors and chaplains, they experienced their parishioners and clients as dependent upon them for professional pastoral care. The widowed student probably did not think of what she had been doing for thirty years as pastoral care because she was not a pastor. Therefore, whatever wisdom she might have gained from this experience had no value; as a laywoman, she didn't know how to care; she was, at best, an amateur who needed what I possessed in order to become a professional.

John McKnight[2] thinks that this devaluation of non-professionals' abilities and knowledge is the root of oppression in contemporary North America, in which a dominant class of professionals earn their living by serving and caring for others. In order to create and maintain the need for their services, care professionals must convince consumers that they lack the knowledge about, and are unable to perform, what the professionals do for them.

This professional service economy has five tragic effects. First, the devaluation and destruction of nonprofessionals' knowledge and abilities. When we do not recognize and value our knowledge and abilities, we do not share them. When we die, our knowledge and abilities are lost. Because society did not value the widowed student's knowledge about and abilities to care, she did not know she had them and had no way of talking about them, sharing them with, or passing them on to others. In many and perhaps most mainline churches, parishioners are convinced that care is a professional service, requiring specialized knowledge and training. As a result, parishioners are hesitant to visit people who are sick, grieving, or troubled. When they don't visit, they begin to lose the knowledge, built up in their communities over generations, about how to care for others. They become, or think they are becoming, disabled and in need of professionals to provide services they once gave to each other.

My illumination in Mamre opened me to the abilities and wisdom of those I had tended to discount. As a result, I have become increasingly aware of the irreplaceable knowledge that students bring with them to seminary, knowledge of the particularities of how people relate to and care for each other in different subcultures. For instance, in the ranching communities of western Oklahoma and Texas, laconic speech is often far more caring than the "reflective" responses I had learned to equate with skilled care. I have changed my understanding of my role as a teacher. Instead of giving students knowledge or equipping them with skills, my task is to help them uncover the wisdom already present in their own day-to-day experiences and to receive and affirm the wisdom of those with whom they care.

According to McKnight, when professionals disable nonprofessionals, they destroy communities—the second tragic effect of the service economy. Mutual care, which people give to and receive from each other, is the defining characteristic of communities.[3] The service economy replaces the mutual relations that constitute communities with relations between knowledgeable professional providers and disabled, needy consumers—the relations characteristic of institutions, such as hospitals and jails.[4] In the service economy, the church ceases to be a community in which people

---

[2] John McKnight, *The Careless Society: Community and its Counterfeits* (New York: BasicBooks, 1995), 16.

[3] Ibid., xi.

[4] Ibid., 108.

recognize and meet each other's needs and becomes an institution that provides services to laypeople.

Having received my training as a care professional in "caring" institutions, hospitals and clinics, I initially treated Mamre as a small institution, in which I served the poor. The poor participants, however, did not act on the premise that Mamre was an institution in which they were "guests" and I was a "host" who was supposed to serve them; rather, they assumed that they and I were members of a community, that all of us needed each other.

In churches, the professional provider of services is usually the pastor. Locating the knowledge about and ability to care in the pastor leads to the third and fourth tragic effects of the service economy. No professional, even if he or she is aided by a group of specially trained laypeople, can meet the needs for care of even a small congregation or community.[5] We all need each other's care on a daily basis. When we cease to seek care from and to provide care for each other and instead focus our needs for care on a limited number of people with special training, we make care into a scarce commodity, something that we cannot get enough of to meet our needs. Our churches, like other institutions, become places in which we compete with each other to get the affirmation and care we need. We become lonely, alienated, sensing that we are somehow cut off from the sources of life, caught in cycles of rage and pain. This anomie, which I experienced before my illumination, is the third effect of the service economy.

Making care into a scarce commodity increases the demand on those professionals who seem to possess "care." Such professionals' livelihood and prestige rest on their meeting these demands. Self-interest (maintaining or increasing their income), self-esteem (maintaining and increasing their status), and altruism (maintaining and increasing their sense that they are doing something of value by serving others) conspire to drive professional care givers to serve more and more people, to give more and more "care." As they do so, as they become the focus of more and more need, often expressed in desperate terms, the danger of burnout increases.

Most care professionals deal with this danger by making clear differentiations between their professional and private lives. Most of them work in offices. At the end of the day or a week, they can lock up and go home, leaving the demands of their work behind, at least for a time. Their clients and others do not expect them to provide services when they are not in the office. Many professionals specialize in a particular "problem" and so limit the kind and number of clients who come to them, without jeopardizing their income (specialists can charge higher fees).

Parish ministers are especially prone to burnout because they are different from other care professionals. They usually can't specialize. And they don't stop being pastors when they return to their homes. They expect

---

[5] Ibid., x.

themselves, and parishioners expect them, as leaders of institutions of faith, both to exemplify a faithful life and to represent God, or mediate God's grace, or interpret God's word. In the terms of the dominant service economy, pastors are supposed to be both perfect consumers of faith, never needing or desiring anything because of their confidence that God will provide, and representatives of God as The Perfect Service Provider, the one professional who can and will meet all needs. People tend to flood the pastor, as the representative of the One whose care is unlimited, with their pent-up needs for care. When they realize that the pastor (and his or her specially trained lay helpers) cannot meet their needs, they tend to devalue him or her, sometimes in very hurtful ways. The pastor, overwhelmed by the demands for care, and injured by the devaluation, can easily burn out.

Initially, I experienced the poor members of the Mamre community as demanding care from me and the other members of the mission group. My despair after the black members of the mission group left was a form of burnout. I identified myself as a pastor to these poor, needy people, and I did not have enough to give them. I did not realize that the poor members of the Mamre community were not treating me as a service provider. Generally, they had not had good experiences with service providers. The service economy tends to overwhelm especially those care givers who work with the poor. They, like pastors, frequently burn out. In their despair, they defend themselves against those they are supposed to serve. Poor people thus often experience service providers as frustrated, rigid, withholding, insensitive, and judgmental. They don't expect to receive care from service providers. They know they need to get care elsewhere. In the Mamre community, the poor members didn't expect me to take care of them; they took care of each other and, when I needed it, they took care of me. In so doing, they liberated me from the causes of burnout.

While, following McKnight, I have discussed the service economy as the source of these four tragic effects, the tradition of pastoral care has had similar effects. In their classic text, William A. Clebsch and Charles Jaekle offer the following summary of how the church has thought of and practiced pastoral care since the second century:

> The ministry of the cure of souls, or pastoral care, consists of helping acts, done by *representative Christian persons*, directed toward the *healing, sustaining, guiding,* and *reconciling* of *troubled persons* whose troubles arise *in the context of ultimate meanings and concerns* .[6]

Clebsch and Jaekle write that the church has always located the authority to care in a limited number of specially trained "representative Christian persons" and has devalued the care that laypeople give to each other as lacking the "dignity" characteristic of pastoral care.[7] By so defining

---

[6] Clebsch and Jaekle, 4.

[7] Ibid., 7–8.

care as a scarce and sacred commodity possessed and distributed only by authorized christians, the church has weakened the bonds of care between ordinary people and so has helped to create the conditions in which parishioners flood pastors with their needs. Recently and currently, dominant voices in pastoral ethics and theology continue this tradition. They state or assume that care or healing requires "traditionally structured dyadic relationships between a[n]...expert and a less knowledgeable, less powerful, and/or less healthy...person."[8]

In summary, this case taught me that the theological devaluation of ministerial and lay practice and its effects are results of much more pervasive assumptions that both characterize current economic relations in America and are rooted in central christian traditions. These assumptions legitimate power-over relations between powerful care givers and powerless care receivers.[9] In the world constructed by these assumptions, care receivers are ignorant and helpless. According to one prominent pastoral ethicist, they even lack the ability and knowledge necessary to make moral decisions.[10] In this world, the poor members of the Mamre community were and are unable to care; the widow was right—she knew nothing about care; the students who are ignorant of their own wisdom are right—they have no wisdom; I was right when, before my illumination, I thought of the poor people of the Mamre community as empty of resources and wholly dependent on me.

The paradigmatic character of this understanding of care explains why my experience in the Fellowship Hall of the abandoned Tabernacle Baptist Church was so profound it involved a change of worlds. Before, I lived in the world in which there were two types of people, those with resources and those without. After, I lived in the world in which everyone both lacked and gave. In McKnight's terms, before, I lived in an "institution without walls"; after, I lived in a "community."[11]

I marked this change by changing the name of the required course I taught from "Introduction to Pastoral Care" to "Care in the Christian Community." I realized that the word "pastoral" implicated the course in an understanding of "care" as a professional skill practiced only by authorized representatives of the church, pastors. I changed the name of the course in order to suggest that care is constitutive of community; it characterizes the activities of everyone. I increasingly sought to help students identify not only how they care for others, but how laypeople care for each other, including their pastors, in their communities.

---

[8] Heyward 1995, 9.

[9] Ibid., 9.

[10] Marie M. Fortune, *Love Does No Harm: Sexual Ethics for the Rest of Us* (New York: Continuum, 1995), 28.

[11] McKnight, xii.

CHAPTER 3

Condescension and Mutuality

During the last fifteen years, as the two events described above, and others, have changed me, I have repeatedly returned to reading and thinking about the story of Jesus and the Syrophoenician woman:

> Then he left that place and went into the territory of Tyre. He found a house to stay in, and he would have liked to remain unrecognized, but this was impossible. Almost at once a woman whose young daughter was possessed by an unclean spirit heard of him, came in, and fell at his feet. (She was a Gentile, a Phoenician of Syria by nationality.) She begged him to drive the spirit out of her daughter. He said to her, "Let the children be satisfied first; it is not fair to take the children's bread and throw it to the dogs." "Sir," she answered, "even the dogs under the table eat the children's scraps." He said to her, "For saying that, you may go home content; the unclean spirit has gone out of your daughter." And when she returned home, she found the child lying in bed; the spirit had left her.[1]

This story parallels my experiences of teaching and of being in community with the poor. I entered both practices consciously identifying with or following a Jesus who heals or teaches; I was the one who acted upon others. In both, the recipients of my activity, the widowed student and other students and the poor in Mamre, did not remain passive. They, like the Syrophoenician woman in relation to Jesus, took the initiative; they acted upon and changed me. But reading this passage has not simply reflected the changes in my practices of teaching and care; turning and returning to the story have also shaped these changes. Reading the story thus constitutes the third case in this account of how I came to a different understanding of care.

---

[1] Mark 7:24–30 (NEB).

The story fascinates me for four reasons. First, the Jesus it presents is decidedly a human being with flaws. The "difficulty" interpreters have had with the story lies in Jesus' harsh rejection of the woman. Interpreters have offered numerous and contradictory explanations for why a loving and divine savior would act in such a way. Some say that the story isn't really about Jesus; it is a Markan creation and reflects the difficulties Jewish christians had in accepting Gentile christians.[2] Others attempt to understand and so to excuse a flawed Jesus; they say that, in rejecting and insulting the woman, he was responding in an expected Jewish way to an unknown Gentile woman who violated his honor by intruding upon his privacy.[3] Others, uncomfortable with the image of Jesus as participating in the injustices of his culture, say that Jesus really didn't mean to insult or even reject the woman; he was just joking with her or provoking her in order to test her faith.[4] All these responses deflect our attention from the cruelty of Jesus' response to a desperate plea from a suffering woman. For me, however, this "difficulty" draws me into the story. A perfect Jesus, who wholly transcends his culture, who never acts cruelly, is unreal; no human being, no being of any kind, except an imaginary one, is so perfect. The story, precisely by presenting Jesus as a human being like me and the other humans I know, makes Jesus accessible. A Jesus who gets tired and angry, who is sometimes insensitive and even cruel, who unconsciously participates in the evil ways of his society—only such a Jesus is fully human and so has something to say to me.

The second reason the story fascinates me lies in the portrayal of the woman. Again, most interpreters have had some difficulty with her assertiveness. Only one I have read, Robert Fowler, simply affirms what is clearly the case, "The woman takes up the figures of speech Jesus uses and turns them against him. In this instance he who lives by the metaphor dies by the metaphor. [She bests Jesus] in this contest of wits and words."[5] Most other interpreters, and perhaps even the writer of the story, treat the woman not as a person in her own right, but as reflecting something about Jesus. They say that her intrusive and shameless request is the occasion for Jesus to discover and display his healing mission to the Gentiles, as well as to the Jews; that her witty response confirms Jesus' discernment and so joking provocation of her; or that her persistence is an example of faith in Jesus as the divine savior.[6] These interpreters miss what Fowler recognizes: The woman is the star of the story. She initiates the turns of the plot. Because she importunes Jesus, Jesus responds with an insult. Because she turns the insult on its head, Jesus changes his mind. From the beginning, she

---

[2] *Interpreter's Bible*, 1951, s.v. "Mark 9. The Syrophoenician Woman (7:24–30)."

[3] Ched Myers, *Binding the Strong Man: A Political Reading of Mark's Story of Jesus* (Maryknoll, New York: Orbis, 1990), 203–4.

[4] James A. Brooks, *The New American Commentary* v. 23: Mark (Nashville:Broadman, 1991), 121.

[5] Robert M. Fowler, *Let the Reader Understand: Reader-Response Criticism and the Gospel of Mark* (Minneapolis: Fortress, 1991), 117.

[6] Brooks, 121; *Interpreter's Bible*, s.v. Mark 24–30.

consistently does what is necessary to heal her daughter; she is the leader and teacher, Jesus the follower and student.

Again, my fascination with the story grows precisely out of the difficulties the interpreters have had with it. In shifting the focus from an initially retreating, retiring, irritable, mistaken, and cruel Jesus to a vital and smart woman who was wholly committed to saving her daughter's life, the story rings true to life. When I read the lives of great healers, leaders, and even saints, I do not find people who were always the stars, always the initiators, always the ones who knew or did what was right. Rather, I find gifted, needy, and flawed people who, at key points in their lives when they could have gone astray, met other gifted people who corrected and guided them. Jesus and the Syrophoenician woman were both gifted, needy, and flawed. The story has them meeting, and out of this meeting comes healing.

The third and fourth reasons for my fascination may have primarily to do with an accident of translation and what I brought to the story. In other words, I have not found much support for the following insights in the work of biblical exegetes. Nevertheless, I share them here because they shaped this passage's impact on me. When I first read the story, I learned that Jesus said, "For this saying, go thy way."[7] I was struck by the thought that the story did not end with the woman following Jesus—going "his way." I understood the story as saying that Jesus was respecting and even commending the woman's different and separate religious way. I grew up in South Asia. While I identified with christians, I knew and respected Buddhists, Hindus, and Muslims. As I became more involved in christianity, I searched for and, I must admit, had difficulty finding authorization within christianity for this simple affirmation of non-christians. The notion that Jesus had commended the Syrophoenician woman's different religious way was very appealing to me.

I also noticed that the story changes Jesus. In the Gospel of Mark, Jesus returns to his ministry of healing after his meeting with the woman; he does not go back into hiding. When I asked why Jesus might desire to hide, I noticed that, before his meeting the woman, Jesus was healing people and talking with the disciples. No one understood him. He was wholly alone in his own self-understanding, even when he was with his followers. Such isolation drains and destroys people. No wonder Jesus sought to retreat from those to whom he thought he was called; he was empty, exhausted, burnt out, probably near despair and doubting himself and his faith.

When the Syrophoenician woman violates his honor and privacy to demand that he, once again, sacrifice himself for others, his frustration and rage ignite. He lashes out at the woman with a demeaning insult, essentially calling her daughter a "puppy"[8] and so implying that the woman is a dirty "bitch" (in the worst American slang sense of the word). His healing power

---

[7] Mark 7:29 (ASV).
[8] Brooks, 124.

(nearly gone) is for Jewish "children" (obtuse, thick-headed, and ungrateful though they may be), not unclean Gentile "dogs."

The woman, however, refuses to accept his insult. Retaking the initiative in the conversation, she reverses his meaning. "Children" drop "scraps" to "dogs" and especially "puppies" who lie waiting under the table. In her speech the woman does what no one else, according to Mark, does. She does to Jesus what he does to members of the temple elite. Just as he turns what they say against them, so she turns what he says against him. She understands what Jesus is saying and doing so well that she not only plays his game, she wins.

With the woman, Jesus is no longer an isolated, lonely hero surrounded by stupid followers and greedy, demanding crowds. In the woman he finds a companion with whom to play, someone who meets him as an equal— not in power, but in dignity, intelligence, creativity, and commitment. In other words, the woman heals Jesus of his isolation. And in this healing, he discovers that he is no longer drained, no longer despairing. He discovers that healing is not a power that flows out of him, it is not something he does to or for the woman and her daughter. Rather, healing happens in a meeting in which all participate fully. In healing, everyone changes. The child becomes free of the demon. Jesus revives and discovers a clearer sense of his mission. The woman throws off the shame of being a dirty bitch and asserts herself as an insightful and compassionate mother, companion, and leader.

The traditionally "difficult," along with the other, aspects of this story suggest a movement between two very different kinds of relation and two associated understandings of care. At the beginning, Jesus dominates and the woman submits; she "falls at his feet," he rises above her. He possesses

Figure 1: Condescension

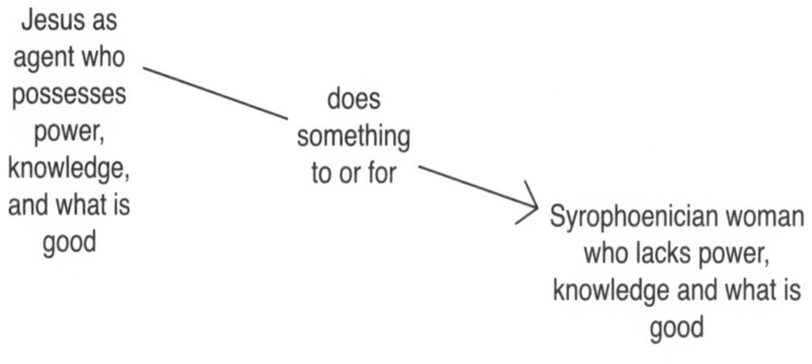

Jesus as
agent who
possesses
power,
knowledge,
and what is
good

does
something
to or for

Syrophoenician woman
who lacks power,
knowledge and what is
good

the power, knowledge, and ability to heal; she lacks them; care is a commodity, like bread, which he owns and distributes or does not distribute. The woman asks Jesus to *condescend*, to come down (*descend*) from his place of high status, cleanliness, holiness, and power in order to share his power with (*con*) her and daughter, who are unclean, unholy, and without power—lowly. In his insulting refusal, Jesus confirms his domination and her submission by refusing to care for the woman and her daughter. At this point, were the mother to continue the relation as it is, she would have to give up her request; the source of power, as well as sacred, social, and moral propriety, has spoken and refused her; if she had any manners, if she knew her proper place, she would, like a kicked dog, slink, whining, away.

Instead of slinking away, the woman stands up (figuratively and perhaps literally; the text doesn't say), throws off her submission, and confronts Jesus. With a bit of rhetorical judo, she flips Jesus' argument. Stunned, Jesus recognizes her as a worthy opponent or partner in the definition of what he must and should do. He grants her original request, but no longer as a superior condescending to an inferior. Instead, he recognizes her essential participation in the healing. In other words, Jesus assents to the woman's redefinition of their relation as a mutual one. They heal the daughter together. And, at least in my reading, they also heal each other. In other words, by the end of the story, Jesus and the woman have constructed an instance of normative mutuality, a relation in which all who participate bring out the best in each other and help each other to live fully.[9]

Figure 2: Mutality

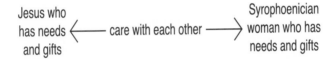

Jesus who has needs and gifts ← care with each other → Syrophoenician woman who has needs and gifts

---

[9] Carter Heyward 1995, 97.

CHAPTER 4

The Reality of Mutuality

The last two case studies reveal that the differences between condescension and mutuality are signs of differences between the ways we construct reality. In "Illumination," I described the movement from condescension to mutuality as a conversion from one world to another. In the story of Jesus and the Syrophoenician woman, the movement transforms all who are involved—Jesus, the woman, and the woman's daughter. The first case study, "Teaching and Learning Care," reveals that the failure to recognize the radicalness of this change creates a contradiction, which roots itself in four related mistakes shared by those who, like me when the student confronted me, lift up mutuality as an ideal for certain relations, while continuing to assume that condescension characterizes caring relations.

The first mistake is to think of condescension and mutuality as mutually exclusive in any particular meeting. By the time I met the student in the hall, I had moved away from condescension as the model for teaching about care. I was attempting to treat students as mutual partners in the quest for care. I assumed that, to the extent that I succeeded, I would not condescend to students. I did not realize that, in assuming the equation between condescension and care—that students, as pastors, are care givers and their parishioners care receivers—I tacitly perpetuated condescension between myself and students; they experienced me as more like a condescending pastor than a mutual colleague. The student faced me with this contradiction in my practice in that she asked me to give to her the knowledge about counseling skills she assumed I possessed and she lacked; in other words, I experienced her as asking me to condescend to her. In response, I explicitly affirmed our mutuality by saying we could learn from each other, but did so in a condescending way, in that I assumed that, as the teacher, I had the sole responsibility to define and to control what happened in the class. And so I ended our conversation by condescendingly not responding to her request because I thought it threatened my commitment to mutuality. Ironically, even as she spoke, I was already thinking about changing my teaching methods in response to her, confirming what I implicitly denied and explicitly affirmed, her mutual participation in, and responsibility for, creating the class. This analysis shows that mutuality and condescension can intertwine in the same meeting.

The second mistake is to think of mutuality in and of itself as an ideal to move toward or to be achieved, that mutuality is only good. The reason I denied my condescension to the student was because I thought condescension was incompatible with mutuality as a moral ideal. But mutuality and condescension can coexist because mutuality is not an ideal toward which we move. There are good or normative and bad or not normative ways of being mutual. Mutuality names how we human beings exist, as continually co-creating each other and the reality we share. Children and parents, students and teachers, friends, lovers, workers and bosses, clients and professionals, parishioners and pastors, consumers and providers— all of these are complementary; they mutually need and create each other. From birth to death, we mutually shape each other and what happens, just as the student and I shaped each other and the reality of what would happen in the class. I—my existence, who I was—became uncomfortable when she made her request; she exposed and called forth my condescension. I, in turn, confirmed her sense of herself as lacking even the correct knowledge of what she was lacking; we mutually constructed condescension.

Condescension is a particular kind of non-normative mutuality, in which those who participate construct some people as giving and active agents and the others as passive recipients. In its more extreme forms, condescension is the denial of the mutuality it presupposes. I moved toward this denial when I explicitly dismissed the widowed student's statement as in any way shaping what would happen in the class. Jesus enacted this denial when he rejected the woman and her daughter as "dogs" who were unworthy of interacting with him.

The third mistake lies at the heart of condescension, the definition of power, knowledge, agency, responsibility, and other immaterial realities solely as measurable quantities with comparable values, as, in fact, commodities. The widowed student presented counseling skills as a commodity which I possessed and she lacked; in paying for the class, she was buying these skills. In response, I offered her a different product, the one that I had in stock.

Commodifying activities erases the differences between them by reducing them to their exchange values. The contradiction that the student and I constructed rests on our reducing her thirty years of experience and my academic and clinical knowledge to commodities with comparable exchange values in the service economy. Her experience was worthless (no one would pay her anything for it) in comparison with my knowledge, which was valuable (people paid me for it). Therefore, she became the consumer and I the provider of a valuable commodity.

Implicitly, we also constructed other relational realities as commodities, all with comparable exchange values. We equated my more valuable knowledge with my greater power, agency, and responsibility as a teacher. We counted as without value or weight not only her knowledge, but also the power, agency, and responsibility she displayed in confronting me with her needs.

Associated with this commodifying of relational realities is an assumption that power means the capacity to control events, that if I have more power and you have less, then I control, act upon, or give to—condescend to—you; only if we have equal power and so equal control can we be mutual.[1] Given such an assumption, my thought that I, a teacher, could be in a mutual relation with the widow, a student, was a dangerous illusion, in that it tempted me to abdicate my responsibility for what I did to or for her. Following this argument, the student exposed this illusion with her comment about what she expected to receive from the class. My response can either be read as my attempt to maintain the illusion that she had as much knowledge and so power, as I did, or as my tacit admission of my power over the class and so over her.

This last argument for the descriptive adequacy of condescension ignores the fact that the student exercised power and agency in confronting me with her knowledge of what she needed she didn't fit the portrayal of her as merely a recipient of my knowledge, agency, and power. She displayed the reality of knowledge, power, agency, ability, value, and responsibility as different from commodities. All of these apparent "commodities" are qualitatively different ways or aspects of relating; they have to do with how we construct ourselves, each other, and our shared reality.

While I do not know exactly what was going on in the student's mind, I can imagine a probable scenario: After more than thirty years of entering into caring relations with congregational members, the student was comfortable visiting people who were sick and troubled, but she also knew that she received little if any recognition for this work, and that those with "counseling skills," gained through graduate education in counseling or ministry, did receive monetary and other kinds of recognition for the same kinds of work. Moreover, she knew that she had been relatively alone and sometimes overwhelmed by the demands of caring; she lacked others with whom to share her difficulties and to discuss her care; as a result, she had a sense that she might not have cared as well as a professional would have. Professional care givers and others, including ordained ministers, named what she lacked "counseling skills." Both her knowledge and her lack did not lie *in* her; rather, they were qualities of her relations to others, ways of naming what was happening as she visited, as she talked with others about becoming an ordained minister, and as she entered seminary.

---

[1] Fortune, 11.

When she encountered me prior to her first class in Introduction to Pastoral Care, she spoke out of this ongoing relational reality. She articulated her need for that which would allow her and others to recognize her care as valuable. In speaking, she exercised power and agency; she initiated an activity that would shape and affect me. Again, neither this power nor this agency was a commodity she possessed more or less of; each was a function of her activity in response to seeing me; each was a relational reality. In stating what she needed, the student took responsibility for her part in the class; she was letting me know what she was seeking and so how she would be participating. Again, this responsibility was not a commodity she possessed; it named the shape and direction of her activity in relation to me.

How she entered into relation with me, the way she knew me, the rhetorical power and agency she deployed as she spoke to me, the responsibility she exercised—all these were responses to the differences between her and me. I had been trained as, and had worked as, an authorized care giver. As a pastor, she would be an authorized care giver and she wanted my help in doing authorized care well. I was a professor. She expected me to be able to teach her something about care. And, in fact, I assumed that I would. After two years of teaching Introduction to Pastoral Care, I had begun to figure out what students actually need to improve their practices of care. What I knew about teaching care was different from what she knew and so thought she needed. I responded to her with this different way of knowing, and so exercised my power, agency, and responsibility as a professor to inform her about what I intended to do with the course. And she, in turn, responded by reiterating her alternative claim, her power, as a student. We were negotiating what we would be doing together with the course.

This close analysis of our encounter does not wholly displace the analysis of it as condescending. In the condescending economy, which is a reality, I was a provider with valuable power and goods, which she lacked. But the reality of condescension was part of a larger reality, in which she and I (and others) continually and mutually participated by exercising our different ways of knowing, different powers, different agencies, and different responsibilities. Within this larger reality, power, knowledge, agency, and responsibility were not quantifiable commodities, reducible to their exchange values; they named qualitatively different ways we related, participated, and created each other and our shared reality.

The difference between remaining in the realm of condescension and moving into a more inclusive mutual world emerges most tellingly when I attempt to imagine how I might better have responded to the student. If I assume that condescension is the governing reality, I am left with brutal honesty (from this perspective), "I know you think you need counseling skills, but what you really lack is self-knowledge, which I will teach you in this class." Such a response avoids the dangerous (in this view) illusion of possible mutuality, lets her know what she lacks, and how I will fill this lack. But such a response also ignores precisely what was crucial in the encounter, her thirty years of experience. At least in my original response, I addressed this reality.

On the other hand, if, assuming that mutuality was the encompassing reality, I had more clearly discerned the differences between our knowledge and ways of knowing, and the play of power between us, I could have said, "I know that you, with thirty years of experience doing pastoral care, know a great deal about counseling and caring for others. What good trained counselors know, the skill they possess and what I can teach you, is how to learn more about how to care by closely examining your own experience. I know that, as we in the class examine our experiences of care together, we will learn more from each other about how to care." Such a response would have addressed and affirmed what she knew, both about care and about her needs, while inviting her into the class as a forum in which she and I and the other students could learn from each other's differences.

In summary, in response to the events I have discussed in the last four chapters (and a host of other events), I changed my thinking about care. My original way of thinking about care as condescension failed me as I thought both about my own experiences and about the cases students brought to me, while thinking about care as mutuality helped me.

CHAPTER 5

Thinking and Practicing

When we do research, we deliberately think about a subject. When we think about an activity in order to improve our performance of it, we *practice* it. When we think about care in order to become more caring, we construct a *practice* of care. This chapter and this book are about how to think about and practice care.

We engage in two kinds of practices. First, we can learn how to do something we don't know how to do by practicing it. For example, one learns how to play the violin by practicing. In such practices, experts—for instance, a violin teacher—usually direct our learning. Most texts present care as this kind of practice, implying that, unless we have previously practiced care, we don't know how to care and must learn how to do so from an expert. The student in the first case assumed that she did not know how to care and needed me to teach her about it.

Second, we can practice something we already do in order to improve how we do it or for some other reason. For example, most contemplative disciplines begin with practicing breathing. One attends to one's breathing and it changes, one relaxes and one's breathing slows down and gets deeper; as one continues the practice, one becomes more aware of different ways one breathes and the effects of these different ways, one learns how to use one's breathing to achieve these different effects. I think of care as like breathing. All of us already care. Care, like breathing, is essential to living. We practice care in order to improve how we do it, to become aware of the different ways we care and the effects of these different ways, and thus to become more deliberate in our utilization of these different ways.

Notice that this understanding of care has already emerged in this book. I wrote about asking students to bring in cases in which they were called to care, my presupposition being that the students were already caring. I also conclude that mutual care is not an ideal to be achieved, but is the way we already live with and construct each other and the reality we share.

We begin to think about an activity we've already been doing because something happens that causes us to become aware of it. I began thinking about care because the seminary hired me to teach students to do pastoral care. With our awareness of an activity usually come three questions: What is happening? Why is it happening? Do I, or we, need to do something about what is happening and, if so, what? These three questions initiate the three fundamental movements of this research method: the *description* of what is happening, the *analysis* of why it is happening, and the *imagining* of what we could and should do about what is happening.[1]

Notice that I was "uncomfortable" when I began thinking about care. Research, at least about care, almost always begins with discomfort. We discover that we can't simply continue to do what we've always done. We're asked to do something new, and we have to think carefully about how we're going to do it. Or we discover that usual practices don't work, they aren't caring, or that what had worked in the past doesn't work now. I discovered that neither the usual ways of thinking about pastoral care nor the ways I had learned to think about cases in my training to become a psychotherapist proved very helpful when I began thinking about and working with others to understand actual care situations in churches and communities.

This discomfort persists and takes different forms depending on the particular focus of the research, the personality of the researcher, the contexts of the situation being researched, and where one is in a particular research project. As, through description, we gather more and more data, we may feel as if we are drowning in information that doesn't fit together; everything is in bits and pieces. As we analyze the data, we may become frustrated as we try out different ways of making sense of what is going on and each theory proves wanting in some way. Finally, as we imagine responses, we may be anxious because we realize we don't really know ahead of time what the effects of our activities are; we may be deeply pained by the limits of what we and our communities can do and by the knowledge that even our most considered and best-intentioned care is ambiguous; it will result in some hurt.

Description

We become aware of a situation because it challenges us. We describe it in order to find out what is happening. We carry out this purpose by performing three tasks. First, we identify what the situation is, what we are doing in it, and what questions and issues it raises for us. Second, we open up our awareness to gather in as much information as possible about all the contexts of the situation. Third, we focus our awareness on the details

---

[1] For a more detailed discussion of the tasks, steps, and categories that make up the method, see appendix A, 198–210.

of what happens in particular events, ones that raise the questions and issues in especially powerful, intense, or provocative ways.

Remember three insights throughout this descriptive movement: First, we begin a research project because our usual ways of making sense of the world and what we are to do in it are not working. Most of the time we care without thinking about it much. We've unconsciously organized our perceptions so that we become aware only of those signals that indicate that we need to adjust our responses. The student approached me in the hall, and I became aware of her. Before she had spoken, I had remembered the significant fact that she had been practicing pastoral care for thirty years. With my awareness came a corresponding response. I looked at her, gestured with my eyes and face that I recognized her and welcomed her. But all these responses were automatic; I wasn't deliberately thinking about her or about how to respond to her. Only when she spoke and I experienced the incongruity between what she was saying and what I knew about her did I begin intentionally to think about what to say to her. My automatic understanding and ways of responding broke down, and I didn't know quite what to do. To reiterate the point, research on care begins with the breakdown of comfortable, automatic ways of doing things, with the outbreak of chaos, the sense of being lost, of not understanding, of being incompetent, of not knowing what to do or how to do it, with the threat of suffering.

Notice that at this point in the case study, I began to identify just what the situation was, what were the key issues and questions I had. I explored what had been happening with pastoral care, the broader understanding of care as a professional service, and theological education. I focused specifically on what happened in the encounter, first on what she said (for instance, her equation of "care" with "counseling skills"), and later on how I responded (the contradiction between my explicit affirmation of her knowledge and ability and my tacit rejection of her statement about what she needed). In other words, I engaged in the three tasks of description: identification of the situation, description of its contexts, and focusing on a particular event.

What this and other case study reports usually disguise is the second insight about the descriptive movement in research. Because one's usual ways of ordering the world have broken down, one initially does not know what information is going to be significant and what isn't. Experience doing such case studies shows that what often proves to be the key to understanding what is happening in the situation is something the researcher initially ignored as irrelevant. For instance, notice that before my illumination in Mamre, I had unconsciously dismissed my awareness that the "guests" were, in fact, bringing food and caring for my family and me; this information was irrelevant to my initial understanding of what was happening with Mamre, yet it proved to be central to constructing a new understanding that enabled me to change my practice to make it more responsive and caring. In the movement of description, gathering even seemingly irrelevant or insignificant data is important, which means that one needs to tolerate and even value the sense of being overwhelmed by information.

Third, researchers must remember that their purpose is to strengthen their own and their communities' practices of care. Even if the overall focus of the research is on the community's practice of care, the researcher must realize that he or she can only realize this purpose by changing his or her own practice. The researcher must describe this practice; he or she must raise questions and issues about it, gather data about its contexts and effects, and focus on what he or she is or is not doing in particular events.

Good description is detailed, textured, vivid, evocative, and comprehensive. It does not rely on generalities, but on the specific details of the described event, aspect, or situation and its contexts. It builds out of these details an almost tangible texture that evokes what happened in the event or situation. Such a description is only helpful if it includes and even highlights those details that stand out, that call into question the initial common-sense understanding of the event or situation, or that, while being seemingly irrelevant, persistently appear in one's awareness and memory. Such a description draws the reader or listener into the place the researcher occupied; the recipient of the description "experiences" the situation and events for him- or herself.

Analysis

The repeated question "Why?" initiates the second movement, analysis, of this research method. Analysis begins with the identification of "cracks." Cracks are what specifically in the events and the situation give rise to questions. One cannot arrive at a new understanding that answers one's questions about a practice without first breaking open one's prior understandings. One does so by identifying the tensions, incongruities, outright contradictions, gaps, or ambiguities in the descriptions. For instance, the conversation with the student turned on the seeming contradictions between her long experience doing care and counseling and her expressed lack of knowledge about how to do counseling, and between our expectations about the class. These cracks opened up questions about theological education and my assumptions about care.

One can open up cracks only if one's attention is free floating. If one focuses initially on making sense of one's practice, one will simply reconstruct one's prior understanding and will be unable to identify where it doesn't make sense. Rather than being focused on understanding the practice, one, in this task, needs to attend to what seems to resist being understood. One needs to attend to the description to discover: the blank spots, what remains unclear or fuzzy; the contradictions or discrepancies, the stray details that don't seem to fit in; emotionally charged images or phrases or words, especially if they are repeated and seem incongruent with the rest of the description; discrepancies between the tone of the description, the effect of the description, and the content of what is being described; contexts that are left out.

I kept identifying the sources of my uneasiness in my encounter with the student and kept asking why she and I spoke as we did. Repeatedly asking "Why?" about such "cracks" opens us up to heretofore hidden relations or realities that give rise to new insights that may answer some of our questions or pose new ones. The exploration of these hidden realities and insights is the second task of analysis. Coming back again and again to the specifics of what happened between the student and me opened up previously unperceived differences and connections between condescension and mutuality.

Pulling these insights together to reconstruct our overall understanding of what happened in an event or a situation as a whole is the third task of analysis. I reconstructed my conversation with the student as an instance in which we constructed condescension with each other.

The analytic movement concludes with the identification of just how care has happened, or is happening, in the events and situation one has described. I identified how the student and I had imperfectly negotiated, in other words, mutually and caringly constructed, our conversation and what would happen in the class.

In analysis, we both discover and construct a theory or conceptual map that guides our thinking. I write "discover" because this map or model is implicit in the situation and events one has described. As one discovers this model, one constructs it as an explicit, more elaborated, and clearer way of thinking. As I examined the three cases, I discerned and then articulated a conceptual map of the relation and movement between condescension and mutuality.

Suggested by my discussion thus far is a certain allegorical model of the research method—a drama. I begin with an image of our everyday life as a surface that usually appears to be uniform and smooth. We can rely on it and walk on it without thinking about it. But sometimes the surface cracks open and we stumble; we no longer can trust the surface or our own abilities to move on it; our living becomes something unknown, difficult, and dangerous. As the surface shatters and breaks apart, we fall into chaos. The image I have often used with students is that we are "in the soup." Walking doesn't work anymore. We have to learn how to swim in, perhaps how to sink in, or maybe how to eat this soup. No matter what we learn to do, this education will only happen if we attend carefully to what this soup or stuff we have fallen into is—we have to describe it. As we collect this information, we come to understand this new reality; we identify its nature and dynamics. On the basis of this new understanding, we identify how we are already responding to it, how we are already swimming, sinking, or eating. Using this new knowledge about our activity, we can imagine how to improve it—how to become better swimmers, sinkers, or eaters.

In this drama, the analytic act recapitulates the drama as a whole. Parallel to the movement of description are the first two tasks of analysis, identification of the cracks in one's prior understanding and attending to the hidden realities perceived through these cracks. Parallel to the movement of analysis is the reconstruction of our understanding. Parallel to the movement of imagination is the identification of the way care is already happening. Another way of thinking about analysis is as the transition between description and imagination. Analysis begins with the description of what happens and reconstructs this description in order to provide us with the basis for imagining how to care in a better way.

Imagination

At the end of the fourth chapter, I imagined a better response to the student. The movement of imagination, which leads from thought back into engaged activity, differentiates this research method from most others; its purpose is to help us imagine better ways of caring. Replacing "better" with its implied synonym in this context, "what I should have done" or "what I should do," reveals the ethical thrust of this imaginative movement. To imagine better care is to construct an ethic of care.

In any actual case study, the three movements—description, analysis, imagination—cannot be wholly differentiated. As we describe, we are also asking and answering the question, "Why?" As we analyze, we also identify and describe heretofore unperceived details of the situation and events. And as we describe and analyze, we also evaluate, which means we compare what is happening with what is "better," what should be. In fact, this crack between the way things are and the way they should be motivates our thought in the first place. We think about, do research on, or begin practicing care because we have a sense that something is not as it should be.

Sometimes we don't understand what we feel we should understand. Even in such instances, more is at stake than understanding. We seek understanding because we *desire* it; *desire* both creates and bridges the distance between the *is* and the *ought*; ethics are the effects of *desire*. For example, when the student confronted me, she did so out of the fusion of what she desired and what she thought the class should give her: counseling skills. I responded out of the fusion of my understanding of what should happen in the class and my desire for this mutuality. The distance between what happened with the student and what I desired and felt should happen moved me to think about what happened.

"Desire" and "imagination" intertwine. Imagination is the capacity to form and retain an image (not necessarily a visual one; it may be an auditory, olfactory, gustatory, tactile, or proprioceptive one), to select out of the chaos of stimuli that reach our brains ones that have, and to which we give, a certain coherence or unity. From the beginning of our lives, we imagine what we desire, initially our mother's face or breast or warmth. We also imagine what we desire to avoid, although initially only as a chaos outside the desired world. We hold on to and, in our imaginations, combine and recombine elements of desired forms into more and more differentiated and complex images, some of which we find in the external world (our mother's face), some of which we make and then find (we draw our mother's face, put the drawing on the wall, and then discover it when she is away), some of which remain real only as images in our mind (an image of our mother's face and warmth that we retain in our hearts even after she dies). The student desired and so imagined herself with counseling skills. I desired and so imagined a class in which students and I would mutually work on how to care.

To practice imagining as part of a practice of care is to be deliberate and intentional about moving between actuality, desire, imagination, ethics, and activity. The actuality of the discomfort between the student and me gave rise to the desire to end it, to imagine a way to negotiate the differences between what we desired. This imagining required more detailed description and analysis to determine what was happening and why it was happening. Exploration of this actuality opened up different ways of imagining or constructing what happened, as condescension or mutuality. These explorations were also of what the student and I desired and why we desired what we did. In other words, the distance between actuality and what we imagined was itself part of the actuality I described and analyzed. Toward the end of the case study I differentiated as better, as more fully satisfying my desire for understanding, the image of care as mutuality; correspondingly, I combined what was undesirable into an image of condescension as a self-contradictory form of mutuality. On the basis of this conception, I imagined specifically how, in the actual encounter with the student, I might have more fully realized, made real in my activity, the image of mutuality.

Assumed throughout the case studies completed thus far is that care is a desired reality that we should, ethically, seek to strengthen or to make more real. Also emergent in the case studies is the image of care as the necessary mutual attention, concern, and confirmation we give to, and receive from, each other. As mutuality, care exists on both sides of the relation that desire constructs. Care is both the actuality of how we live together and the image we desire. Like the mother's face, care is the both the beginning and the end of our imagining. Because we experience care and its absence, we seek it. Going a step farther, as mutuality, care is the basis and the goal of ethics. Ethics arises out of our experience of living together in caring relations, out of our suffering when such relations are truncated, and so out of our desire to make care more real. Ethics is the imagining of how we can live more fully in reality by more fully caring for, and with, one another and, in fact, the whole of creation.

Understanding the play of actuality and desire, the *is* and the *ought*, in the imagination points to the three tasks implicit in imagination as the last movement of the method of practicing care. The first task builds upon the last task of analysis, the identification of how care happens in a situation or event. Implicit in such identification is an image of care, which one can abstract from the particular events and situation. Lifting out this image of care from the description and analysis of the situation and events is the first task of imagination. When I defined care as a fundamental mutuality, I was engaged in this first task.

Once one has abstracted a certain image of care, one needs to identify the obstacles to its fuller realization, that is, specifically what in the situation and the events prevents care from happening. Here, one deploys the capacity to imagine what negates or hurts one, what one desires to avoid. I identified condescension as the obstacle to a fuller realization of care. In my conversation with the student, I showed how condescension specifically led to my implicit denial of care as mutuality, even as I explicitly affirmed it.

Finally, one imagines how one could have acted in the events or situation, and could act in the future, to more fully realize the care one has identified. I imagined a different response to the student that would have more fully realized care as mutuality. Assumed by this task is that the imagined response will deal with and, in some way, at least partially overcome, or get around, the obstacles to care in the situation. This method is my imagined response to the situation I discussed in the first chapter, how to teach about care. In the discussions of condescension and, later in this book, in the discussion of how we bar suffering, I identify ways students and I have found to overcome the obstacles to care as mutuality.

Notice that the final measure of the movement of imagination and of the method as a whole is whether or not it helps the researcher to respond more caringly in actual events and situations. In this method, one successfully performs the imaginative movement when one imagines specific responses that, when one enacts them in the particular situation, result in better care. In other words, the individual researcher returns his or her attention to his or her own practice. I come back to such a focus because, only through the initiatives of individuals, acting in relation to others, can a larger community's practice change.

PART TWO

From Sacrifice
to Resistance

CHAPTER 6

The Case of Christ Church

In this chapter, I introduce a case study that demonstrates how to use the method. This case is partially fictional. The "student" who presents it, "Les Nodale," combines features of myself, some students, and a few others I have known. Similarly, the events of his life and his responses to them are like ones I or others I have known have experienced. His church, "Christ Church," is an amalgam of a number of churches I have attended, and its ministers are based on ministers I have known. The city "Sandford" combines features of a number of midwestern cities with which I am familiar. I experienced the three worship services "Les" describes or events very like them.

I have decided to construct this partial fiction for a number of reasons. First, bringing together in one case three of the originally disparate events that taught me that care is a communal activity allows me to use my discussion of these events to present the method for thinking about care in one situation. Second, while these events occurred in different communities and were separated by significant periods of time, they are closely linked in my mind as revealing features of most of the churches with which I have been involved. They could easily have occurred as I present them, in one church in a six-month period of time. Third, the original events involved significant suffering for numerous individuals and communities. The separation between the factual events and what I am presenting allows these individuals and members of these communities (if they happen to read the book) the choice to recognize or not to recognize themselves in my descriptions. My experience indicates that communities and individuals do much better in practicing care if they intentionally choose to do so, rather than if they find their activities exposed by someone else (though I recognize that such exposure is sometimes necessary to deal with especially destructive individual and communal behaviors).

Finally, constructing a partially fictional case allows me to affirm the constructed and even fictional character of experience, memory, and so description.

36

With the Mamre community, I initially experienced and so constructed the poor and myself as "members of different species." If, before what I have termed my "illumination," I had honestly retrieved my memories of Mamre and described what was "really" happening in the meals, I would have written about this experience of two species as the "truth." In the light of my "illumination," I reconstructed my experiences, my memories, and so the "truth" of Mamre; and, in the light of this new "truth," I experienced the prior "truth" that the well off and poor are two species as a destructive fiction, a lie. I also know that my reconstructed "truth" is both partial, in that it leaves some details out, and partially fictional, in that some details that I remember probably didn't happen exactly the way I remember them. In the sense that we construct as much as find what we experience, remember, and describe, all case studies are fictional.

But, still, in constructing a partially fictional case to demonstrate my method, am I not violating the distinction I made between "case" and "example"? Am I not utilizing this case study primarily to illustrate elements of my theory or method, rather than as the source for thinking that leads to theory and as the measure of theory? Not really. For even a total fiction can be a way of describing the impact of certain events and situations. One can still begin one's thought with this "description," and move from it to theories and techniques, rather than vice versa.

The idea that even a wholly fictional case study might be a source for thinking about care is an instance of a more general principle, drawn from, and confirmed in, the discussion of numerous cases. Everything can be data, a source of knowledge and insight. Every bit of information, whether it be a fiction or even an outright lie or a wholly subjective response, a vague or mistaken memory, or a blank spot in one's memory, can, if examined as what it is, throw light on what is happening in a situation. A key phrase in this statement is "as what it is." The best information is as transparent as possible, in other words, we know what kind of information it is.

I have attempted to make this case transparent by identifying it as a partial fiction and stating why I have chosen to present actual experiences in this form. When I construct a fiction, why I am doing it, what I am doing, how I am doing it, and the outcome of my activity all are part of what is happening—in other words, a fiction happens, it is part of, not opposed to, the particular and actual situations in which I exist and about which I think at a specific time. Even the most fantastic fictional stories, novels, television shows, and movies both reflect and affect the particular social contexts in which they are created; they give rise to theories and ways of thinking. For example, Sigmund Freud constructed a highly influential psychoanalytic theory out of his reading of the Greek tragedy of Oedipus; and a number of Freud scholars have discovered in his retelling of this fiction many insights into how modern European and European American society constructs gender and family relations.

Identification of a Situation

A student, Les Nodale, in the class "Care in the Christian Community," introduces a situation in which he feels called to care. He says (generally, his *descriptions will be from edited transcripts of what he said in class; his analyses and imagined responses will be from his final written report):*

Well, there is something about my church—in Sandford—that really bothers me. I'd like to be able to do something about it, but I don't know what. Partly, it's the worship services. Don't get me wrong, I like them a lot; in fact, they're the reason I came to seminary. I feel called to worship leadership. And I'm chair of the Worship Committee in the church. But I've also been hurt by what's been preached or prayed, especially in three worship services. It bothers me because I respect the ministers and other worship leaders a great deal; I know they care about people, and they're really good with worship and preaching; so I feel kind of bad even talking about it. Actually, these worship services are part of a larger concern I have about the church. My church has this reputation for being really liberal, for doing all this outreach and mission work; but—please don't get me wrong, they really do care about people most of the time—sometimes, they don't care. It's weird, they talk all the time about poverty and liberation and all that, but when it comes to someone who has troubles in the church, they drop the ball. I think if I can figure out what's happening in the worship services, I'll be able to get a handle on what's going on with the congregation.

In the above statement, Les has identified a situation which contains the three elements that make it suitable for research about care. First, it is a current context, group, issue, community, or relationship in which he is already doing something; he is concerned about it; he is already thinking about it. Second, the situation raises questions about his own and his community's care. Third, in the situation, there are identifiable time-limited events—meetings, particular experiences, encounters—that focus the questions about the situation. In Les's situation, the events are "three worship services."

Description of Situation Contexts

Les has also already begun, in his discussion of the contradiction he sees in the church, to describe the contexts of his situation. When I asked him to say more about this contradiction, he said:

Well, you know, Sandford is a pretty conservative city, but Christ Church is (and has been since it was started in the twenties) the liberal place in the city; all the more liberal leaders of the Democratic Party are members. And these aren't quiet liberals. You know the pro-choice counter-demonstration a few years back? Got into all the headlines? Our ministers were leaders of it. There's The Center for Racial and Economic Justice; members of our church started it thirty-some years ago and other members are still running it. There are lots of activists in the church. And they give all kinds of money to outreach—about fifty percent of the budget. Maybe that's the issue—with all this history and all these activists in the church, it's like you can't be a real member if you can't give lots of time or money to the church. It's like all the needy and suffering people are out there, and our job is to serve them, to be in mission to them. And there just isn't much room in the church for anyone with any needs. But that's not the only thing. There's something else going on in the worship services. We say we accept everyone in the church, but that just isn't true; but I'll talk more about that when I present the particular events.

I asked Les to say something about how he got involved in Christ Church. He said:

I'm there because of Susan Chance. She's the associate minister. I grew up on a farm about thirty miles west of Sandford, near Jeanne [a small town]. In '86, the bank foreclosed on our farm. It was really rough. My great-great-grandfather homesteaded the land back in 1892. It was handed down to my great-grandfather, and then to my grandfather. He got sick around 1970, and my dad took over the place. He did real well. We bought up a lot more land and equipment in the mid-seventies, ran up a lot of debt. We just couldn't make the payments when things went bust. Everybody was going bust, all our friends—everyone. Even the bank in Jeanne— it went belly-up a year later. But that didn't help my dad any. He blamed himself for losing his father's and grandfather's and great-grandfather's farm. He killed himself, with a shotgun—his grandfather's.

My mom and my sisters and I didn't have anything for a while. Susan Chance was the new minister at First Christian Church in Jeanne. She was going to seminary here at Phillips. She'd begun at the church just before my dad died. She visited us and did the funeral. My mom talked with her. They got to be friends. She and I got to be friends. She was great. I really think she saved my life. I was down, pretty suicidal myself, and she talked with me, not really counseling; I'd just go over to the church when she was there and kind of hang out. She'd let me help out with the bulletins; she'd ask me about hymns and prayers she was thinking of using. That's how I got into worship.

Anyway, Susan didn't need the parsonage, she was living here in Tulsa. So she convinced the church to let us have it for nothing until we could figure out what we were going to do. She left after a couple of years. My mom got a job in Sandford. We moved there and I went to SU. I kind of lost touch with church—any church—after we moved. But then, just after I graduated, Susan became the associate minister at Christ Church. My mom was going to the church and told me about it. So I decided to try it out. I liked it enough to stay.

In the above, Les has alluded to a number of the contexts that constitute the situation. Some contexts are objective, describable by someone outside the situation. The objective contexts are the seven material contexts (the geographic, ecological, socio-ecological, resource, local, institutional, and individual), the three social contexts (the demographic, economic, and political), and the single historical context. The other contexts (the psychological, the cultural, the ethical, and the religious) are subjective, having to do with how the participants in the situation experience and construct it. In the above, Les has indicated roughly where Christ Church is located (geographic context). He has indicated something about the politics of Christ Church (the power apparently belongs to liberal activists). He has alluded to the history of Christ Church and extensively to his own history. He has also alluded to the ethical and religious contexts of Christ Church in his discussion of the value the congregation places on social activism.

I have the luxury of hindsight, which allows me to sift through the description of the contexts of Les's situation and pick out only what turned out to be most relevant to the discussion of his situation. I require all students to write up a detailed and complete description of all the contexts of their situations. What I ask for is in appendix A.

CHAPTER 7

Sacrifice and Violence

Les alluded to three "events" in his situation, the three worship services. By "event," I mean a certain time-limited happening in the situation—a meeting, an encounter, a counseling session or part of it, a worship service, a particular experience. Descriptions of events should be highly detailed and vivid. Les focused in on specific segments of each worship service.

Before giving a detailed recounting of an event, I ask students to identify the event, then set the event in the larger situation by describing its particular contexts, especially if those differ from the contexts of the situation. In the detailed recounting, I ask students to present the event in a dramatic or narrative form. I ask them to include what was said, the non-verbal communication or body language, their ongoing thoughts and feelings during the event, and any changes they noticed in the contexts. I ask them to close their account with a brief description of the outcome of the event, its impact on the researcher, others, and the contexts.

After a student describes an event, she or he, usually with the help of the class, analyzes it and gives an imagined response to it. As a reminder, analysis involves identifying and opening up the cracks, exploring hidden realities, reconstruction, and identifying care; imagination includes abstracting an image or conception of care, identifying the obstacles to care, and imagining a response that can at least partially overcome the obstacles. Imagined responses may be retrospective, in which case the researcher imagines what he or she could have done differently in the described event, or prospective, in which case the researcher imagines how he or she would behave in a similar event in the future.

Description

Identification
The first event happened during a sermon by this big shot, visiting preacher; I'll call him Dr. Hollerein. I didn't like the sermon much—all

41

about sacrifice and faith—but then he quoted Luther, something like, "Show me that for which a man is willing to sacrifice his daughter, and I will show you that man's God." He was serious. I couldn't believe it. I've got a daughter. I walked out.

Contexts

Dr. Hollerein was in town doing some lectures at SU. He's real liberal politically, but theologically—well, Dr. SteinhoffSmith would call him a "new sectarian"; he wants to clearly define the church's identity against the world [*religious context*]. Anyway, Dr. Milton Hightower (or "Milt"; he's the senior minister at Christ Church) knows him and invited him to preach [*historical and political contexts*]. Even though I didn't like what I'd heard about this character, I went to the service. I figured it couldn't be that bad [*psychological context*]. Anyway, I go every Sunday I can—or at least I did. This service was about six months ago [*historical context*]. About then, I had begun to realize that I was having more and more trouble with worship, mainly with falling asleep. I had taken to sitting near the front of the sanctuary to try to stay awake; it hadn't helped much, but I was still trying; I was sitting in the second pew. But I still don't remember anything leading up to the sermon, not even the scripture reading [*material and psychological contexts*]. When I think of what happened during the sermon, that painting "The Scream" comes to mind; I felt like the person in that painting [*cultural context*].

Recounting

Dr. Hollerein was preaching about sacrifice and faith. He was talking about the founder of Habitat for Humanity, who had "sacrificed" a large income for his work. I think I've got this right, but I'm not sure about all the details. He said that this founder had moved with his family into the poor neighborhood where he rebuilt the first Habitat house, and how (this part I'm clear about), in making this move, he was sacrificing not only what he valued, but also his family's comfort and security.

I remember getting uncomfortable at this point. We, my family and I, live in a pretty poor neighborhood. There's a Habitat house down the street. We don't make much money. My wife's an artist who earns an income by teaching as an "artist in the schools." I'm a seminary student who's driving a cab to make ends meet. But "sacrifice" is not the word I'd use to describe our life. We've never had the stuff to sacrifice. But it 's more than that—we've got more than enough, even when we have trouble paying the bills. We're doing what we want to do and what we think is important to do. Our daughter's doing fine. Other people think the neighborhood is dangerous, but we've never had much trouble in it. Anyway, I was thinking that this guy doesn't know what he's talking about. I was getting mad as he went on and on about how much faith the founder of Habitat had because he was willing to sacrifice so much. It seemed like a real put-down of me and of my family's life. I mean, he was making it seem as if we were living some kind of deprived life, and we weren't.

I was good and awake, though, really listening to him. He was leaning out over the pulpit, holding on to the sides of it, his elbows up in the air, looking down at me and the other members of the congregation, speaking intensely, loudly, and very deliberately. And I was sitting straight up, leaning forward, looking intensely back at him. Then he said, really seriously, something like, "Luther said, 'Show me that for which a man will sacrifice his daughter, and I will show you that man's God.' He [the founder of Habitat] was willing to sacrifice his daughter—her comfort and possibly her future—for the God of justice."

I saw red. I lost it. I felt as if I were in some kind of nightmare. I knew that if I stayed, I would do something I'd regret, maybe stand up in the service and yell at the bastard. I have a daughter. I love her. Cyn and I are doing the best job we can of raising her. The notion that , because we aren't making a lot of money, because we are doing what we believe in, we are sacrificing her, is ludicrous, it's incredibly offensive. I stood up and walked out—not down the center aisle; I used the side aisle. A friend of mine was sitting at the back. I muttered to him as I went by, "I thought we gave up child sacrifice a long time ago." Once I got outside the sanctuary and was alone, I took some deep breaths and quieted down.

Unfortunately, because I was sitting near the front, my leaving was very noticeable. After the service was over, I talked with a few people about the sermon. People generally thought it was great. No one seemed to understand why it upset me so much. A few days later, Milt called me into his office to give me a lecture about hospitality to guests and the like. I told him that I would have been a lot less hospitable if I had stayed, and besides Dr. Hollerein was being highly offensive. Milt didn't get why I was upset, but he realized that he wasn't going to get anywhere with his lecture, so he dropped it.

Analysis

Cracks

The first crack in this event is why I went to the service in the first place. I had heard enough about Dr. Hollerein to know that I didn't like his theology. I guess I went because I thought that, somehow, because it was a worship service, it would be okay. That thought both does and doesn't make sense. It makes sense because worship has been really important to me. After Dad died, the services Susan led were times of comfort and insight during which I could feel and deal with what had happened. But, as I said, at Christ Church, I've been having more and more trouble staying awake during worship. When I think about that, I realize that, even before this worship service and the others I'm focusing on, I was either bored, mad, or in a lot of pain, emotional pain, during most of the worship services over the past year and a half or so, ever since I began coming to seminary. I'm not quite sure why. Anyway, there's a real crack between my reasons for going to this service and what I should have known might happen.

The second and third cracks lie in the sermon itself. Second crack, Dr. Hollerein is talking about doing something good for the poor, but his attitude is so patronizing, as if the poor are these lesser beings to be pitied. He acts as if parents who live in lower-middle-class or working-class neighborhoods, which is where a lot of Habitat houses are, are somehow depriving or sacrificing their children. Even if he is talking about a really poor neighborhood, where kids *are* deprived, the idea that those who live there are sacrificing their children is pretty insulting; most parents in those neighborhoods work really hard to give their kids what they need. What does it tell your neighbors if you say that moving there means that you've sacrificed your children? It tells them that you think they are somehow terrible and that it's okay to deprive children.

Now I have to give the founder of Habitat credit. He really was, and is, trying to change the conditions that lead to poor kids' being deprived. And I think that, when he moved into the poor neighborhood with his family, he probably wasn't thinking, "Oh, I'm sacrificing my children." He was probably thinking what a good experience it would be for him and his children to get to know poor kids and their parents and to work with them to build up the neighborhood. "Sacrifice" probably didn't enter his mind.

But maybe I think that sacrifice didn't enter his mind because of the third crack, which is that I still can't make any sense of how sacrificing children, even in the sense that Dr. Hollerein meant, has anything to do with faith or love. I can understand, though I still have some trouble with it, the idea of self-sacrifice or of sacrificing something I own as perhaps good, but I don't own my daughter and she's not me. I understand how my decisions and commitments are sometimes hard on my daughter and wife, but that's different than sacrificing one of them.

The fourth crack is the strength of my reaction to the comment about sacrificing daughters. I've heard some pretty bad things in worship services, especially in sermons. I've been hurt and mad and just plain disgusted, but I've never reacted this way, never with the violence I felt. The issue is not my strong rejection of what he said; it's how I felt it, as if I had been violated.

The last crack is everyone else's reaction. Maybe I'm just being stupid, but I just don't understand how anyone can not be offended by the notion of sacrificing daughters as a measure of faith. But almost no one shared my response. Mainly, people were upset with me for walking out. My friend to whom I made the comment as I left the sanctuary just shrugged it off. "Why did you expect anything different from him?" And I've told you about Milt's response.

Hidden Realities

I began my thinking about these cracks by wrestling with what was going on with me in worship in general. I realized that I've tended to think of worship, especially at Christ Church, as a special time, a holy time, in some ways a safe time. But for a couple of years it hasn't been that way. The more reading and work I've done in seminary, the more I've come to see worship as not awfully different from other times. I used to think that, when we prayed or preached or wrote a communion liturgy, somehow God or Christ or the Spirit took over, at least enough so that we wouldn't be hurting each other the ways we do in the rest of our lives. But that's not true. My wife, Cyn, works with the children rather than attend worship because the language of the hymns and the understandings of God and faith expressed in most of the services are hurtful to her. What this event shows me is how much I still want worship to be what it once seemed to be, so much so that I go to a service where I know I'm going to be hurt, angry, and offended. So much so that I sit right in the front in an effort to make the worship be what I want it to be. And still I go to sleep, rather than feel just how painful worship has become to me.

In this particular service, I really came up against the connection between my dad's death and the whole issue of sacrifice. I still haven't got all of it. Dad worked hard on the farm, day in and day out. And farm work was hard on all of us. We all worked, everyday; we kids worked in the morning before we went to school and when we came home. We worked especially long and hard when it looked like we might lose the farm. I suppose you could say we "sacrificed" ourselves for the farm. But we didn't call it that; we were just doing what we could to try to save the farm.

The preacher seemed to think that "sacrifice" is a good thing. But if you call what we lost trying to save the farm, the time my sisters and I lost at school, the time with friends, the time with each other, a "sacrifice," it doesn't make those losses good. Maybe someday I'll be able to look back and say that what we did was a good thing, but right now I can't get it out of my mind that, maybe, if we had stopped, even for a day, and thought about what we were doing, we would have realized just how stupid it was, that there was no way we were going to hold on to the farm. Of course, it's easy to say that now. We didn't know that then. But maybe, if we had talked some more, we would at least have realized that what we were doing might not work, maybe we would have been able to realize and to get Dad to realize that it wasn't his fault that things were so rough.

But we didn't, and I'm not even sure that Dr. Hollerein would recognize what we did as a "sacrifice." I'm having a hard time getting my mind around what he did mean. He seemed to be saying that a sacrifice, or at least a good one, is something a person chooses to give up. When you come right down to it, he made it sound as if only a rich person could really sacrifice. The founder of Habitat could sacrifice because he had a lot of stuff. He could choose to give it away. But that means we didn't sacrifice when we gave up everything trying to save the farm. As I said, doing that wasn't something we chose; we just did it because we felt we had to.

But it's more than that. When I read the biblical stories about sacrifice, they're about killing people. I know something about that kind of sacrifice. Dad killing himself—that was sacrifice, that was a real loss, that hurt like hell. And I know, I know, Dad thought he was doing the right thing, that by getting rid of himself, he was getting rid of a load of guilt and pain and loss and rage so big that he thought it was going to crush all of us—my mom, me, my sisters. He was wrong. All he did was make the load bigger and leave it for all of us to carry. We had to carry what he couldn't. I've hated him for what he did. But I also love him.

Giving up a cushy job in order to move into a poor neighborhood—that's not sacrificing your kids. That has nothing to do with sacrifice, at least sacrifice in the Bible. Sacrifice is bloody, sacrifice is hell. Sacrifice means someone dies, they're gone, they don't come back. Sacrifice is what happened to my dad and us. It's not anything good. It has nothing to do with faith. It's about destroying lives. It's about killing and being killed. Sacrifice is what Abraham almost did to Isaac and what Jeptha did do to his daughter. It's what the Romans did first to Jesus and then to the whole Jewish people. It's what Hitler and his cohorts, with most christians looking on, did to the Jews and gypsies and homosexuals and disabled.

There's something else here, something that made it especially hard for me to take what the preacher was saying. I live with this terror that I'll do something like what my dad did; not kill myself, but that, for some crazy, selfish reason that seems really good or important at the time, I'll just up and leave my daughter and wife. It's a terror that reaches into all kinds of places. People at Christ Church tell me with a lot of admiration, as if they're saying something good, that my family and I are sacrificing so much for me to go to seminary. And, in their sense of the word, they're right; my family and I are giving up some things for me to go to seminary. But, as Cyn will remind me if I forget, there's nothing noble about it. I wanted more than anything to go to seminary; going to seminary is not a "sacrifice" for me. Similarly, Cyn's given up a lot to do her art, but it's what she wants to do. Together, we don't make an awful lot of money, but we make enough to give our daughter a good life. If we really were depriving our daughter, or if, because I was going to seminary, Cyn couldn't do her art, the "sacrifice" wouldn't be good; it would be tragic and unjust. But when the preacher commends the founder of Habitat for his "sacrifice" and when people at Christ Church talk so admiringly about what my family and I have "sacrificed," they are implying that it would be okay for me to deprive Cyn and my daughter and myself of what we need to live in order to do what I consider most important; they are basically saying that I should abandon consideration of my family in the pursuit of what I feel called to do. This implication is why I walked out, why what Dr. Hollerein said was so offensive. I am not abandoning and sacrificing my family by going to seminary. It terrifies me to think that, because of some misguided, fanatic understanding of faith, I might do so.

Reconstruction

When I put this event back together, I realize that I identified with the "wrong" people. The preacher assumed that the people in the congregation would identify with the founder of Habitat. It makes sense; most of the people at Christ Church are well off. But I identified with the daughter and the people in the poor neighborhood. I'm the son of a man who "sacrificed" and I've been poor. And when I listened to the preacher from this position, what I heard horrified me, made me feel worthless because I didn't have enough to sacrifice or because I might be sacrificed.

My strong reaction grew out of the fact that I am also in the position of the founder of Habitat. I do identify with him a bit. I am doing something that I believe in, even though that means my family and I don't have as much stuff as we might otherwise. I experienced the sermon as a kind of demonic temptation to me as a seminary student, the temptation to consider what I'm doing so important, so holy, so godly, that I would be justified in "sacrificing" my daughter or wife to it. I know, in my bones and gut, just how destructive giving in to that kind of temptation is.

I realize, looking over what I have said and written, that I have not dealt with how the congregation and Milt reacted. Thinking about that, I realize something I did not include in the description. Because I was so mad, I did not just unobtrusively leave the sanctuary—I shot up out of my seat and strode out. Even though I went down the side aisle, a lot of people, probably most of the congregation, got the message that I was upset, I was walking out! I think that the people in the congregation were primarily responding to the strength of the message I gave. They and Milt didn't see how anything Dr. Hollerein said, which was, after all, standard christian stuff, could have upset me that much. They were probably mad at me for disrupting the welcome and honor they felt they owed this famous man, and they were probably uncomfortable with their own anger at me.

Care

I don't think Dr. Hollerein had any idea about the effect of what he was saying on me or people like me. From his point of view, he was giving a middle- and upper-middle-class congregation a model of effective christian caring for, and commitment to, the liberation of the poor, a model that is realistic in that it recognizes the costs of such commitment. And almost everyone in the congregation probably received the sermon as he intended it, as encouraging them in their care for the poor.

My friend cared for me by responding to the comment I made by dismissing the preacher. He was saying to me, "Don't let this guy get to you. He's not worth it."

Milt was clearly concerned about me and the congregation when he called me into his office to talk with me. And he was even more caring when, after expressing his concern and not really understanding my response, he didn't continue to pressure me; he just let it drop.

I cared for myself, for the congregation, and for the preacher by expressing, however ineffectively, just how much hurt he was doing with his remarks, and by getting out of a situation in which I felt abused and in which, if I had stayed, I might have reacted in a very hurtful way.

Imagination

Image of Care

Habitat is caring in that it provides opportunities for privileged and poor people to work together to do something that really does alleviate some of the suffering of poverty. In the work, the privileged people come to learn that the poor are not lazy, disabled, and passive—the stereotype—they are just people. If the privileged workers keep on and open themselves even more, they may learn a great deal about what it means to be poor, and even how much in common they have with the poor. The poor families who work on the houses get to shape and participate in the building of, and then to own, their own homes. They also make valuable acquaintances with people who may be able to help them get good jobs and access to other resources. In short, what makes Habitat caring is that poor and privileged people interact, get to know each other, and work together on changing things for the better.

Similarly, all that was caring about what happened in and after the worship service involved me, the congregation, and others coming up against each other and expressing our concerns about each other and what we knew and felt from our different perspectives. In this event, I learned that care requires that different people with different perspectives let each other know when they are hurting and that people listen, especially to those who are hurting; and that privileged people recognize that the poor are talented, able people with whom one needs to work to make the changes necessary to alleviate poverty.

Obstacles

The obstacle to care in this event is a certain conception of sacrifice that separates people into those who do the sacrificing, those for whom the sacrifice is done, and those who get sacrificed. In the act of sacrifice, the only one who does or says anything is whoever is doing the sacrificing. In the story Dr. Hollerein told about the founder of Habitat, the poor and the founder's children didn't say or do anything. What hurt me most about what he said is that it put me in one of two positions, both of which were intolerable. Either I was one of the ones being sacrificed or for whom the sacrifice was done, in which case what I thought, felt, did, or said didn't count, or I was the one doing the sacrifice, in which case I violated my family. Care requires that everyone be able to speak and act; sacrifice, in this conception, disables and silences everyone except the one doing the sacrificing.

In the event, this idea of sacrifice appeared to be part of a larger reality. The sermon, the reactions people had to me, and the lack of reaction to what Dr. Hollerein said all revealed a failure, an unconscious unwillingness, to deal with real violence, pain, and death. Dr. Hollerein didn't deal with the real violence and pain of poverty, nor the horrifying violence and pain associated with the biblical stories of sacrifice. The congregation, Milt, and even my friend effectively dismissed or ignored my pain, and they tried to reject my violent response to the preacher. The cutting off of the voices of the poor and the children who are sacrificed also silences their cries of pain. Dr. Hollerein only talked about the relatively minor losses of the founder of Habitat, and even these losses were less the founder's than they were his children's. This way of thinking about sacrifice seems designed to maintain the illusions of privileged people that only their experiences and voices count for anything, and that, when they really do give something of themselves, their pain over these losses (even when the real losses and pain are borne by others) is somehow the only real pain, that they deserve to be praised and honored for what they are doing. In other words, this idea of sacrifice appears to be part of a larger conceptual system through which the privileged seek to deny the impact of others' pain and to glorify themselves. While the denial may temporarily alleviate the suffering of the privileged, it afflicts those, like the poor and the sacrificed children, who are really suffering. It is an obstacle to care.

Imagined Response

When I look back at the worship service, I really wish I hadn't gone. I learned a lot from thinking about what happened, and that is valuable; but I was already on the way to those insights. What I learned doesn't justify the pain I went through and the alienation from Milt and the congregation I have experienced since.

In order not to have gone to the worship service, I would have had to take my misgivings about Dr. Hollerein much more seriously, to realize just how much views like his hurt me, and to overcome my sense of worship as always, or even usually, a safe, comforting place. With some sadness, with help from Cyn, who's much farther along on these tasks than I am, I am working on how to take my own apprehensions and limits seriously and to examine why I have held on so tightly to worship, when it has so often hurt me.

Given that I went to the worship service, what could I have done differently? Quite simply, I could have quietly and unobtrusively left, as if I were going to the men's room. Such a departure would have created much less fuss and spared me the reactions of Milt and the congregation. But, as I think about it, I'm not sure that my original disruptive response wasn't more caring, in that it at least let me express my pain and anger and let Dr. Hollerein and the congregation know that I was upset.

Neither of these imagined responses really deals with the central insight about care coming from this event—that care requires interaction with, working with, and listening to the poor and those who are suffering. Thinking about how to carry out such care at Christ Church carries me well beyond this event. I'll talk about it later.

CHAPTER 8

Tithing and Devaluation

Description

Identification

The second event was, again, a sermon, this one by Milt, the senior minister, on Stewardship Sunday. He was talking about tithing and said that if any of us didn't tithe, it was a sign of our lack of faith and "financial mismanagement." Any of you remember the farm crisis? In 1986, over half the farms in Jeanne County, including ours, were up for foreclosure. And almost all the small-town banks, the ones we depended on, went under. You know why? If you listened to the news and all the experts, it was because of "financial mismanagement." My father killed himself because of "financial mismanagement." He thought losing the farm was totally his fault. It didn't matter that everyone else his age went under, too; it was all "financial mismanagement."

Contexts

Again, I had some doubts about going to church that Sunday. I don't like Stewardship Sundays. I always feel bad [*psychological context*]. I mean, everyone seems to think everyone has all this money to give. After we lost the farm and Dad died, we didn't have anything. And when Mom finally got a job in Sandford, it still didn't pay much. And, as I said, Cyn—my wife—and I, we've always just scraped by. Actually, we give a good bit away to some homeless friends of ours, probably not ten percent, but a good bit. We give what we can to the church, when we can [*economic context*]. But every year, on Stewardship Sunday, somehow it's like I'm bad or wrong or something because I don't tithe [*ethical context*], like I don't have any faith [*religious context*].

Recounting

Up to the sermon, I didn't pay much attention. I was trying not to fall asleep again, sitting in my usual spot in the second pew. I don't remember the content of the prayers, what hymns were sung, or even what the scripture was. When the sermon began, I sat up straighter, leaned forward, and focused on Milt. I often like his sermons—challenging liberation stuff. If you haven't seen him, he's tall and slim, distinguished looking, dark hair. He had his black robe on. He kind of stands back from the pulpit, his voice is like that, too—reserved, formal; he doesn't get excited, doesn't move around much, kind of thinks through his sermons with us. He began by commending the church for its outstanding commitment to mission. He talked about how, through their donations of money and time, the members of this church were working with poor people to build communities in which they could meet their own needs, provide education and health care for themselves, and participate in truly democratic forms of government. Then his tone changed and he began the part of the sermon that really hit me hard.

He straightened up even more and spoke slowly in a low, clear voice, "But I'm here to tell you that we are not doing enough."

"Here it comes," I thought, and I leaned forward again and focused on him. I probably nodded. I thought he was going to talk about how we need to care more for those in need in and outside of the church—probably I was really wishing that was what he was going to say.

"Overall giving to Basic Mission Finance has been declining. It's down again this year."

I sat back in my seat thinking, "Oh well, it is Stewardship Sunday."

And as it declines, we have to reduce our support for some of the programs I described. A number of them are perilously close to being shut down for lack of funds.

And that's not just tragic, or unjust, it's a sign of a failure of faith on our part. We in this nation are rich. Fewer than one in twenty people in the world are Americans. But we consume more than a third of the world's resources.

At this point, I breathed a sign of uneasiness. Milt didn't seem to realize that these statistics were meaningless to a generation that was downwardly mobile. Some of us might be rich, but many of us were less rich than our parents, so we didn't feel rich, and some of us weren't rich at all, at least not in American terms.

And our wealth is not due to our virtue. People in other nations work longer hours, have less violence and crime, stronger families, and display more compassion toward each other than we do. Our riches are a product of historical accidents.

The God of the Bible and our economists tell us that there is plenty in the world for everyone to have more than enough. But not if we, who have more than enough, don't share. When we don't share, millions of others suffer and die young.

Now, let me tell you something else. A researcher asked a large number of people how they were doing financially. No matter what their actual financial situation was—whether they were poor, middle class, or wealthy—the vast majority answered the same thing: "We need about ten percent more than we have." Ten percent more! If I'm trying to support a family of four on twenty thousand a year, I need two thousand more. If I'm living alone on two million a year, I need two hundred thousand more.

I wanted to tune out at this point. This was going the way every other Stewardship Sunday sermon went—guilt-tripping. Milt didn't know what he was talking about.

There's something wrong here. What this researcher measured was not need, but desire. We're so mixed up, we think that what we desire is what we need. That's not true. I know a lot of people in a lot of churches, including this one. And I know that the percentage of their income people give to the church has nothing to do with how much they actually make.

I think the ten percent statistic is interesting. Ten percent of one's income is a tithe, what the church has said, for centuries, we're supposed to give to God. I've done my own survey—from memory. I know over a hundred people who tithe. And their level of income has had nothing to do with their decision. They take the first fruits, ten percent off the top, and give it to the church for God's work. And they have been happier and less desperate—again no matter what their financial circumstances—than the people who don't tithe. They've got faith—faith in the God who creates us all to live abundantly.

At this point, I felt really sad and heavy and alone, as if I couldn't move and, even if I could, there wouldn't be anyplace better to go. Obviously I didn't have faith, and obviously God had somehow messed up, at least with my dad and all those other farmers. Abundance—what a crock!

If even half of the members of Disciples churches tithed, then Basic Mission Finance would have all it needs to fund its projects and more. If half the Christians in the United States tithed and half these tithes were put into mission programs like the ones I described, the world would take a giant step toward becoming the just and peaceful place God created it to be.

> Let me make myself very clear. I am convinced that tithing is
> something every member of this church can do. If you don't tithe,
> it's not because you can't; it's because, in God's economy, you've
> mismanaged your finances. You haven't given God what's due
> God.

I was mad. I didn't get up and walk out this time. I knew Milt, I knew
he cared. He just didn't know what he was saying, didn't have any idea. So
along with the anger, there was this kind of wrenching pain inside me,
tearing me apart—and no one could see it. I had this sense of futility. Milt
knew what had happened to me and my dad. He *knew*, so how could he
talk this way?

The outcome of the event was that I didn't hear the rest of the sermon
and paid little attention to the rest of the service. As soon as it was over, I
exited through one of the side doors to avoid seeing Milt. I just wanted to
get out of the church, to go home or to a movie—anything, just to get away.

Analysis

Cracks

The first crack is the same as in the first event. Why did I go when I
knew what would happen on Stewardship Sunday and how the service
would affect me?

The second crack has to do with the sermon. Why did Milt preach this
sermon to this congregation, which already donates fifty percent of its budget to outreach? But more importantly, why did he preach it when he knew
that there were people like me in the congregation—I know I'm not the
only one—people who are living from paycheck to paycheck, who don't
tithe, although we do give? I know, from talking with him at other times,
that he doesn't really think that we don't have any faith; and I'm pretty
sure that he doesn't really think that we have mismanaged our finances. So
why suddenly is he acting as if we don't exist?

This crack goes deeper. Why is Milt preaching a sermon that alienates
the privileged from the poor, especially when he's so committed to liberation theology? For that's precisely the effect of the sermon. It alienates the
rich from the poor by portraying the poor solely as a source of guilt, which
the rich can buy off with enough money. It doesn't build a relation between rich and poor, it doesn't really build any concern for the poor. And
the sermon totally alienates anyone who, like me, is struggling financially.
Milt basically said that if we have financial difficulties, we don't have faith,
and that we've mismanaged our money. That's a form of blaming the victims of our economy, and right now, even in boom times, that's a whole lot
of people. As I said earlier, it's that kind of blame that drove my father to
suicide. That Sunday, it drove me out of the church.

The last crack is the contradiction in my response to Milt. I tried to get
him off the hook by thinking that he didn't know what he was saying, but

then I wondered how he could have said what he did when he does know me and others like me. In other words, I thought that he both knew and didn't know what he was doing.

Hidden Realities, Reconstruction, and Care

Visible through the cracks in this event is a kind of forgetfulness. I go to church on Stewardship Sunday because I forget how it feels to be there. Each year, I think that I should go, that's what a good member does. I shouldn't just skip out because I don't like a particular service; I think that I really should give more, even though I know I really won't. I forget the reality of struggling each month to pay the bills and falling a little bit more behind. I forget that Cyn and I really do give a lot—in time, but also, proportionately, in money; we just don't give it all to the church. Each year, I go, and I feel guilty, but more than that, I feel ashamed that I don't give more.

If I forget myself and my reality, is it any wonder than Milt forgets me? It's as if, when he's in his office preparing his sermon and then when he gets into the pulpit, all he sees is a congregation full of people trying ever so hard to let each other know that they're doing well, especially financially, because that's what we try to do in this church. It's not that everyone dresses up, it's just that financial matters don't come up, except in discussions about "poverty" as an "issue," and then it's only discussed the way Milt did in the sermon; poverty is something we rich folks could fix, if we really decided to; it's not something that threatens us. In a way, there's something comforting in the sermon; Milt basically said we're all okay financially and that we have control over poverty, which is what we'd really like to believe.

But this comfort, this forgetting, costs us, especially those of us who have suffered or are suffering financially. It sets up an anguished contradiction in us, though most of the time we don't feel it. On the one hand, we feel guilty that we haven't done more, aren't giving more. On the other hand, we feel deeply ashamed if we have any fears about or any real economic struggles. In our shame and our guilt, we feel totally alone. Cornel West said that, in an oppressive capitalistic economy, everyone knows, deep in themselves, no matter how rich they are, that a twist of fate can render them poor, without any value, ashamed and struggling to live.[1] We do everything we can to forget this threat that we live with all the time, and we feel ashamed when we fail, either to forget or to be economically successful. Our forgetting cuts us off from the only real way we could address this struggle, by talking together about it, by finding ways to help each other. Instead, we afflict each other and ourselves with a loneliness that turns our shame into despair and terror.

There's a liberation form of this privileged forgetfulness and Milt expressed it. The poverty that threatens us isn't here, and, if it is, well, we

---
[1] Cornel West, Scott Lectures, Phillips University, Enid, Oklahoma, 1987.

have control over it, we can manage it. If we really wanted to, we could get rid of it. Because we don't, we are guilty. What Milt forgets is that "the poor will always be with us"; poverty is not something we can, by will power, get rid of. Its causes reside in the fundamental ways we organize ourselves into societies; they are even in the loneliness and alienation between the privileged and the poor constructed by liberationists seeking to forget their own poverty. Guilt is another sign of privileged forgetfulness.

And I reacted to his sermon because I am too close to the pain and the terror. In a few months, my family went from seemingly happy, secure, and well off to devastated and poor. Losing the farm and my father's suicide destroyed my ability to blind myself to the reality of the threat.

But part of me still buys into the notion that the only reason I feel this threat is because I'm doing something wrong. I'm financially mismanaging, I'm not faithful enough, I'm not giving enough. I want to believe that I or someone can control and get rid of the terror.

I think that this desire is why I try to give Milt the benefit of the doubt. When my dad was alive, we all relied on him as the one who made life secure. I think I want to rely on Milt this way. I want to believe, against the evidence, that he both knows what he is doing and that what he is saying is true—in other words, that he represents a God who is omniscient, omnipotent, and all loving. But that makes what happened to the farm my dad's fault, since such a God wouldn't cause such suffering. Such a theology doesn't make any sense to me anymore, but I still feel it. I still want my life to be secured by someone bigger—be it my dad, or Milt, or God.

When I clear away these illusions, I find a very different reality of care. I realize that I was giving Milt the benefit of the doubt because I really do know he cares, and I care about him. I've talked with him and seen him in tears over the failures of the church to respond to the real suffering of some of the people in the neighborhood. I really do know that he doesn't judge me for my financial struggles, but is very supportive of me. And I really care about him. He relies on me to talk through his struggles and I am very willing for him to do so. We work together.

His sermon and the theology that lies behind it are both tragic and ironic. They bring about the suffering they try to alleviate. When I see through the illusions, I find that, rather than being angry with Milt and the rest of the congregation and myself, who buy into this junk, I feel sad. Blinded by our desire to be free of all the pain and fear, we wander up a blind alley.

But at least we are wandering together. Just as, together, we make this illusion of a secure place, protected by "immortal, invisible, God only wise," we also sometimes, as in the conversations between Milt and me, begin to work together to change our affliction.

Imagination

While there is care even when we construct our illusions of being secure and protected, these illusions also contradict the possibility of care. More effective care requires a rending of the illusions about ourselves and others.

The primary illusion that obstructs such care is the division of people into those who are privileged, who are supposedly in control of what happens to them, and who are therefore wholly responsible for their own and others' suffering, and those who are afflicted and must be liberated or helped. God supposedly protects us, the privileged, from poverty and suffering and expects us to free others from these scourges. If we fail, either by becoming poor and suffering ourselves, or by not freeing others of affliction, it is our fault; we should be ashamed or guilty. Because, in fact, we actually all do fail in both these senses, we live always in shame and guilt.

This illusion prevents us from clearly perceiving both our own and others' suffering, from identifying the causes of suffering that can be alleviated, and from working together to address these causes. Tithing, especially if the money is spent in such a way that it maintains the illusion, does not address the causes of poverty.

The only way to address these causes, the only way to care effectively, is to realize that the privileged and the poor are citizens of one society. Both of us make, and are subject to, our economics and politics. We can escape neither the pain and suffering—epitomized by death—over which we have little control, nor the pain and suffering we construct together. If we blame those who fail to make it in our society for whatever reason, if we say that they have not earned their living and deserve to have their lives cut short in various ways (by poor medical care, faulty nutrition, violence, inadequate housing, despair, and meaninglessness), we are blaming ourselves. Even if we say that those who are poor can't help themselves and thus we must take total responsibility for them, we are, ironically, setting up the conditions for our failure, our own participation in making poverty, and so for our own helplessness. We can care effectively only by facing, together with the poor, the reality of what threatens us, by recognizing our limits, needs, and suffering, by affirming each others' gifts, by helping each other. The "we" here cannot be just the privileged. The "we" must be all of us, privileged and poor, healthy and ill, currently suffering and currently comfortable.

If I had listened to Milt's sermon with this understanding of care in mind, I might have felt the same, but my attitude would have been different. Rather than being wholly subject to the twists and turns of my reactions to his words, I would have been able to recognize these as responses to the struggle between two ways of constructing the world, as divided between the privileged and the poor and as shared by all of us. After the sermon, rather than leaving the church, I would have stayed and talked with Milt and others about how we experienced the sermon and about ways we could work together with others to bring about the more effective care I've described. In other words, rather than supporting the illusion by allowing the shame and guilt it produced to isolate me, I would have built upon the more truly caring relations that I had with Milt and other members of the congregation.

CHAPTER 9

Communion and Exclusion

Description

It was another Sunday service, just a couple of weeks ago, the Week of Compassion [*identification of the event*]. This time, I was looking forward to the service. Susan was leading it, and I usually loved what she did. But, even though I felt pretty good about going, I also was struggling with the weekly communion [*psychological context*]. One of my closest friends at Christ Church is Ruth. She's Jewish. Her husband's a member of the church; he's really involved, thinking about going to seminary. They attend synagogue together on Friday and church on Sunday. She's really active in the church. She was one of the first to welcome us when we began attending. She helps put the bulletin together for the services. I always like seeing her [*historical context*]. Anyway, this Sunday, I was sitting next to her, in the middle of the sanctuary [*material context*]. My daughter Zoe—she's four—sat on the other side of me throughout the whole service [*material context*], she didn't want to go back to Children's Church after the Children's Sermon; she didn't say why, but it probably had to do with not wanting to share her mother with all the other kids (Cyn was—is—the adult leader of Children's Church) [*psychological context*].

Anyway, I was—am—struggling with communion. I had read Burton Mack's *A Myth of Innocence: Mark and Christian Origins*,[1] and I was having difficulty with communion as a ritual enactment of Mark's passion narrative, which blames the Jews for Jesus' crucifixion. At the same time, I was excited about communion as a reenactment of the meals in which some of the Jewish followers of Jesus ate with everyone. I had talked about this struggle with Susan and knew she'd been thinking about these issues [*historical and religious contexts*].

---

[1] Burton J. Mack, *A Myth of Innocence: Mark and Christian Origins* (Minneapolis: Fortress, 1989), 304–5.

The children had brought their baskets of money and placed them on the communion table. Before that, the service had opened with an appeal—so much would provide three months of food for a refugee family, so much would provide inoculations for so many children. Susan had done the sermon on the agape meal, picking up on what so attracted me to communion, the understanding of it as a ritual that tears down all the barriers between us, a meal to which everyone, no matter what her or his station in life, is invited. One thing she said bothered me some. She said that what makes the meal possible is agape, which overflows from God to all of us and so fills us that we can love each other without regard for that which usually divides us, a love that doesn't grow out of need or dependency or desire, but is the simple delight in the other. I liked this vision of love, but it didn't quite ring true—setting up the contrast between, on the one hand, God's love and, on the other hand, human need and desire and dependency. But what she said didn't bother me a lot.

After the sermon and a prayer, Susan introduced the communion by asking the congregation to remember all the unseen people, represented by the gifts, gathered around the communion table—the least of these. She went on with the words of institution, "On the night before he died, Jesus gathered with his friends. . ." And she concluded, "All Christians are invited to eat this meal."

At this point, I went cold. I was sitting beside Ruth. I knew that she would not take communion. We had talked about it after I had gone to a Seder at her home. I had commented on their welcome of me, a Gentile, as an honored participant in the Seder; and on the difference between the Seder and the communion service, where non-christians were not invited. Susan had said that she felt part of Christ Church, except during the communion ritual. It didn't bother her much; she recognized that the communion service was just for christians. She might not have been bothered, but I was. The contradiction that I had been reading about was real, now, in my face. Susan had said that the communion meal was open to everyone, but then she only invited christians. Ruth, even though she wasn't christian and wasn't a member, was as much a part of Christ Church as I was. How could the meal of love not include her?

As the deacons passed the trays of cups and bread, I squirmed, in my mind, if not my body. The trays came to Ruth first. She didn't eat or drink but held the trays for me to take some, looking at me with a welcoming smile. I shook my head, took the trays without eating or drinking and was passing them across Zoe to the adult sitting on the other side of her. Zoe caught my arm, and whispered loudly, looking up at me, "I want some!" I shook my head and mouthed a firm, "No," and passed the trays on. Zoe gave me an angry look and scrunched as far away from me as she could without pushing up against the next person.

This event tore me up. I haven't been able to take communion since. I just can't get over the contradiction. I don't like not taking communion. I feel cut off from the church. But I can't figure out how keeping children or people who believe something different from eating and drinking the elements has anything to do with being loving. It seems like the opposite.

Analysis

Cracks

I have already identified the first crack, the contradiction between Susan's inclusive intention and the performance of the communion as a ritual of exclusion. This contradiction runs through the content of her invitation. Her opening words envisioned the whole of humanity, especially children in need, no matter what their faith, gathered around the communion table. Her closing words confined the meal to professed christians, who, in this church, were adults who had confessed Jesus as Lord and Savior. Her intentions were universal, but she participated in the performance of a ritual that drew a clear boundary between christians and non-christians.

The tension between these two meanings of the service emerges clearly from the perspectives of the children and Ruth. On the one hand, they were welcome in the worship service. The children opened the service with their offerings. Ruth was a regular attender, affirmed by the members of the church as a valued participant; she helped with the layout of the bulletin. On the other hand, she and the children were excluded from the central moment in which the congregation participated in worship, the sharing of the communion.

The contradiction came into focus when the trays came to Ruth and then to me and then past Zoe. As Ruth refused the elements and then I rejected Zoe's demand for some, it became clear to me that the ritual was as much about inhospitality as anything else. What host would invite children and guests to a meal, only to refuse them food and drink?

The second crack is why I am the one who responds to this contradiction, while Ruth, who is subject to the exclusion, does not.

Hidden Realities and Reconstruction

Hidden by the communion service, but becoming perceptible through the first crack, is the devaluation of those not considered to be full christians. The absent needy ones were empty vessels into which the church poured its wealth; they neither spoke nor participated in the service. Similarly, while the children and Ruth did participate in the service, the rest of us viewed their actions and voices as peripheral; we did not see them as shaping the service.

Recognition of this reality seems to resolve the contradiction. The church was universal in that it served all those in need. It was exclusive in that it limited effective participation to confessing adult christians.

But this resolution is superficial—false. For the communion service was a symbolic sharing of what is necessary to live, food and drink. This ritual was seductive. Through Susan's words, the congregation first offered to share the necessities of life with all, including non-christians, but then reneged, saying only christians could eat and drink.

The contradiction is deeper. For the primary need human beings have is for relations in which they are confirmed as full and effective participants. A baby who is given enough food and drink, but is not given this kind of confirming love, will die. An adult who is cut off from the network of confirming relations will often withdraw and die. When a community refuses the gift of effective participation to someone, it denies her or him the love that is as necessary to life as are food and drink.

I felt this contradiction and Ruth didn't because she, as a non-christian, is primarily subject to it, while I, as an active adult member, a christian, and as Ruth's friend, Zoe's father, and one who has been suffering and poor, am both subject to and an agent of it. In other words, in Christ Church, the ministers and formal members possess the power to include or exclude nonmembers like Ruth; she doesn't get to choose. As a member, I wield this power, but I also have been subjected to it. In the first two events, I experienced myself as alienated from the church because of my experience of losing the farm and my father's death, my experiences of suffering. My reading of Burton Mack's book increased my sense of being an outsider. Sitting between Ruth and Zoe, I found myself both dominated by this alienation and still, as a member of the church, one of the ones who was doing the dominating; the contradiction was in me, rather than outside me.

My alienation uncovers another, somewhat paradoxical reality. The differentiation between christian and non-christian does not fully define the boundary between insider and outsider at Christ Church. The exclusion of children, like Zoe, from the service suggests other dimensions of this boundary. When asked, members explain that children shouldn't take communion because they are not old enough to understand its meaning. But Zoe and other children can understand what it means to be included in or excluded from a sustaining meal or loving gathering. Something else is at work here. I felt alienated from Christ Church partially because of my history of suffering and poverty. When Susan opened the communion with a recognition of all the people gathered round the table and represented by the gifts, she also tacitly observed that, in the perception of the church, the poor, the suffering, and the needy are invisible; they are not really here. The analyses of the first two events reveals that, in Christ Church, those who are poor and suffering are indeed invisible; The boundary between christian member and non-christian outsider appears to be fused with the boundaries between adults and children and between the privileged and those who are afflicted. Adult privileged christians exercise the power to accept or not to accept children, the poor and suffering, and non-christians.

Care

Susan's intended inclusive message remained, eclipsed though it may have been by the performed ritual. It remained in her initial words and in her omission of "on the night he was betrayed" from the words of institution. As Burton Mack observes, the theme of betrayal in Mark's passion narrative lies at the heart of christian anti-Semitism, in that it leads to the portrayal of the Jews as Jesus' betrayers and killers.[2] The presence of children and the Jewish woman in the service also made the theme of inclusion real. Excluded from the table, their participation devalued and not recognized, they still tacitly shaped the event.

Susan stated what is essential in this inclusive way, recognition that the least of these (the poor, children, suffering people, and non-christians) are already gathered around the communion table, not just or even primarily as recipients of help, but simply as full and active human participants in shared life. The radicalness of the contradiction between the two understandings of communion stands revealed: the ritual of inclusion requires the active participation of children, non-believers, and the suffering; the ritual of exclusion requires at least their passivity and anonymity and, preferably, their absence. I, ironically, participated in the ritual of inclusion when I joined Ruth in the company of the excluded; I participated in the ritual of exclusion when I refused to let Zoe eat and drink the elements.

Imagination

In this event, I learned that a community defines how and for whom it cares by how it defines its boundaries, often through its central rituals. A caring community is one that includes and affirms the participation of strangers, including nonbelievers, children, those who are suffering, and the poor [*image of care*].

The primary obstacle to the realization of this care is the use of boundaries to prevent active participation in communities. Communities, like Christ Church, can use religious boundaries—for instance, the differentiation between christians and non-christians—to disguise other boundaries—for instance, the differentiation between privileged and poor [*obstacles to care*].

During this service at Christ Church, I could have been more caring by allowing Zoe to eat the bread and have one of the cups. In so doing, I would have been honoring her desire to participate in the communion and, through the communion, in Christ Church [*retrospective imagined response*]. In the future, I will take my lead from children, Jews, and other nonbelievers, the poor and the suffering; I will do what I can either to be with them in their exclusion or to facilitate their inclusion [*prospective imagined response*].

---

[2] Ibid., 304–5.

CHAPTER 10

Suffering, Domination, and Resistance

After students describe, analyze, and imagine events, I ask each of them to analyze and imagine the situation as a whole. Such reflection on the situation includes and integrates what they have learned through their reflection on the events. Following is Les's analysis and imagination of his situation at Christ Church.

Analysis

Cracks

From the beginning of my discussion of Christ Church, I describe a contradiction between its liberal and even liberation commitments and its performance of sacrifice, devaluation, and exclusion. In each event, I find this contradiction existing in myself. As an active and even central member, I find myself both tempted to sacrifice and the one being sacrificed; I feel both guilty as a privileged person and ashamed of my suffering and financial struggles. I both exclude my daughter and join Ruth in being excluded from the communion. It's as if Christ Church and I dwell in and help make two worlds that coexist and yet contradict one another, one world in which sacrifice, tithing, and a communion service that excludes non-christians are good and loving; and one in which these same acts are destructive and hurtful obstacles to care.

Hidden Realities

In each event, suffering initiates the movement from the first to the second world. I experience as abhorrent the sacrifice that the visiting preacher lauds, because of my experience of losing the farm and my father's suicide. The sermon on tithing hurts me because I know firsthand the suffering caused by charges of "financial mismanagement." The communion service tears me in two because I have suffered the exclusion that afflicts Ruth and Zoe.

In each event, suffering signals the de-idealization of what is considered most holy in the first world. Dr. Hollerein idealized sacrifice, Milton Hightower idealized tithing, and Susan Chance idealized communion. With the admission of suffering, sacrifice, tithing, and communion become at best ambiguous and at worst demonic realities.

An implicit theology connects the three events. In the first, Dr. Hollerein says that sacrifice discloses the God to whom the sacrifice is given. In the second, Milt says that tithing is a sacrifice we give to God. And Susan portrays God as emptying or sacrificing Godself for us; in the communion we both receive God's love and join God in giving or sacrificing ourselves for others. In each event, the admission of suffering betrays the way this sacrifice constructs a world in which there are privileged, powerful, holy agents and suffering, passive, unholy recipients of the agents' activities. The sacrifice, in each case, locates and creates suffering in the recipients, while seemingly emptying the agents of this suffering.

With the admission of suffering, those who had been passive become participants. This breaking in of those who had been excluded occurs in two ways. First, it occurs as I find myself one of them, one of the sacrificed or poor or excluded. In finding myself, I cry out and so affect what is happening. In the first event, this cry takes the form of my walking out of the service; in the second, it comes later as I realize that I must confront others with the reality of how they are afflicting me; in the third, I resist the exclusion by joining the excluded.

Second, the cry occurs as those who were seemingly passive, powerless, and excluded break into my awareness as powerful participants in my reality and in Christ Church. I responded the way I did to the sermon on sacrifice because I could not get my daughter's voice out of my head; she emerged as an agent driving me to act. In the service on tithing, I resisted the message because I realized that not only my father but also all the other destitute farmers and, in fact, all those who are blamed for their affliction and poverty were not and are not passive objects; they resist, they act, even if by destroying themselves; they cry out, and their cries shape me and others and the reality that we share. In the communion service, Ruth and Zoe, by their presence and actions, and the invisible company of the poor, even in their absence, decisively shaped what happened in the service, at least for me, and I think for others.

Reconstruction

Behind the idealization of sacrifice, tithing, and communion as a ritual of exclusion lies the theology to which all three ministers alluded. Susan articulated it when she described *agape* as flowing from God to us and from us to the world. In this theology, God is the bottomless source of power and love. To the degree that we christians are empty and receive this power and love, we are able to give them without need or desire to the world. The world then is the empty vessel into which we pour power and love. This theology was implicit in Milt's assertion of abundance as the reality underlying tithing: tithing is the way christians participate in God's abundant love. This theology makes sense of Dr Hollerein's view of sacrifice. I sacrifice my daughter to God because I know that this God is the source of all love and all life. In sacrificing her, I open her and myself to abundant life and power; I receive her back as no longer mine but God's.

This theology displaces suffering and blame for suffering downward, into the poor, children, those who are already suffering, and nonbelievers. It displaces power upwards, into privileged, comfortable, adult believers. When these greater ones tithe in order to increase their status, their holiness, their religiously authorized power, they do so by sacrificing their possessions, including the lesser ones. The lesser ones cannot be holy because they have no disposable possessions; they are, by definition, empty, the vessels that carry the suffering and need that the greater ones seek to deny in themselves. The communion in this system is a gathering of those who have been purified by their possessions of need, desire, suffering, and lack; their giving is the sign of their holy abundance, their participation in the God who only gives. Unable to sacrifice, the lesser ones become sacrificed objects, the vehicles through which the greater ones work out their salvation. Unable to tithe, the lesser ones become the empty recipients of charity, the means by which the greater ones work out their ethics. Excluded from communion, from sharing what is necessary for life, the lesser become the world dominated by death, from which the greater escape by communing with the God of abundance.

This religious system emerges in, and legitimates, a political and economic system of kingdoms, empires, and colonies. God is a supreme or dominant Ruler, to whom one must pay tribute—sacrifices or tithes—and to whom one confesses one's loyalty, one's belief in the Ruler. If one pays tribute, then one receives blessings, the food and drink, shelter and protection, care and love that are necessary to life. If one does not or can not pay tribute, then the Ruler withdraws his favor and one suffers and dies. This ideology justifies and disguises an imperial system in which rulers exact tributes of raw materials, cheap labor, and taxes from colonies; they process these tributes into products with which they bless those in the colonies who are loyal to the rulers and so willingly participate in the imperial exercise of power; these native participants buy these products and so increase the wealth of the rulers.

Under different names—"international capitalism," "the market economy," "development," "export economies," "consumers"—the same system rules today. Multinational corporations and their political counterparts "develop" markets in "undeveloped" areas by buying up or in other ways taking control over the human and material resources of those areas, utilizing the resulting cheap labor to produce material and immaterial products, which are then sold back to those laborers who most willingly participate; but all the profits accrue to the multinationals. Those who resist or cannot participate in this rule of the market literally suffer and die.

People at Christ Church know all the above, but only in theory; they don't see how they are participating in it. They feel terribly guilty about being U.S. citizens who benefit from this political and economic system, but they assuage this guilt through their sacrifices and tithes, and the illusion of an inclusive communion that, in practice, is exclusive. They don't see how, through these religious acts that seemingly have nothing to do with what they tend to see as the dirty, brutal economic and political world, they maintain and participate in this system. Nor do they see how their seemingly private failures, their hidden suffering and struggles of which they are so ashamed, their pain and alienation and rage that continually threaten their sense that they are saved, part of the religiously privileged "people of God"—all these "problems" that they so often successfully project into children, nonbelievers, the poor, or a few afflicted "antagonists" are the signs that they are also the victims, the raw materials, the objects that this system consumes.

I see and feel these contradictions because I have experienced them directly. Whenever I have talked about what happened to my family and me, I have said we "lost" the farm. That's the lie that killed my father. We didn't "lose" the farm, any more than almost all family farmers over the last seventy years have "lost" their farms. At least since the thirties, in a series of "farm crises," first a few large landowners and then agricultural corporations have bought up family farms. Most "farmers" now work as managers and laborers on these large farms. Because we could not pay our "tribute" in taxes and interest payments, this system took our farms.

At the same time, this system constructs the ideology that it doesn't exist, that individual farmers and individual rural bankers and individual store owners were and are wholly responsible for losing their farms, banks, and stores. My father took this ideology into himself and it destroyed him. He believed that his and our suffering was caused by his failure, his fault, his sin of "financial mismanagement." Under the load of this shame, he got rid of what he believed was the cause of all this suffering—he killed himself; he did to himself what the system told him he was already doing to himself.

As I write this analysis, I experience again the nightmarish combination of despair, helplessness, and rage that I experienced after his death and which I know he experienced before his suicide. And this nightmare returned in each of the three worship services I have described. But, having analyzed and named this demon, I no longer feel the terror of it. I am aware that it retains its power through an illusion, which is that there is no resistance possible to it, that those who don't pay tribute are indeed powerless. I have experienced the power of my daughter, and of Ruth, and the power that lies in my own suffering. I know that, contrary to the ideology of the demon, we "lesser" ones also make things happen, we participate, we can and do affect and change this system of domination. So, with the nightmare, I also experience a grim determination to resist it.

Care

The care in this situation is both fundamental and fragile. It resides in all the relations through which people often unconsciously sustain each other. For me, it resides in the relations with Cyn and Zoe, with Susan, Ruth, the friend I talked to as I walked out of the first worship service, and Milt, with homeless and poor friends, and with the people in the congregation. All of us, some more fully and consciously than others, consider and rely upon each other; all of us, through how we interact, co-create each other and the world we share. In this fundamental sense, care is synonymous with our life together.

But, in another sense, care is fragile. In all three events, and in the church as a whole, the oppressive system I have described destroys our ability to name and strengthen these bonds of care. This destruction of awareness breaks apart the bonds that sustain our lives together. While I found sustaining care in each of these services, I did so only by overcoming their alienating effects. In each case, this alienation is both internal and external. Externally, the events broke or at least strained the relations between me and people for whom I cared and upon whom I depended for care: Milt, Susan, my daughter Zoe, the other members of the church. Internally, they ignited violent conflicts within me that initially threatened to paralyze me.

When I look around Christ Church, I see widespread evidence of this alienation and lack of care. There are a number of homebound members of the church who could come and participate in the church if we used the van the church owns to pick them up, but we don't even think to offer homebound members this service; they have fallen into the category of those we serve, those whose function it is to receive what we have to give, to be passive receptacles; but we don't even visit them very often. We do have a lay care program, Stephen Ministers, but increasingly these lay ministers comment on how drained they've become as the congregation members have focused their many ongoing needs on this handful of people; the program, after an enthusiastic beginning a few years back, is now barely functional. Members who go into the hospital, who are grieving or going through "personal difficulties," complain that, while Susan and a Stephen Minister visited them, no one else did, including those they considered their friends; they felt betrayed and isolated. The church is losing families with children. Cyn says it's because members aren't really interested in children, even though they say they are. Cyn has real difficulty recruiting reliable teachers and aides for the children's classes; almost no one is willing to commit to teach for more than a few weeks. Cyn and I have brought homeless friends to the services once or twice but have stopped doing so because, while everyone is polite on the surface, no one really welcomes them; certainly no one considers them prospective members. As our friends look around, they don't see anyone else who looks even working class, no one like themselves; they don't want to come back. The church is much more effusive in its welcome of the occasional middle-class black person, who, taking the liberal reputation of the church seriously, wanders in; but such visitors rarely return; the church has no black members. Some members and the ministers express a willingness to examine the reasons for the homogeneity of the congregation, but when anyone actually comments on the ways church members tend to stereotype anyone who is not white and middle class, the ministers and congregation members attack the one making the comment for being too critical and "angry," for creating conflict, for not recognizing the "complexities" of the situation.

In my experience, instances of resistance to this widespread destruction of caring relations are isolated, rare, and weak. They don't cohere into a movement or a space in which even a few members of Christ Church can work together on how to strengthen our care for each other, not to mention others in the church and the surrounding community.

Imagination

Image of Care and Obstacles

How is it that care can be both fundamental and so fragile? In college, I decided to try to understand what had happened to my family. I began reading about agriculture. I found my way into what C. Dean Freudenberger calls agro-ecology.[1] The capacity of the earth to grow plants is fundamental. But this capacity is actually a complex network of relations among water, soil, air, climate, and a huge number of interacting and interdependent plant and animal species. As long as a sufficient number of these relations or certain crucial ones, remain, this complex ecological system will survive.

But disrupting critical relations can lead to the destruction of the ecosystem and even to the destruction of the land's capacity to support life. Near Tucson, Arizona, in what is now a desert, there used to be a flourishing agricultural civilization, dependent upon irrigated land. Probably in one decade, this civilization disappeared because the salt brought by the water reached such concentrations in the soil that the farmers could no longer grow crops; the land became a desert. A number of agro-ecologists say that a similar fate awaits the midwestern United States today. Dams along the eastern rim of the Rockies are draining water out of Oglala aquifer, which supplies the Midwest with water. Sand dunes are already spreading in parts of southwest Kansas. The consolidation and mechanization of farms leads to the creation of large fields with no windbreaks. The fertile top soil is blowing off. In well under a century, there will be none left if it continues to erode at this rate.

---

[1] C. Dean Freudenberger, *Global Dust Bowl: Can We Stop the Destruction of the Land before It's Too Late* (Minneapolis: Fortress, 1990).

I think care is like an ecosystem. It resides in the complex interdependent relations we have with each other and the other beings in our world. The system is remarkably resilient, residing as it does in the ways we sustain each other, the very fabric of our society. Most of the time we are unaware of this web of relations through which we co-create each other and our world.

This lack of awareness can blind us to the ways we, even as we attempt to sustain each other, also destroy the relations that make our life together possible. In my thinking about the three worship services at Christ Church, I have begun to become aware both of the care that sustains us and of the ways we are destroying ourselves. The primary way we are breaking the bonds of care is through our adherence to what I have called the system of domination.

When I talk about the fragility of care at Christ Church, I am referring to my experience of there being little, if any, social space or openness in which members and others there can become aware of, identify, and work to resist the system of domination that is breaking up the caring relations that sustain us. By alienating us from each other and even ourselves, the system of domination destroys our capacity to care for each other and ourselves. So far, we have not wholly destroyed our capacity to care.

Right now, my hope lies is the resilience of life. The desert near Tucson may no longer support agriculture, but it is an ecosystem and a rather beautiful one. My homeless and very poor friends suffer greatly, but they also find ways to live together and sustain each other. But mostly, as an American, I find hope in the communities of African Americans and indigenous peoples. My ancestors subjected both to the most horrific, death-dealing domination. When my ancestors enslaved African peoples and cleared Indian peoples off the land, they intentionally, repeatedly, and systematically destroyed the family, communal, material, and cultural ties that made life possible for these subjugated peoples. Today, we, the descendants of these European colonists, continue this destruction through racist and other systems of domination and subjugation. Yet, in a number of religious, artistic, economic, and political communities, African Americans and Indians have constructed spaces of resistance to the system of annihilating domination.

As a middle-class, white American man, I have not yet found such a caring community or space in which I can intentionally work with others to resist the system of domination. Christ Church is like the other middle-class white communities I know. The leaders and people in these communities are generally unaware of how they, and we, participate in this system and how it is destroying us.

Imagined Response

While I do not currently have community of resistance, I do have friends with whom I share, partially or wholly, my growing commitment to resistance to the system of domination: Cyn, Zoe, Sarah, a homeless man named Sam, my friend to whom I spoke at church, a few students and a couple of the professors at seminary, and, to a lesser extent, Susan and Milt. Thinking about my experiences with Christ Church has awakened me to how important these friends are to me, how they sustain me. As a result of this thinking, I have already begun to attend to these friendships and to be more intentional about discussing my commitments.

This thinking has also alerted me to how crucial it is to identify and confront the system of domination when I see it. At Christ Church, I plan to be much more consistently vocal in this work of naming and resistance. Rather than blowing up and leaving services, I am working on how to be more intentional about talking with people who see and are concerned about the destruction of care. I hope, at least, to build more and stronger friendships with such people.

I will continue to look for such people where I have most often found them, among those who are suffering, especially those who are suffering because of the system of domination. Through an art class she taught in a prison, Cyn has befriended an inmate; they exchange insights about how to survive in the face of the beast. I continue to find friends among those who, in the system of domination, I am supposed to be serving—the poor, the ill, those who have been abused, members of subjugated groups. I find that such friendships are much more helpful to both them and me than my "service. " Through me, they can sometimes access resources that would otherwise be unavailable to them. Through and from them, I come to understand both how the system of domination destroys people and means of resisting it.

From my own experiences of affliction in Christ Church and other communities, from Cyn and others like her who have suffered much more extensive injury than I have, I am also learning to respect my limits and apprehensions. I am learning to pick my battles. As I indicated earlier, I probably would not go to hear Dr. Hollerein again, unless it would be because I had decided to find a way to confront him and others with the effects of what he has been saying. I am probably not going to the Stewardship Sunday service next year, unless, after talking with Milt about why I have such difficulty with this service, I find that he is going to make enough of a change in it that it becomes more meaningful than hurtful to me.

Whether I attend services at all remains a question. Doing this project has uncovered the pain and anger that lie behind my drowsiness in worship. I find it most difficult to be in the sanctuary during the communion service, most beset by the painful contradictions in it. It's not just services at Christ Church. I've been to services here at the seminary and at other churches, and I find myself less and less willing or sometimes even able to participate; it's just too painful. Like Cyn, I feel abused by most of the services I go to. Part of the struggle I have is that, even as I feel this pain, I also really want to be in worship. In any case, I am resigning as Worship

Committee chair. I need to be able to be free to attend or not to attend worship as I work out my struggle with it.

There's a broader question for me that I'm just beginning to face. My real desire is to find or to help construct a community of resistance to the system of domination. So far, Christ Church is not the place for me to carry out this work. I'm less and less sure any church is. So my whole relation to the church or Church is in question. At the same time, I do find here at the seminary, if not a community of resistance, at least a community in which people are open to the questions, in which I can really learn; so I plan to stay in seminary. Where I will go once I finish my degree I do not know.

PART THREE

Analyzing Care

CHAPTER 11

Cracks and Triads

In the first chapter, I discussed how most books about care, including most texts in pastoral care, counseling, and psychotherapy, focus on analyzing the person who is suffering. A few texts enlarge this focus to families, groups, or communities in trouble. Most of these analyses implicitly assume that care is rightly condescending, that the causes of suffering lie solely or primarily within a disabled individual, family, group, or community, and that the care giver is the active and able agent who relieves suffering. To the extent that these texts focus on the care giver, they tend to do so in order to equip him or her with the knowledge, skills, and abilities needed to intervene in situations of suffering. They tend to define the care giver's suffering, needs, and desires as obstacles to the practice of care that need to be cleared away, if the care giver is to be effective.

I have deliberately selected the case studies so far presented in this book because they trace a movement away from this understanding of care and the premises underlying it. In each of the cases so far presented, the causes of suffering do not lie solely within a disabled other, or unit, for whom an able person must care. Rather, suffering is a result of the relations and network of relations in which we all participate. In other words, while suffering does come from within us as individuals, families, groups, and communities, it also comes from outside us. More precisely, suffering is an effect of how we, and all beings, constitute each other in our relations. To need or to suffer is not to be disabled. No one, in any of the case studies, was wholly disabled by her or his suffering and need. On the contrary, close examination of what happened in each of the case studies revealed the caring and able participation of those who were most needy and suffering.

While focusing on the knowledge and abilities of those who were most needy and suffering, the case studies exposed the participation in causing

74

suffering of those initially defined as expert care givers or authorities. The case studies traced this participation in causing suffering not to the intrusion of these experts' needs and suffering into their care, but to their unintentional condescension and so participation in patterns of domination. In fact, these experts' admission of their own needs, suffering, and desires into their caring relations was essential to their identification of the relational and systemic causes of suffering and to their participation in effective mutual care.

These case studies thus raise broader questions about care and suffering. How do relations cause suffering? How does domination work and how does it cause suffering? In what ways do condescending care givers unintentionally participate in larger systems of domination that cause suffering? How do we resist such oppressive systems?

Finding some answers to these big questions is essential, not to caring (which everyone does), but to the intentional practice of care. It is especially essential for those of us, which I assume includes many if not most of the readers of this book, who are care professionals or are preparing to be care professionals: ministers, therapists, counselors, chaplains, social workers, community organizers, and teachers. The case studies presented thus far implicate us as powerful, if unintentional, players in the systems of domination and condescension that cause suffering. These systems authorize our use of dominating and condescending power in caring relations. If we are to use our power to support and construct communities of mutual care that alleviate suffering, rather than to dominate and condescend, then we must explore how these oppressive systems work, how they determine what "care" means and how it is practiced, and how to resist them.

Thinking about care in this way produces discomfort for two reasons. First, it leads into territories that are unfamiliar to most care professionals or would-be care professionals. In order to answer the questions introduced above, we require an analysis of the material or economic and power or political dimensions of caring relations. Most texts about care deal with the psychology and theology of care, a few with the sociology of care; it is rare to find a text that explores the politics and economics of care.

Second, political and economic analyses of care tend to be disillusioning. Most of us who seek to practice care professionally do so because care giving seems to be inherently good. The case studies presented thus far call this idealization of care givers as essentially benevolent into question. Pursuing these disillusioning insights into larger and unknown territories of political and economic systems calls into question how we define what is good, our own practices as good, and our assumptions about and motivations for becoming care professionals.

While I cannot promise that you who continue with this research will not experience this discomfort (it comes with the territory), I can reiterate what I wrote earlier. While such explorations are disillusioning, difficult, and disorienting, those who have undertaken them have also learned how to care more effectively *with* others and have discovered great joy in these mutually caring relations.

Discomfort while doing this kind of research is usually an indication of the presence of cracks. Notice that each of three questions posed above grows out of the crack between care as condescension and care as mutuality. In this part of the book, I explore these questions. In this chapter and the next, I explore suffering as relational and how domination causes suffering. In chapters 13 through 15, I analyze condescension as an ideologically shaped practice that legitimates and enacts economic and political domination. In chapter 16, I discuss ways of resisting domination and condescension.

Other Cracks

Four cracks other than those described above emerge in my reading of what I have written thus far. The first is the relation between the discussion of care as mutuality in the first part and the emergence of suffering and how we respond or don't respond to it as central to care in the second part. The second crack is the tension between the privileged denial of suffering and the ubiquitous reality of suffering. The third is the relation between care as a foundational and fragile reality and care as what we desire, an ethical norm.

The fourth crack lies in my use of the image "cracks." I have implied that, in order to practice care, we need to get beyond our assumed, everyday understandings by identifying and opening up the "cracks" in this "surface." The realities and insights with which we need to grapple lie "below" this "surface." Once we have explored these realities, we can reconstruct a modified "plane" which includes them; we "surface" them.

The danger of condescension lurks in this image. If I think that, with this method, I can dig into others' unconscious lives and motivations, diagnose their difficulties, and then treat these difficulties, I fall into condescension; I meet these others not as knowledgeable agents with whom I live in co-creative relations, but as objects of my care.

The danger is acute, and slipping into tacit condescension is perhaps inevitable, given the prevailing system of domination Les Nodale discussed. In the worlds we imagine and construct under the sway of domination, our everyday lives are empty of real meaning and order, which come from someplace else. A pastoral counselor unintentionally expressed this assumption: "Poor people seek meaning in their lives just like everyone else, and they are willing to pay for therapy in order to get it." In the therapeutic version of the system of domination, our presumably empty everyday selves are raw materials which therapists, counselors, and pastors, using their abilities to crack us open and see into our depths, convert into meaning which they then sell or, if they are generous, give back to us. Meaning comes from professional care givers' knowledge and skills.

The case studies so far presented in this book, as well as others, support John McKnight's claim that "the power to label people deficient and declare them in need is the basic tool of control and oppression in modern industrialized societies."[1] This power lies at the heart of condescension as an ideological justification of the system of domination. Using this power to deny people's agency, their power to participate in the decisions that affect their lives, to define themselves and their needs, is a primary cause of preventable suffering in our lives. In the professional service economy and the condescending therapeutic culture that both reflects and maintains it, we tend to idealize this power, to think, as the pastoral counselor implied, that meaning, and healing, and all manner of necessities come from it. Caught up in this ideology, we miss how this power denies and so undermines the meaning of our everyday lives, how it renders us anonymous, objectified raw materials, desperate consumers of the meaning we are told we lack, and driven and guilty professionals providing this idealized, immaterial, and esoteric meaning to others, even as we feel that we ourselves somehow lack it.

The fourth crack emerges with the question, Why, if it suggests this ideology, which I reject, do I use the metaphor of "cracks" in "surfaces"?

Dualism

I begin my exploration of the cracks and what lies hidden in them with this fourth crack. To be honest, I began using the image of "cracks" before I had isolated condescension as an issue. But I retain it because it remains useful, in that it identifies a crucial and sometimes obscured reality. The ideologies that reflect and legitimate the system of domination do construct reality both as a uniform "surface" and an esoteric "depth." A closer look at these ideologies uncovers (see how the metaphor extends even into critical discussions of it) the image of "depth" as another "surface" or "plane." For example, Milton Hightower, in his sermon, seemed to assume that the truth is like a plane that intersects and reveals the superficial character of our everyday lives, as in figure 3:

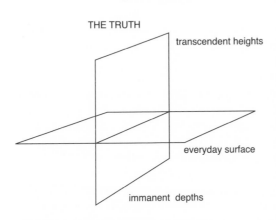

Figure 3: Dualism

THE TRUTH

transcendent heights

everyday surface

immanent depths

When Milton Hightower discussed "tithing," he placed it on the intersection of the two planes. He sought to reveal both the superficiality of our

---
[1] McKnight, 16.

everyday attitudes toward tithing (its position on the horizontal plane) and *The Truth* about it (its position on the vertical plane).

A crucial differentiation between the two planes characterizes Milton Hightower's discussion, as it does the thinking of others who fall into condescension. For Milton Hightower, the everyday surface is not "true"; it is a tissue of superficial observations, distortions, illusions, and convenient lies. Condescension joins the domination system in this presupposition (here expressed in terms of the metaphor) that truth lies on a vertical plane that cuts through everyday reality. For those who condescend, only the horizontal plane contains cracks or flaws; the vertical plane is wholly homogeneous, united, perfectly consistent, smooth.

This image points to the dualism inherent in condescension and the domination system. To put it theologically, when we condescend, we assume that the everyday world, the horizontal world, is a flawed reflection of the vertical reality, which God orders. In this divinely different vertical plane, we find *The Truth*, or meaning, that connects the immanent depths of our lives with the transcendent heights. The everyday surface of our lives is filled with cracks that trip us up. Only that meaning and truth and power and love that come from outside, above and below, this mundane surface can save us. Les Nodale and I have already discussed the destructive effects of this dualism.

Collapsing Dualism

While my use of the "cracks-in-the-surface" analogy may imply that I am proposing an alternative dualism, that this method gives us access to *The Truth* about *The Truth*, such an implication ignores one insight, emergent in repeated case studies, which is that the cracks are ubiquitous; no plane of experience, thought, feeling, or reality exists without them. In other words, no wholly homogeneous, unified, consistent, universal plane of *Truth* unites the essential depths of reality with the transcendent heights. Reality, at least as we know it, is cracked, and comparing it to a plane upon which we walk only works until we stumble into a crack. Then the "plane" fragments, and we can no longer "walk." Les Nodale discovered this truth in the experiences he described, which shattered his understanding of worship as access to a flawless and so perfectly comforting *Truth*. His insight was more radical, that the attempt to assert such a perfect *Truth* constructs and legitimates suffering and oppression; his painful experience of the plane of *Truth* was the crack into which he fell and which shattered his image of reality as two intersecting planes.

Les mourned the loss of this exalted sense of worship, which, while he maintained it, seemed to be healing. He had discovered in worship the idealized images of comfort and of a father who would not abandon him, who would secure his world in the face of suffering. In his mourning, the nature of this conception of *Truth* as a uniform, united homogeneous plane stands revealed. It is an image born, like all our images, of desire. To put it theologically, in the light of this insight, the vertical relation between our essential being and God collapses into the horizontal relations in which we continually desire, imagine, and construct each other.

If one were to take the diagram of dualism and collapse the two planes into one; if one were to assume, then, that one could not rise above or sink below everyday reality in order to observe it from a privileged external point; if one imagined oneself as walking on this plane, then the place where the two planes had been collapsed would initially appear to be a tangle of lines, cracks, or barriers. If one walked around this tangle, one would discover pairs of opposed terms, each pair linked by a barrier or bar. Some of these oppositions would be recognizable from the earlier discussions—for instance, *"The Truth"* versus "everyday reality," "transcendent heights" versus "immanent depths"; others would be new. If one climbed over, broke through, or walked around a barrier, one would discover what is hidden behind it. The two opposed terms with a bar between them and lines connecting each of them to the hidden reality would form a triangle. And so one would construct an analytic model my students and I have found useful in identifying the cracks and hidden realities in our descriptions and previous thinking. For example:

Figure 4: Two Triads Analyzing Dualism

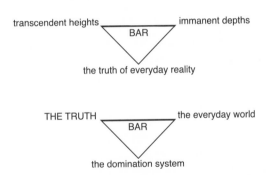

The "bar" in this model is another way of thinking about the "crack" in my earlier discussions. "Bars," like "cracks," indicate discontinuities, often between seemingly opposed or contradictory realities; they also, like "cracks," signal the presence of hidden realities.

This model diagrams both a dichotomous construction of reality that some thinkers say characterizes systems of domination, or at least Western patriarchal ones, and a way of thinking, also common to many of these critics, that opens up what is obscured by the dichotomous image. The model intentionally does not identify the specific character of either the bar between the two poles or the lines connecting these two poles to the barred reality. Given different elements, the relations among them are also different.

This model offers another response to the question implied by the last crack, the crack of cracks: Is there a way of thinking ethically that does not involve a condescending evaluation, from a transcendent height, of the hidden depths of a presumably superficial everyday reality? I moved toward an answer when I implied a triad (see figure 5) by writing that what I am proposing in this method is neither a "phenomenology" nor a "science" of care; rather, it is useful "bric-a-brac."

Figure 5: Phenomenology, Science, Bric-a-Brac

In using "phenomenology" and "science," I refer to perhaps the major dichotomies in modern Western thought, between *interpretation* and *explanation*, between *culture* and *nature*, between *meanings*

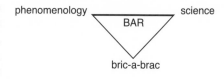

and *causes,* and between *relativism* and *universalism*. While there are exceptions to the following characterizations, phenomenologists tend to interpret the particular or relative meanings of cultural phenomena and scientists tend to explain the universal causes of natural events. The battles between what I am somewhat simplistically calling "phenomenologists" and "scientists" obscure an assumption they tend to share, that the meanings or causes they seek lie on a different and truer plane than the phenomena or events they examine; both interpretation and explanation tend to be means of getting at something hidden below or above everyday reality, taken as a superficial plane. In other words, both phenomenologists and scientists tend to be condescending. In using the word "bric-a-brac" to characterize the tools with which I think about care, I am seeking a different image of thought and research, one that does not so easily become condescending. "Bric-a-brac" refers to items I find or construct, tools that help me find a way to live. I am evoking a topographic image here. Rather than *mining* reality for the *gold* of *meanings* or *causes*, I am seeking a *way*. The criterion for a good theory in my way of thinking is not that it is meaningful or true, but that it is useful. I am not seeking what is hidden *by* the everyday surface of reality. When I fall into a crack or come up against a wall, I am seeking what is hidden by this particular crack or barrier *in* or *on* the surface. The analogue for a good theory in this image is a compass, a map, or, sometimes, a machete. In this model, ethics are not so much a matter of understanding or explaining what is good or right; ethics are what help us find ways of living fully that cause as little suffering as possible.

While different triads work in different ways, I have sensed that this model is useful because it points to a common tendency, at least in the West, to construct dichotomies to avoid suffering and its causes. When Les Nodale deconstructed the dichotomy between worship as safe and comforting and the everyday world as not, he discovered, lying behind his idealized image of worship, the domination system that was a cause of his and his family's suffering. To move beyond the bars constructed by the dichotomies is to move into the place of suffering. When we deny or bar suffering, we also deny or bar the participation of those who suffer in making our world. We cannot admit them as mutual co-creators because their voices inevitably awaken us to the reality of the suffering we seek to avoid. And so the link between care as mutuality and care as responsive to suffering reemerges. If we are to respond to suffering, we must confirm the mutual participation of those who suffer. If we are to realize the mutuality which is our life together, we must respond to each other's, and our own, suffering.

A map, a compass, or a machete is a limited tool, sometimes useful, sometimes not. Similarly, the theories I present in this book are not *Truths*; they are provisional truths I have found to be useful in my explorations of the topography of care. I have signalled the provisional character of these conceptual models in various ways. In the case studies, I kept and will keep coming back to the events to discover cracks in earlier understandings, which themselves were based on an exploration of the cracks in the description of the events. Similarly, in the discussions of the method and theories and metaphors I construct and use, I repeatedly point out the flaws, the cracks, in these constructions. Coming back to, identifying, and exploring new cracks in previous understandings, theories, and metaphors is not just a single step in this method; it is, as are the other tasks and movements, an ongoing work to which we repeatedly return as we think about care. Through this repeated examination of how I am thinking and composing this book, I have attempted to make my thinking and this method as transparent as possible. In other words, I have repeatedly called attention to the cracks in the plane of my own thinking.

CHAPTER 12

Heaven and Hell

Dualism, domination, and condescension are realities. As Les Nodale and I have explored them, they cause real suffering and then hide this suffering. If, as I propose, one definition of care is an ameliorating response to suffering, then, in order to care, we need to explore the topography of dualism, domination, and condescension. To switch metaphors, we need to see how they work and what drives them.

Les Nodale provided a valuable insight into how they work when he observed that the reason he held on to an idealized sense of worship was that, in this image, worship was a comfortable and safe place, where he seemed to be protected from the overwhelming suffering and insecurity of the rest of his life. Even as he was de-idealizing worship, he clung to this image, despite some wariness, when Susan Chance clearly articulated it in her sermon. This sermon exposes the desire lying behind dualism. Susan Chance said that Godly love or *agape* secures the communion service as unconditionally inclusive. She contrasted *agape* with human *eros*, in which we need, desire, and so hurt and are hurt by one another; *agape* is love purified of suffering and its causes.

The promise of dualism, which lies behind and motivates domination and condescension, is that we can have lives wholly filled with joy and wholly free of suffering, in other words that we can live in heaven and avoid hell. A modification of the two-planes image illustrates this promise (see figure 6).

Figure 6: Heaven and Hell

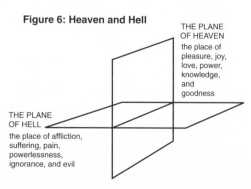

THE PLANE OF HEAVEN
the place of pleasure, joy, love, power, knowledge, and goodness

THE PLANE OF HELL
the place of affliction, suffering, pain, powerlessness, ignorance, and evil

Heaven is the plane of all that is good and of the knowledge and power to achieve and maintain this life of pleasure, joy, and love. Hell is the place of all that is evil and of the powerlessness and ignorance that keep us mired in affliction, suffering, and pain. In hell, we need and desire because we lack what we need and desire. In heaven, we do not need and desire because we have all that we need and desire. In hell, our love is always tinged by self-interest, while, in heaven, we love freely, with no self-interest.

Two insights lie in Les Nodale's disillusionment with worship. First is the contradiction lying at the heart of the construction of heaven. Heaven is a construction of desire, to maximize joy and eliminate suffering, that seemingly excludes desire; to live in the heaven one desires, one must not desire it; desire brings suffering and so contaminates heaven. Some misguided theologians and mystics have attempted to turn this contradiction into a paradox by locating the contradiction within desire, by saying that desire can only fulfill itself by extinguishing itself.

Second, the contradiction remains because of the failure of the attempt. The degree to which Les Nodale successfully idealized worship as heavenly was the degree to which he found himself in a hell of denied and unaddressed suffering. He discovered that the heavenly suppression of suffering does not eliminate it; rather, it intensifies it by alienating the suffering self from others and itself. The irony in heaven is that, in the attempt to build it, we construct our everyday lives as hell. As Les found, this hell is a social and material reality. In the desire for heaven, we attempt to isolate suffering and its causes—violence, disease, poverty—in certain groups of people. While this attempt fails to extinguish our suffering, it intensifies the suffering of those in whom we seek to locate our suffering, such as the farmers and their families during the farm crisis.

Unfortunately, the resulting contrast between those who seemingly live in heaven and those who reside in the hell of intensified suffering reinforces the impression that heaven is an achievable reality. The attempt by dominant elites to control access to the material and immaterial commodities necessary to life and so to that which brings pleasure, joy, and love and fends off pain, suffering, and affliction partially succeeds. In middle-class and wealthy suburbs as opposed to poor inner cities, in the first world as opposed to the third world, in communities as opposed to institutions, people generally live longer, do not suffer as much from physical want, do not afflict each other with as much violence, are healthier, have much greater opportunities to explore their own subjectivity and experience the joy of being co-creative agents, and have more time, energy, and freedom to devote themselves to loving and being loved. Socially, no matter where they live, within the physical "heavens" or "hells," those who are socially privileged, the citizens of "heaven," the elites, those who dominate—in America at this time, young and middle-aged adults as opposed to children and the aged, whites as opposed to people of color, Anglos as opposed to Hispanics and indigenous peoples, the middle class or wealthy as opposed to the working class or poor, professionals as opposed to nonprofessionals and clients, heterosexuals as opposed to homosexuals, the healthy as opposed to the ill, the able as opposed to the disabled, men as opposed to women—retain the benefits of "heaven" wherever they are, while the citizens of "hell" tend to remain relatively afflicted even if they migrate to a "heaven."

Still, in the social and material realms, the realizations of "heaven" and "hell" are partial. Even in the most "heavenly" physical places, "heavenly" citizens inevitably experience pain, suffering, and affliction. All have been children and have suffered some abuse. All will face pain and death. Almost all will become ill. All, at some times in their lives, and almost all throughout their lives, will occupy non-elite or subjugated positions in which they will suffer denials of their agency and subjectivity; they will be clients in relation to professionals, employees in relation to employers, the weaker in relation to the more powerful. On the other hand, even in the worst "hells" of our world, afflicted citizens experience a measure (however tiny) of pleasure, find joy (however transient) in co-creativity, and love (however ambivalently, ambiguously, and partially) each other. Given that pleasure, joy, and love are the signs of human life, if people still live, hell is not total.

Despite this partial failure of the realization of the two-planes ideology in the material and social realms, the domination system, in the form of global capitalism, uses it to great effect. Representatives of global capitalism represent the world as caught in a single movement from "undeveloped" economies, societies, and nations, the material and social manifestations of "hell," to "developed" ones, the manifestations of "heaven." The contrast between the relative riches of developed areas and the impoverishment of undeveloped locales supports the claim that the reason for the disparity is that those who are "developed" have got hold of a superior, universal, and unitary Truth, Power, and Goodness, and that those who are "undeveloped" are caught in inherently self-destructive and false ways of living and thinking. As the ethicist and theologian M. P. Joseph observes, in India as well as in the U.S., this understanding of "development" is so powerful and ubiquitous that even people committed to seeking alternative analyses and visions find no available common languages or popular cultural images through which they can effectively construct these alternatives.[1]

In the psychological realm, unlike the material and social realms, the ideology of a heaven as opposed to a hell can be fully realized, at least for a time. Neurologists, psychologists, and contemplatives from various traditions have observed that an individual or group is capable of experiencing periods of pure pleasure, joy, and love, in other words, of experiencing as empirically real a state of heaven, in which there is no pain, suffering, and affliction. According to developmental psychologists, all children

---

[1] M. P. Joseph, unpublished conversations with the author, Phillips Theological Seminary, Tulsa, Oklahoma, May 1998.

experience such heavenly states, both in the natural course of life and as a defensive response to experiences of abuse. Neurologists have traced the physical sources of such states to the release of endorphins, neuro-transmitters associated with experiences of pleasure. Group psychologists have studied how groups and communities can effectively project all pain, suffering, and affliction into one or more members of the group or outside the group, and so can experience the time and space in which the group meets as a realized "heaven." Contemplatives have observed that the perceptions and conceptions of reality in these purified states seem self-evidently, absolutely, and unquestionably True, apparently revelatory of Ultimate Reality. Such psychological states provide the experiential ground for the construction of the vertical plane of "heaven," in which dwell absolute Truth, Goodness (pleasure, joy, and love), and Power (to possess pleasure, joy, and love and to banish pain, suffering, and affliction). The group psychological observation that a group can come to associate such experiences with the presence of certain people, specific and regular times, and literal places experientially substantiates the claim, present in ideological justifications of the domination system, that "heaven" is a socially and materially achievable reality or Reality.

The same psychologists, group psychologists, and contemplatives who identify the psychological reality of heaven warn against taking this experience as a sign of the possibility of the final elimination of pain, suffering, and affliction. Neuropsychologists point out that the release of endorphins often occurs during experiences of traumatic or intense pain. While the resulting experience of pure pleasure and elimination of suffering may be adaptive, in that it sometimes protects a severely injured person from overwhelming and wholly disabling pain and so enables that person to do what is necessary to save her- or himself, it can also prevent a person from recognizing the pain as a signal of a threat to his or her life. Drugs that replace endorphins and so initially induce pleasurable states tend to become addictive. The body comes to rely upon them, experiencing no pleasure without them. And, in most cases, the addicted body requires increasing amounts of the drug to produce a high. In the end, drugs that initially produce heavenly states leave the addicted person in a hell in which he or she is nearly incapable of experiencing pleasure, joy, or love. In other words, endorphin-driven experiences, while they are heavenly in and of themselves, have ambiguous effects. They may contribute to terminal injuries, severe pain, suffering, and affliction.

Developmental psychologists and contemplatives join the neurologists in a recognition of both the adaptive and maladaptive uses of experiences of pure pleasure. On the one hand, such experiences establish the conviction necessary to life that the self and the world are, at bottom, good enough—life is worth living. Also, an abused child or adult may need to split the world into an idealized heaven and a hell in order to survive. But this maneuver legitimates abuse, afflicts the victims of abuse with the conviction that their pain and their resistance to it cause their suffering and affliction, binds them to idealized abusers, and so opens them to greater abuse. Contemplatives warn that attachment to experiences of bliss create even greater suffering when they inevitably end.

Group psychologists are the most concerned about the experience of purified pleasure, which, when it occurs in a group, results in "the group illusion," the conviction on the part of the members that the group, just as it is, is perfect. Group psychologists recognize that the group illusion is necessary to the maintenance of group cohesion. But when it pervades all the activities of the group, it results in cruel violence. Like all human beings, group members experience pain, suffering, and affliction, which they seek to avoid, and pleasure, joy, and love, which they seek to attain. As individual members seek to avoid what is negative and attain what is positive, they conflict with each other and with the group as a whole. Under the group illusion, any expression of pain, suffering, affliction, conflict, or violence threatens the group as the source of pleasure, joy, and love. When the group illusion rules, the members of the group respond to this threat with the belief that anything negative is its own cause; they thus seek to locate pain, suffering, affliction, conflict, violence, and their causes either in a particular member or group of members, another community, or the outside world. To the extent that the group is successful in this maneuver, the members experience the group as purely positive. However, in order to maintain this "heaven," the members of the group violate the designated containers of evil. They sacrifice, scapegoat, shun, or psychologically and sometimes physically torture individual containers. In order to defend themselves as innocent against an "evil" community or "world," they often, in highly provocative but seemingly innocent ways, provoke the "evil" community or world to violence, whereupon the good group will justify the use of unlimited violence to stamp out this evil threat. In other words, group psychologists argue that, in attempting to maintain the group as heaven, the group creates hell.[2]

Still, elites use the ability to achieve a psychological heaven to support the ideology of dualistic domination. Recolonization under global capitalism gains its power to extinguish all alternative ways of envisioning reality from the cultural appropriation of all that is pleasurable, joyous, and loving. Under global capitalism, the domination system first identifies, and then takes possession of, not only material resources, but also the particular ways the people of a culture experience pleasure, enact joy, and love each other, the valued patterns of interaction and the symbols, rituals, dramas, and religious visions growing out of them that identify a culture as unique. Multinational corporations transform these cultural resources into commodities provided, for a price, to those who originally created

---

[2] Didier Anzieu, *The Group and the Unconscious* (London: Routledge and Kegan Paul, 1984), 143–59; Roy Herndon SteinhoffSmith, "Euro-American (christian) Dreams of Love and Genocide," unpublished paper presented at 1996 American Academy of Religion, New Orleans.

them, as well as others. Through this transformation, global capitalism materially and culturally impoverishes third world peoples by exploiting their material and cultural resources, employing some of them at very low wages to transform these resources, and appropriating whatever resources they still possess by selling them the resulting material and cultural products. This system relies upon the use of the appropriated means of achieving psychological states of pleasure, joy, and love, now become cultural commodities, to construct a "heaven" that is presented to the impoverished residents. Through media and other means, global capitalism offers and provides these seductive experiences of purified pleasure, joy, and love, through which it convinces those whom it is impoverishing that their "hell" is their own fault and that their hope lies in further subjugation to the "development" that promises them permanent residency in a developed "heaven."

While the elites are seemingly in charge of this exploitation, they are also victims of it. The promise of heaven carries with it the equation of suffering with shame, failure, and evil. For those who identify themselves as members of the heavenly elite, this equation, along with the real intensification of the suffering of the denizens of "hell," makes any suffering wholly terrifying, a demon that threatens to consume and so to extinguish any possibility of pleasure, joy, or love. Driven by this terror and drawn by the lure of a "heaven" without suffering, elite citizens desperately plunder the world for any sources of pleasure, joy, and love that seem to promise a release from suffering. We (I assume that most of you who are reading this book are economically privileged—I certainly am) search the world for material and cultural "goods," consuming more and more material and immaterial resources, impoverishing more and more people who do not have the money to compete with us in buying the material and cultural goods they produce or even the land on which they live, the air they breathe, and the water they drink. We maintain a hellish economy in which even people who, like Les Nodale, awaken to it and seek to resist it, find that they are dependent upon exploitation in order to live. The popularity of the movement toward "simple living" among middle-class whites exposes this tragic irony. In a radio interview, a pair of authors who helped to initiate this movement happily discussed how one can carefully save and wisely invest one's money so that one finally has enough to live on stock dividends and interest and can quit one's exploitative job and have time free to devote to the pleasures of simple and ethical living. The authors seemed to have no awareness that, as they presented it, one can live simply and morally only if one is a member of a tiny economic elite that actually has enough income to save and invest and that, in relying upon investments in the stock market, one is participating in an institution that currently is a major contributor to the increasing global disparity between the very few wealthy people and the destitute masses. Heavenly simple living depends upon supporting and benefitting from an extremely complex and hellish global economy.

I am not intending to create guilt here. Elite guilt maintains the illusion that we privileged people can actually free ourselves from hell by doing the right thing, the illusion that we control our lives, that we are omnipotent.[3] I am reminded of the opening scene of the movie *Platoon*, in which an idealistic white private, obviously well-educated and from a middle-class background, steps off a helicopter at a base in Vietnam. A black soldier, who has clearly been there for some time and is equally clearly not from a privileged background, greets the white soldier and asks him how he got there. The newcomer says he volunteered. The black soldier ridicules him for choosing to come to the hell of Vietnam. It begins to dawn on the white soldier that guilty self-sacrifice might not be an adequate moral response in hell.

In using the word "hell," I also am not saying that there is no hope. Elite despair is the result of the dualism that takes the persistence of suffering to be the sign of the total collapse of the possibility of human meaning—of any real pleasure, joy, and love.[4] Les Nodale discovered that the opposite is the case. When he abandoned the illusion of heaven and faced the reality of hell, his suffering taught him to value his friendships and love with others who resisted what he called the domination system and to find hope in the resilience of those most subject to affliction and oppression, in other words, those most familiar with hell.

"Hell," as I am using it, is not a place of ultimate damnation; it is, rather, the world in which we actually live. I use the word "hell" to describe this place for three reasons. First, implicitly, if not always explicitly, "hell" is the name dualists give to everyday life. They state that we must be saved from this world of corruption and that this salvation must come from outside of it, because anything in this world is ruled by evil. Second, the adjective "hellish" accurately describes the logics through which dualistic elites implicitly seek to locate suffering and its causes in others and specifically the ways these logics rationalize afflicting the afflicted. Third, to the extent that dualistic domination goes unresisted, it constructs reality as truly hellish for larger and larger numbers of people. One does not have to revisit the horrors of the colonial genocide of indigenous peoples, of slavery, or of the Shoah to recognize this truth. One merely has to spend some time with some very poor people, to face the cruel and absurd contradictions they confront in attempting to provide for themselves and their families, while continually receiving devaluing and degrading treatment from those with whom they have to relate in order to live.

---

[3] Sharon Welch, *A Feminist Ethic of Risk* (Minneapolis: Fortress, 1990), 23–47.
[4] Ibid.

reach. From this time forward, she continually shapes her subjectivity and agency around the particular human and non-human others she meets; as she reaches and receives them, she constructs and shapes them and is constructed and shaped by them. She enters into the co-creative relational movement that we name reality or living.[2]

Relation, body, and self are the three registers of human life—all are primary. In the absence of relation, human bodies do not live and human selves do not come into existence. Bodies are the substance, the matter of human existence—without the body, there are no partners in relation. As indicated in the above narrative, the self comes into being as the child's bodily awareness, through the relation with the mother, turns back on and forms itself as a relation; the self is the body's relation to itself, an internal relation that first exists only as an external relation to the mother. More precisely, the child's self at first exists only in the mother's desire, her self, as the imagined other to whom the mother reaches. As the child matures into adulthood, his life is an ongoing repetition of the act through which he was born as a self, a continuous movement in which he reaches out to another, forms himself around this other, reaches back and grasps himself from this different position, and then, having been born anew as a relational self, reaches out to the other with new sensitivities and abilities, new capacities to form himself around the other.

While the external and internal others continually change, and so then does the self, there remain two continuities in human life, two that were once one, one's own body and the embodied self of the mother in whom one was born as a self. As one lives by reaching out to and forming oneself and being formed by others, one traces, in the very capacity for relation that constitutes oneself, the image of the original constituting relation to the mother.

Two irreducible movements constitute life as relation, the differentiation and communion of the self and the other; relation is the communion of the differentiated. One becomes a differentiated self only when one confirms and is confirmed, is in communion with, a differentiated other. In the absence of either differentiation or communion, there is no relation, no life, no self, no other.[3]

Desire, the movement of the human body toward life and away from death, is always double, always a movement toward both communion and differentiation, toward union as a differentiated self with the differentiated other. This double movement constructs a second and paradoxical double movement. Life always involves the risk of death. This paradox begins with bodily birth, in which the bodily separation between the mother and the child carries with it the risk of bodily death for each. Similarly with

---

[2] Roy Herndon SteinhoffSmith, "The Becoming of the Person in Martin Buber's Religious Philosophical Anthropology and Heinz Kohut's Psychology of the Self," Ph.D. dissertation, University of Chicago, 1985, 31–57, 116–46, 169–209.

[3] Martin Buber, *The Knowledge of Man: A Philosophy of the Interhuman*, ed. Maurice Friedman (New York: Harper, 1966), 60–64.

the birth of the self, when the infant grasps itself as a self, he or she breaks, for an instant, the unconscious communion with the mother in which he or she had previously lived. In becoming self-aware, he or she also becomes aware of two distances, two absences where there had been presences, between the self and the external other and between the self and the internal other. Psychological birth carries with it the risk inscribed in these absences, of the permanent absence of the relations that make life possible. Once born, the human self lives in a continual repetition of this risk, in a continual reaching for an other who may not be present or who may extinguish one by its overwhelming presence.

The two double movements of desire between the self and other construct the topography of pain and pleasure, suffering and joy, affliction and love. Pain, suffering, and affliction are the signs on the three registers—the body, the self, and relation—of threats to life. Pleasure, joy, and love are the corresponding signs of the movement toward life. Because human life is continually lived on all three registers (one is always an embodied relational self) and always involves the risk of death, each of these terms names a quality of human experience that has been abstracted from the whole lived event, in which all are present. One of these qualities may so dominate one's awareness during a certain period that the other qualities seem to have been extinguished, but they remain as realities that are inseparable from the abstracted experience one is having.

Pleasure is the bodily sign of the movement toward life. One experiences pleasure as a vitality, a surge or flow or release of energy, that accompanies the meeting of physical needs—for food, shelter, drink, health, comfort, elimination—or the exercise of the vital bodily and sensory functions and activities—perception, movement, breathing. Erotic pleasure, the sensory pleasure of the other, points to the inextricability of pleasure from life as relational.

As bodies, we experience pain as the sign of potentially life-threatening injury. For instance, we experience as a painful "ache" the possibly fatal effects both of a blow to the head and of hunger. The physical pain of grief over the loss of another points to the inextricability of pain from life as relation.

Joy is the psychological sign of the movement toward life. As the self is inherently relational, so is joy. We experience joy when we are confirmed by others or confirm ourselves as unique and differentiated agents and when the space of our subjectivity opens wide to include and delight in all manner of others. Joy is always accompanied by a measure of pleasure, in the forms of exhilaration, alertness, exuberance, or relaxed openness.

As selves, we experience suffering as a diminution of our capacity for action and of our awareness. While such psychological suffering often results from injury, deprivation, or pain, the experience of suffering itself is quite different from that of pain; psychological suffering eats us from within, gnawing at or tearing apart our sense of being someone, narrowing and sometimes nearly extinguishing the space of our awareness, limiting our ability to act. As selves, we experientially measure the intensity of physical pain by its capacity to cause us psychological suffering, to so contract our subjectivity and agency that we are aware only of the pain and lose any capacity to choose our actions.

Love is the relational movement toward life, the delight in the other, and the reception of the other's delight in us. With the experience of the communion with the other as differentiated, love opens subjective space wide and energizes agency as the reaching toward the other; love produces joy and so bodily pleasure.

Affliction is the effect of threats to the relations that sustain life. These threats may come from the self which, in the assertion of its own agency or the desire to grasp and hold on to the other, may either push the other away or deny the other's difference. Or the threats may come from the other, who is absent when one needs him or her, refuses to confirm one as a differentiated agent and subject, affirms one not for whom one is, but for what one is not, or directly attacks one as an agent and a subject. Such threats, whether they come from the self or the other, tend to collapse the space of subjectivity and to drain the self of its sense of ability or agency. Either directly, as in physical abuse, or indirectly, as in the depression that accompanies isolation and rejection, they cause physical pain.

The above discussion points the connections among, on the one hand, love, joy, and pleasure, and, on the other hand, affliction, suffering, and pain. Affliction by others is the cause of pain and suffering. Even when pain comes from a disease, say a heart attack, one experiences it as an affliction, an attack by that which is other than oneself, outside the sphere of subjectivity and agency. Similarly, while we experience psychological suffering as a destruction from within, we also experience the sources of this destruction as alien to ourselves—depression or madness *descends* on us. Psychological suffering is the measure of the intensity of either pain or affliction. When affliction directly or through the intensification of pain collapses subjectivity to a point and extinguishes agency, suffering is radical.[4]

Similarly, love is the source of joy and pleasure. We experience both joy and pleasure as signs that we love and are loved. We also tend to measure love and pleasure by the joy we feel. In the absence of joy, even the most intense bodily pleasure can come to seem empty, exhausting, and even painful, and we begin to question whether we do indeed love or are loved. This insight reveals why the attempt to turn pleasure, joy, and love into commodities eventually fails, why the attempt to construct a heaven in which these commodities are abundant results only in a sense of emptiness and increasingly desperate consumption. A commodity is not and

---

[4] Scarry, 27–59; Dorothee Soelle, *Suffering*, trans. Everet R. Kalin (Philadelphia: Fortress, 1975), 13–16; Simone Weil, "The Love of God and Affliction," in *Waiting for God*, trans. Emma Craufurt (New York: G. P. Putnam's Sons, 1951), 117–25.

cannot be a differentiated other, with whom I am in relation, whom I love. The attempt to commodify pleasure, joy, and love cuts people off from the everyday relations that are the presuppositions of these positive realities. In other words, to the extent that we commodify pleasure, joy, and love, we destroy the possibility of pleasure, joy, and love.

Recognition of the relational register as determinative reveals the inevitable interweaving of pleasure and pain, joy and suffering, and even love and affliction in human life. When one reaches for another, to the extent that the other is truly different, one's reach will always be somewhat clumsy and may be destructive and painful. A child gleefully grasps a butterfly in her hand and opens it to find the beautiful wings crushed and the butterfly dead. She cries out, not only because she has lost the beauty she so desired to know but also because this unintentional act of destruction rebounds upon herself, in a bleak rejection of herself, a distrust which she almost immediately projects onto the butterfly, throwing it to the ground and calling it "Stupid!" The vicissitudes of relational life involve continual experiences in which, because of the very newness of each meeting, we, even with the best of intentions, hurt others, isolate ourselves, and open ourselves to unintentional and intentional rejection and affliction. And we all, like the child, inevitably construct defenses, through which, while trying to protect ourselves from hurt, we increase the hurt to ourselves and others. A life of love, joy, and pleasure is, in the best of circumstances, also a life of affliction, suffering, and pain.

This theoretical narrative provides a map for how the logic of abuse emerges in all infants. The logic of abuse is a result of the child's remarkable resilience in maintaining the relations that sustain him or her, even in the face of intense affliction, suffering, and pain. A young child is physically and psychologically vulnerable to abuse. Physically, because of neurological and psychological immaturity, a child sometimes experiences as intensely painful what an adult would identify as mild discomfort. Psychologically, because their nascent sense of self is formed around others' ongoing confirmation of them as good and competent, young children are extremely vulnerable to any signs of the withdrawal of this confirmation; such withdrawals, or sometimes even indications of them, cause severe psychological suffering. When a child experiences a person upon whom he or she depends for confirmation and so whom he or she desires, in other words, a person whom he or she loves and looks to receive love from, as inflicting intense physical pain and severe psychological suffering on him or her, she or he, in order to protect the needed and desired relation to the abusive other, divides the world in two. In one world, the idealized one, the presence of the loved and loving other brings bodily pleasure and psychological joy; the child experiences pleasure and joy as gifts from the other. In the other world, what Les referred to as the "nightmare," severe pain and suffering are signs of the absence of the loved and loving other; he or she experiences his or her pain and suffering as the cause of the absence and so as the cause of his or her pain and suffering. Because all children sometimes experience their parents and other nurturing adults as inflict-ing intense physical pain and severe psychological suffering on them, this division of the world into a heaven in which the loved and loving other rules and a hell seemingly created by one's tortured self sometimes charac-terizes the psyche of all young children. In other words, at certain times in their lives, the logic of abuse orders the psyche of all children.

In most children's lives, good, loving, trusting experiences, those in which the presence of a loved and loving other allows the child to inte-grate pain and suffering into a world that remains fundamentally good, predominate over the experiences of the world as divided into heaven and hell, and so the logic of abuse remains one among a number of ways of responding to reality. But it does remain, in the adult as well as the child, as an available perceptual, conceptual, and behavioral pattern or drama that certain circumstances, especially the experience of suffering, can activate. One of these circumstances is being a parent. As parents nurture and inevi-tably afflict their children, they experience abuse from the other side, as abusers. This experience can tempt the parent into the idealization of power and identification with the abuser and so into the appropriation of the logic of abuse from the position of power.

Group psychoanalysts have observed that, in groups, people often ex-perience and construct each other as players in dramas that replicate the experiences of young children.[5] A group can and often does assign the role of victim to a person who has not previously been seriously abused, and this designated victim then experiences the group's psychological attacks as what they are, abuse. In other words, groups, such as churches, can and do severely abuse people and so awaken and strengthen the logic of abuse in these people's lives. In such a group or community, those who perpe-trate the abuse also experience themselves as abusers, even if they deny this experience and are not abusive outside the group; through the group, the logic of abuse becomes unconsciously and sometimes consciously ac-tive in their lives. This theory makes sense of why Les Nodale experienced the worship services, in which the congregation gathered as a group, as abusive and himself as occupying both positions, that of victim and of perpetrator.

The group psychoanalyst Didier Anzieu observes that large groups (from twenty to about two hundred members) are where internal indi-vidual psychological reality and external social and historical forces meet and shape each other.[6] Moving from individual experiences to social move-ments, through the replication of early childhood experiences in large groups, what had been internal psychological or familial dramas become communal ones. Freed from their sources in childhood experiences, the characters and logics of these dramas come to characterize the ways those

---

[5] Anzieu, 100–142.
[6] Ibid., 255–61.

not connected by family ties act toward each other. People find themselves experiencing, acting toward, and constructing each other in ways that replicate the logics established in childhood. Groups then enact these logics in relation to other groups; they become social realities. For instance, the childhood relation between a powerful, nurturing, and at least sometimes abusive parent and a vulnerable, dependent, and sometimes victimized child comes to characterize some relations among members of communities, such as churches, and some relations between communities, for instance, between some churches and their surrounding neighborhoods. In other words, insofar as the logic of abuse pervades these communities and society as a whole, these communities and the society they constitute become abusive.

The movement between individual experience and social reality also works in the reverse direction, from society to the individual. The social enactment of these dramas reproduces and reinforces them as real and powerful. For instance, the relation between the all-powerful abuser and nurturer and the dependent one who is both nurtured and victimized becomes a drama that adults experience as just the way things are—reality— and so they socialize their children, they bring them into this drama, by both nurturing and dominating them in authorized and assumed ways that are sometimes abusive. The children take this drama in as reality, and so the cycle repeats itself.

But replicated childhood experiences are not the sole determinant of social interactions. Individuals, groups, communities, and societies also seek access to and possession of material resources that are necessary for life—food, water, and shelter. These individuals, groups, communities, and societies organize themselves to distribute these resources by constructing social dramas. These dramas contain a limited range of characters and certain fixed patterns of interaction. Governed by a drama that they experience as reality, the members of a community assign each other, nonmembers and other communities roles in this drama as they enact it.

One common way people organize themselves to distribute resources is through the domination system Les Nodale described. In this system, a certain group of individuals takes and maintains sole possession of resources and access to them and distributes the resources to themselves and others. Such a system tends to transform the relational prerequisites of life— bodily pleasure in the presence of the gratifying other, joy in one's exercise of co-creative agency with and in being a subject in relation to others, and love as the relation to desired others who also desire one—into commodities possessed by the privileged elite. These rulers appropriate childhood dramas of dependency on, and abuse by, nurturing parents to legitimate their power over others. In using parental images and metaphors to legitimate their rule, those who dominate make their power over others seem wholly natural, the way reality is, and good, in that these rulers portray themselves as like those who have given us life.[7]

But as those who dominate utilize the parental drama, they also change it. The drama only serves the interests of the rulers if it is purified of mutuality. In other words, reconstructing "being a parent" as an ideological defense of an economic and political system of domination requires the conception of "parents" as possessing a power purified of any evil and any cause of suffering and the conception of "children" as both passive recipients of "parental" nurture and as sources, or containers, of suffering and its causes. So reconstructed, the "parental" drama effectively legitimates the domination system; it associates superior power with goodness and lack of power with suffering and evil; it constructs those who dominate as the source of all goods and others, "children," as either consumers of such goods or recalcitrant, but finally and ultimately, powerless agents of evil. Communities enact this reconstructed "parental" drama; their members take it into their own lives as descriptive and normative, as the way parents do and should treat children. Through the ideological appropriation and reconstruction of the parental drama (now the "parental" drama), the dominating class reinforces precisely those elements that result in the establishment of the logic of abuse, the experience of suffering as its own cause and the purification of abusive power.

Les Nodale identified and resisted the reconstructed "parental" drama implicit in the three services he attended. The drama emerged most clearly in the sermon about sacrifice. The preacher performed the reconstructed drama. A good or faithful parent was one who appropriated all agency, subjectivity, and power in himself (the founder of Habitat is a man) and treated others either as the recipients of his goods (the poor who received homes and the beneficent presence of the founder living among them) or as obedient and powerless objects of his activity (the sacrificed daughter). Out of his experience of being a parent of a daughter and of being the child of a father who sacrificed, in other words, of being in both positions in the parent-child relation, Les protested that this portrayal of parenthood both violated his experience, which included recognition of parents as sometimes abusive and of children as agents and sources of good, and, by justifying abuse, tempted him and other parents to become more abusive.

To summarize this part of my analysis, the logic of abuse has its sources both in experiences of being abused and abusing and in ideological justifications of economic and political domination. These two sources construct and strengthen each other through the mediation of groups or communities that replicate, reconstruct, and enact abusive parental and "parental" dramas, as in the following illustration:

---

[7] Roy Herndon SteinhoffSmith, "The Boundary Wars Mystery," *Religious Studies Review* 24:2, April 1998, 131–42.

Figure 7: The Logic of Abuse

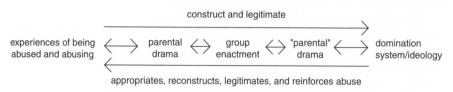

This discussion of the logic of abuse clarifies the pattern formed by the cracks I have identified. The issue of idealization links the "crack of cracks" and the relation between care as reality and care as ethical norm. In Les's experience, idealization or the splitting off of "heaven" from "hell" emerges as a necessary and adaptive response to the fused experience of abuse, powerlessness, and responsibility, that fusion which defines what it means to be a "victim." For a victim, idealization defends the experiences of nurturing, power, and good, which are necessary for life, from the overwhelming and annihilating experiences of abuse. Idealization also, by emptying the victim of anything that resists the abuser's will and intensely focusing the victim's attention on the abuser's behaviors, can, in some cases, help the victim to avoid lethal abuse; in other words, for a highly vulnerable victim, idealization can spell the difference between life and death.

Idealization constructs the dualism discussed in the "crack of cracks" discussion. It creates the two planes of reality, the horizontal hell in which victims bring their own abuse upon themselves and the vertical heaven in which the Ruler is the source of all good. Because it constructs those who possess greater power as both innocent and the sources of all good, members of the dominating class can and do appropriate idealization as legitimating their domination. One way they do so is by locating ethical norms on the vertical or idealized plane, just as Susan Chance did in her sermon on *agape*. They promulgate the ideology, born of the logic of abuse, that only if our values are rooted in a supreme and dominating power that is purely good do we have any hope; or, in Susan Chance's sermon, only an *agape* purified of desire and need is finally reliable. According to this ideology, the evil that dominates this world will eventually overcome an ethic that finds its source in this mundane horizontal and ambiguous surface of life. In other words, ethical arguments that rest on strictly differentiating the *is* from the *ought* (or, in this book, what care is from what care should be) tend to root themselves in and to legitimate both domination and the logic of abuse.

Les Nodale's account and the above analysis point to contradictions in the two-planes ideology that we have not yet identified. The "goods" that this ideology locates in "heaven" are actually derived from everyday life, what the ideology construes as "hell." As we have seen, everyday relations create the ethical ideals and purified states of pleasure, joy, and love that characterize "heaven." Perhaps more significantly, our discussion of the logic of abuse, which constructs the two spheres, reveals that those heavenly beings who apparently possess all power, knowledge, and good depend upon the power, knowledge, and goodness of their victims. The contradiction in both abuse and torture is that, even as abusers apparently seek to annihilate the agency and subjectivity of their victims, they also require this agency and subjectivity. Only a victim who is an agent can confirm the abuser's power by his or her act of acquiescence; a wholly objectified, passive, or dead victim cannot do anything.

In fact, surviving as a victim requires great subjective strength, evident in the capacity to control the body's most fundamental responses to pain. It also requires a nearly unlimited capacity for moral agency, as the victim takes upon her- or himself responsibility not only for her or his own suffering but also the suffering of the abuser. Finally, surviving as a victim requires close attention to and incisive and detailed knowledge of the abuser and the way the abuser constructs the world.

I am not intending to romanticize victims here. Being a victim means utilizing one's power, moral agency, and knowledge in the service of the domination system. But recognition of the presence of these "heavenly" attributes in the victim is important for two reasons. First, it reveals the dependency of those who dominate on those who are dominated. "Heaven" is not an autonomous realm, as its ideologues claim.

Second, and most importantly, it points to the inherent instability in the domination system and the openings for subversion of it. The degree to which a victim survives by nurturing these virtues will be the degree to which he or she can identify and utilize opportunities to throw off his or her status as a victim and subvert the domination system. The Syrophoenician woman displayed these virtues when she subverted Jesus' domination. Asserting her power, she defied his characterization of her as a cringing and unclean "dog." Asserting her moral agency, she implicitly rejected as morally wrong his refusal to heal her daughter. Asserting her incisive knowledge of his rhetorical strategies, she utilized these same strategies to present her argument. Les Nodale's story is similar. Through his close attention to (born of his idealization of) those in power in the worship services, he awakened to the inconsistencies and contradictions in what they were saying; idealization resulted in de-idealization. He mobilized his moral agency—developed partially as he wrestled with his sense, born of domination, of responsibility for his father's death and so for his own and his mother's and sisters' suffering—in his evaluation of the worship leaders' actions and words and of his own participation in the domination system. He displayed his power when he resisted the domination system by acting against it in and after each service. From these cases, then, we learn that, even as the domination system constructs "hell," it also constructs breaches in the walls of "heaven" in which the denizens of hell can construct ways of living that resist the abusive system.

Les tacitly established an ethical alternative to the dualistic ethic that grounds morality in heaven. Notice that, for Les, what he imagined as good, his measure of care, his ethical norm, was born out of his experience of care and of what extinguished it. He could engage in ethically imagining care because he knew that care was both foundational to life and fragile. Numerous developmental psychologists, sociologists, political theorists, and anthropologists confirm this connection between the *is* and the *ought*. The experiences of what sustains life are the source of the ability both to identify when these conditions are absent and to imagine how to make them present again. For example, recently, National Public Radio reported on a study of Gentiles who hid Jews during the Shoah. All had experienced, throughout their lives, close and affirming relations with people very different from themselves. These Gentiles knew, from their experiences, that relations with different others sustain life; they correctly identified the Shoah as extinguishing such relations, and they did what they could to protect and extend such relations.

The reason the ethical imagination is fragile is the same reason life is fragile. We can and do neglect, abuse, and destroy these webs of caring relations that sustain life. When we do so, we diminish the capacity for ethical imagination and so for moral activity. Still, where there is life, there are also the mutually caring relations that sustain life, and so the ethical imagination lives.

CHAPTER 14

"Fixing" Suffering

The above discussion has prepared us for a detailed examination of condescension as the predominant ethic of the service economy. Condescension is a dualistic ethic that rationalizes, through idealization, the power of those who dominate, by locating suffering and its causes in others. A critique of condescension requires de-idealizing it by exploring the political and economic interests that it both obscures and supports. Such political and economic critiques are essential to the construction of a practice of mutual care that effectively resists domination and condescension.

In the case study "Teaching and Learning Care," the student wanted counseling skills because she thought they would help her respond to the people for whom she cared. She and I both assumed that these parishioners were the ones who were suffering, and we were not. Yet hidden in our conversation were traces of our own suffering. Her suffering was evident in the urgency with which she approached me. Somehow, she felt, she had not been as effective as she should or could have been in alleviating the suffering of those for whom she cared, and this failure was gnawing at her. And, in my understated insistence that I knew that she knew how to care, and so in my very denial of her indirect confession of suffering, in my desire to fix her up with what she really needed, I betrayed my own defensive denial of the persistent ubiquity of suffering, in those for whom she (and I) cared, in her (in her failure), and in myself (in my own failure to fix up those for whom I cared).

A closer examination reveals a pattern in our responses to suffering. We both assumed that suffering was fixable, using either the correct techniques or methods. We took the persistence of suffering to mean that we had somehow failed, betraying our assumption (and also our discomfort with this assumption) that we could eliminate suffering. Connected to the notion that suffering is fixable is the idea that it and its causes are located or isolated in someone else. So the student tended to assume that suffering was located in her parishioners, and I tended to assume that suffering was located in the student's sense of failure and lack of recognition of her own abilities. The pattern of condescension emerges with the realization that we both assumed that we could, or should be able to, fix this suffering in someone else. We can only fix something we can control. To consider another's suffering as fixable is to construe that other person as an object we control, in other words to dominate that other by denying her or his subjectivity and agency.

The ubiquitous and uncontrollable character of suffering means that we often fail to fix it. One way to control something we can't fix is to get rid of it. But suffering is unlike garbage (or seemingly unlike, but actually very like it; as ecologists point out, we never get rid of garbage); we can't just throw suffering away— it does persist; and so the attempt to "get rid of" suffering is a denied denial of it. We deny it in thinking that it is something that can be got rid of, and then we deny it in thinking that we have got rid of it.

In saying that the student had successfully cared, I both denied her suffering in her failure and denied this denial; I, in essence, implied that, if she were going to remain in my class, she would have to discard her conception of herself as failing, herself as suffering. The consequence of this denied denial becomes evident in the fact that, if the student had failed my class (she didn't; she did very well in it), I would have been able to dismiss any concern about her with the ironic judgment that, since she had failed to learn my way of getting rid of suffering, she wasn't "fixable" or "good seminary material." This seemingly innocuous phrase is the expression of a horrifying assumption. While we cannot wholly eliminate suffering and its causes, we can get rid of people, especially if we have already tacitly construed them as "material" with a flaw, in other words, as containing unfixable suffering and its causes.

This exploration turns up connections between care as mutuality and care as responsive to suffering, and between the ubiquity of suffering and its denial. Overwhelmed by the ubiquity and persistence of suffering, we construct condescension as a way of denying it. When we condescend, we construe suffering as a fixable flaw and then afflict others by constructing them as containers of this suffering and its causes, as objects that can be fixed or discarded. To deny other's self knowledge and agency is to dehumanize them, to deny their mutuality as co-creators, as living participants in the construction of reality. In other words, by denying mutuality, condescension both causes suffering and denies the suffering it causes. In order to respond to this suffering, one must affirm the mutuality of the suffering other.

But doesn't suffering sometimes, even often, conform to the definition condescension gives to it? Isn't it often caused by some internal physical, psychological, or social injury, disease, or flaw? Don't medical and other care professionals often effectively diagnose, treat and, in that sense, "fix" suffering in their patients or clients? If so, wasn't the student correct in her assumption that she might be failing in her caring responses to her parishioners because she did not have the professional skills and knowledge that I, as a care professional, could give her? And wasn't I correct to assume that I could teach her about a more effective way to care?

The answer to all these questions is "yes." But this affirmation does not change the analysis or evaluation of condescension presented above. Even if condescending professionals effectively treat some suffering, they also, to the extent that they deny the agency of their patients and clients, cause it. Examination of therapeutic discourse reveals how this denial happens.

Current discussions among therapeutic professionals commonly pit advocates of a "medical" approach against advocates of a "psychological" or "psychosocial" or "systemic" approach to "treatment" of what are usually defined as "psychiatric," "psychological," "mental," or "emotional" disorders. The medically oriented professionals (currently ascendent) tend to view mental disorders primarily as variations of physical diseases, with physiological causes; they rely on drugs and other physical interventions to treat the resulting "psychological pain" and its presumably physical causes. The psychological professionals tend to view these disorders as caused either by past experiences or current family (systemic) relations. They treat their clients using variations of talk therapy, focused either on intrapsychic or intrasystemic change.

The often vehement debates between representatives of these two groups, and sometimes within the psychological camp between those who focus on intrapsychic dynamics and those who focus on systemic dynamics, disguise what they agree on and what they do not see. In their discussions, these care professionals tend to agree that what ails their clients comes from within the unit they are analyzing. For the "medical" professionals, the causes of suffering come from within the body; for the intrapsychic professionals, the causes of suffering come from pathological intrapsychic relations rooted in the client's individual history; for the systemic professionals, the causes of suffering come from "dysfunctional" relations within the family system. Even if some of them vociferously disagree with their colleagues in their recognition of external political, economic, cultural, or ecological forces, they tend, in their practice, to focus on how suffering results from the pathological effects of incarnations of these powers within the unit they are treating. They almost unanimously agree that the effective response to suffering begins with a professional diagnosing the pathological cause of suffering (be it physical, intrapsychic, systemic, or political) *in* the unit. Treatment involves adjusting the internal dynamics of the unit from the outside, often by temporarily entering the unit. In other words, current care professionals tend to view the client as an embodied self (or, in the case of couples, families, or groups, as a collective body and collective self) that suffers physical or psychological pain; they tend to ignore or discount the constitution of this embodied self (or collective embodied self) by its relations to others and so as vulnerable to affliction.[1] (See figure 8.)

These professionals thus tend to respond to suffering by isolating the unit being treated from relations to other units. This assumption holds true even for those therapeutic professionals who view the "treatment relation" itself as the means of therapy. When these care professionals talk or write about the "treatment relation," they are rarely talking about the "real" social relation between the client and the professional; they are almost always talking about a specially constructed "therapeutic relationship" in which the therapist enters and functions as part of, an other within, the client's self.

Figure 8: Therapeutic Triads

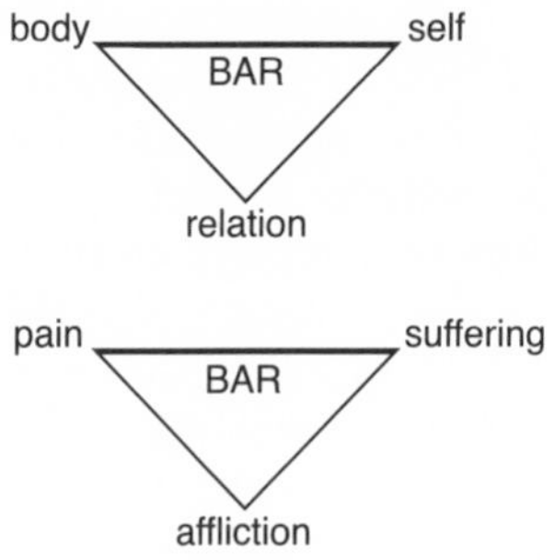

body ———————— self
BAR
relation

pain ———————— suffering
BAR
affliction

In other words, therapeutic professionals tend to be condescending. They tend to assume that care occurs in a relation between a professional with power, skills, and knowledge of what is good and a client (be it an individual, couple, family, or community) who has been disabled by some internal malfunction. They tend to discount the client as an agent in the relation and so the reality of mutuality, as in the following diagram (see figure 9).

Figure 9: Professional, Client, Mutuality

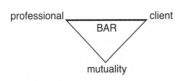

professional ———————— client
BAR
mutuality

When care professionals discount the ongoing relational constitution of the self, they tend, as a result, to ignore the care relation itself as a possible cause of suffering. But notice that, given the definitions of suffering and affliction offered above, condescension, in its devaluation of the client's agency and subjectivity, ability to participate in the relation and knowledge of self, afflicts the client; it is a tacit attack on the client as a co-creative, relational self. The condescending professional tends to locate suffering and its causes in the client, asserts that the client is responsible for his or her own suffering, including the suffering actually caused by the professional's devaluation of the client's agency and subjectivity, and assumes that the client is dependent upon the professional for liberation from suffering. In other words, therapeutic professionals tend to prescribe as the cure for suffering precisely the condescension that afflicts the client.

---

[1] Archie Smith, *The Relational Self: Ethics and Therapy from a Black Church Perspective* (Nashville: Abingdon, 1979), 39–41.

Evidence for the above argument against condescension lies in what we, as care professionals or following the lead of care professionals, do to people whose "condition" is considered untreatable: the chronically ill, the disabled, and the dying. Such people threaten the prevailing professional and condescending understanding of suffering as "fixable." And so we "take care of" such people. We get rid them by abandoning them in institutions, such as asylums and nursing homes, where care professionals, directly or indirectly, through the technicians they supervise, destroy these patients' agency by wholly controlling their activities and crush their subjectivity by severely limiting their relations to each other and the rare visitors they receive and by reducing to a bare minimum those meaningful possessions around which any of us constructs a sense of "my" space. The affliction and psychological suffering in such institutions are palpable; one can feel the isolation, alienation, the subjective impoverishment, despair, powerlessness, fear, and, sometimes, rage when one enters them.

The affliction and psychological suffering are measurable in that those who do not suffer from serious emotional illnesses when they enter these institutions often suffer from diagnosable psychiatric disorders after they have been there a few weeks. Often such disorders go undiagnosed. Sometimes a physician will simply prescribe antipsychotic medication for a patient exhibiting "psychiatric" symptoms. As they are used in these institutions, these antipsychotics are chemical versions of straitjackets, drugs that, especially in nonpsychotics (and most residents of nursing homes are depressed, not psychotic), wholly fragment whatever subjectivity or agency patients might retain. The fact that a significant percentage of the people in such institutions routinely receive less anti-pain medication than is needed to control their physical pain clinches the argument that these institutions of condescension afflict, rather than heal their residents.

CHAPTER 15

The Construction and Uses of Cases

The poor who came to the Mamre meal were, like those we place in institutions, "labeled" people. We who are privileged tend not to see these people as individuals, for instance, not as individual people who happen not to have homes, but as wholly defined by their label, as "the homeless."[1] I suggested another theory that describes the reality of the poor who came to Mamre when I admitted that I initially responded to them as if they were members of "a different species." Such a theory clarifies how we can treat those we place in institutions so inhumanly. We don't really consider them to be human beings like ourselves.[2] Another term that describes this phenomenon is "stereotyping." We stereotype people when we identify them wholly with one of their characteristics, assume that their possession of this one characteristic means that they possess a whole range of other characteristics, and so do not respond to them as different and unique human individuals, like ourselves. I initially stereotyped the poor who came to Mamre as "the least," assumed that, because they were poor, they were also wholly disabled and dependent; and so I did not recognize them as individuals, like myself, with different needs, abilities, and characteristics.

Care, medical, and criminal justice professionals "served" most of the poor who came to Mamre. Yet usually these professionals did not call these poor people "clients"; they were instead "cases."[3] John McKnight's theory

---

[1] McKnight, 103–23.

[2] I believe it was Erik Erikson who identified this phenomenon as "pseudo-speciation."

[3] This use of "case" is different than, but related to my use of "case" as in "case" study. Service professionals generally use "case" to refer to a person, family, group of people, or situation upon which they work. In my method, I remove the boundary between the one who studies or works and the one being studied or worked on. I recognize the researcher or professional as the central figure in the "case"; as a researcher, I study and work on my own practice.

points to the significance of the distinction between "clients"; and "cases," as well as other distinctions obscured by the use of the word "client." We tend to assume that a "client" receives, pays for, and is the primary beneficiary of professional services. McKnight questions this fusion of what I shall call "cases," "consumers," and "beneficiaries." "Cases" are the "raw materials" of the service economy, upon whom the professional works. "Consumers" are those who pay for the services. "Beneficiaries" are those who reap the benefits of the professionals' work. McKnight suggests that the primary beneficiaries of services are neither cases nor consumers; they are the professionals themselves and the service economy as a whole. Professionals transform consumers' needs into disabilities, which only the professionals can identify and treat. Despite ideological protests to the contrary, this transformation often primarily benefits neither the consumer who purchases the services nor the case upon whom the professional works, even if the consumer and the case are the same person.[4]

When McKnight talks about people as "raw materials," he is describing the similarities between service and manufacturing economies. Mapping these similarities on triads clarifies them. The relations in a manufacturing economy are as follows (see figure 10).

Figure 10: Manufacturing Economy Triads

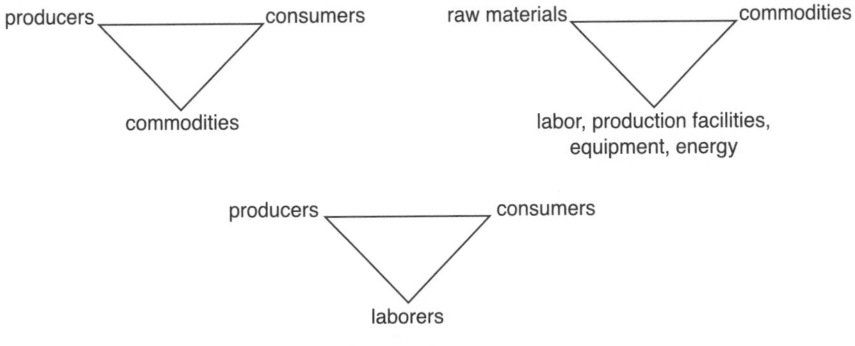

Producers sell commodities to consumers. Production is the transformation using labor, production facilities, equipment, and energy of raw materials into commodities. The human relations are among producers (or owners or "bosses"), laborers, and consumers. Today, in the manufacturing economy, these relations are transparent, there are no bars between them (although there are other bars).

Commodities are something we need or desire that we cannot provide for ourselves or each other in our family or communal relations. Unable to produce what we need or desire for ourselves, we buy these commodities from those outside our family or community who do produce them.

---

[4] McKnight, 36–51.

Communal disability creates the demand for commodities. An illustration: Imperial, colonial, and, now, global market economies produce disabilities out of communal and national material needs and desires. Current development programs focus on bringing "undeveloped" countries and regions into the "global market" by, for instance, transforming fields used for rice production into corporate shrimp farms. This "development" not only provides the previously self-contained rice farming community with a commodity that it can export to those who are unable to produce shrimp; it also creates a shortage of rice among those who had previously fed themselves from their own fields; they become disabled as rice producers; rice becomes a commodity that they must buy from other producers.[5]

In manufacturing economies, human material needs and desires are an essential raw material, which the economy transforms into disabilities and thus the demand for material commodities. In the service economy, nonmaterial or relational needs and desires are the raw materials that service providers transform into disabilities, therefore creating a demand for nonmaterial commodities or services. Often, especially in the service economy, the construction of disability and so demand remains hidden or barred.

The service economy tends to bar recognition of the interplay of disability and demand for three related reasons (see figure 11). The first is the ideology, especially prevalent among medical and therapeutic professionals, that the

Figure 11: The Barring of Disability and Demand

relation between themselves and clients is not primarily economic, but is about the compassionate meeting of human needs. The second is the fact that, in this country, most consumers in the service economy are middle or upper class, in other words, people who do not consider themselves disabled and might not buy the services if doing so meant admitting to disability. The third is the largely barred reality that opened this discussion, the distinctions among cases, consumers, and beneficiaries. McKnight suggests that service workers benefit primarily themselves by charging consumers for their work on cases. The reason consumers pay for work often done on others is that service professionals are very good at using cases to construct disabilities out of potential consumers' needs and desires, then isolating these disabilities and their causes in the cases, separated from the consumers, reframing this act of separation as the effective control or healing of the disability, and then selling this work as a valuable service to consumers.[6] Cases are thus not merely raw materials; they are also the

[5] Joseph.
[6] McKnight, 36–52.

evidence and deposit of service professionals' work. They are the commodities of the service economy.

Exploring the relations among cases, consumers, and beneficiaries in three sectors of the service economy, the medical, the criminal justice, and the therapeutic, confirms the usefulness of this conceptual map and extends it.

The Medical Sector

In the medical sector of the service economy, the differentiations among cases, consumers, and beneficiaries at first seem unhelpful. It appears that most of those upon whom medical professionals work both usually pay for and benefit from the services. If such patients aren't consumers, if they can't or don't pay for these services directly or indirectly (through insurance), as in the case of indigent patients, the medical professional is ethically obligated to act in the best interests of—in other words, to benefit—the patient.

But a second glance at six common medical situations reveals the naivete of this view. I've already introduced the first situation, that of institutionalized patients. Here, even if the patients technically pay for their medical treatment, directly or through insurance or through Medicaid or Medicare, control over these payments usually lies in others' hands, those of guardians, healthy or younger family members, or payees. As indicated by the overuse of antipsychotic medications in these institutions, the purpose of medical treatment in this situation often appears to be the control and pacification of patients. Whose need, turned into a disability, is really treated here, if not the patients'?

For close relatives, the answer appears to be their need and inability to provide care for chronically ill, disabled, or dying relations. The breakup of the extended family and the rise of single-parent families and nuclear two-parent families in which both parents must work make it very difficult for relatives to provide ongoing care for chronically bedridden patients. In addition, the medical profession has convinced us that the overriding ethical consideration in the care of such people is treatment of their physical illnesses, no matter what effects such treatment has on the patients' psychological or social well-being. Given this measure, even relatives who might be able to stay with a disabled, chronically ill, or dying person cannot provide "adequate" care; they are disabled. The medical profession sells them the service of care for their relatives. Medical professionals provide precisely the treatment, focused almost completely on physical injuries and illnesses, that relatives are unable to give. Here the relatives are consumers, the patients are cases.

The second situation is that of indigent patients, including those in institutions without relatives to pay for their care. Many of these patients, especially if they are elderly, receive Social Security payments. Medicare and Medicaid, some state government programs, and a few local programs

pay the costs for their medical care. These funding sources directly determine what care medical professionals can provide to whom. The limits
these funding sources place on this care indicate that they do not provide it
primarily to serve the patients' needs. For instance, while doctors recognize substance and alcohol addiction as physical diseases, many funding
sources will not pay for the care of patients disabled by them. Currently,
most of these sources will not pay for the treatment of many disabled children. For indigent elderly and disabled people who need medications for
multiple problems, the limits these programs place on the numbers of pre-
scriptions they pay for effectively means that these patients often do not
receive treatment for painful and life-threatening illnesses. Only rarely do
these medical programs address the primary causes of disease among the
poor: poor nutrition, environmental and community degradation, and lack
of public health services. The poor are cases, not beneficiaries.

The public, through taxes, is the ultimate source of these funds, and so
is the consumer of medical services to indigents. What need, transformed
by the medical profession into a disability, is the public paying for when it
funds these programs? The answer lies in what these programs do. They
provide just enough care to keep the ill and disabled poor largely out of
sight, to give the appearance that the medical profession is waging a largely
successful battle against illness. But not too successful—the residual numbers of visibly ill people point to the work still to be done. They may also
point to something else.

In order to understand just what disability the medical profession is
constructing and treating here, we need to recognize some facts. Almost all
the increased health and lengthened life spans of people in this country
and the world are not due to better private individual medical care. They
are due to improved nutrition, improved living and work environments,
and improved public health care, in the form of preventative care, vac-
cines, and publicly available treatments for infectious diseases.[7]

For a century, medical professionals have worked to create a larger
demand for their services by convincing those who could pay, primarily
middle- and upper-class families and individuals, that they need private
individual medical care, that publicly available treatments, family and community wisdom and remedies are not adequate. They have been partly
successful, for some good reasons. For while one cannot ascribe overall
advances in health and life spans to their interventions, private and individual medical treatments have more successfully eased many pains and
cured many illnesses than did the remedies they replaced.

But these successes have come with steep costs. In some cases, such as
midwifery, the medical profession has outlawed, or nearly extinguished,
communal traditions that are more effective than the professional medical
procedures that replaced them. I have already described the second cost,
the focus on the treatment of physical pain and disease even if such

---

[7] McKnight, 55–88.

treatment afflicts the patient with severe psychological suffering. The third related cost is the destruction of traditions of family and community care. The last, and perhaps most serious, cost is the failure to recognize, and the resulting withdrawal of funding and support for, the environmental, social, preventative, and public health programs that are the actual sources of better health and longer life-spans. The negative impact of this withdrawal primarily affects the poor. For instance, in this country, reduction in support for prenatal care and antipoverty programs in the eighties directly resulted in increased infant mortality rates.

Probably because of these costs, and perhaps also because large segments of the public, primarily poor and working-class people, were not the primary targets of medical marketing campaigns, the American public as a whole has retained a measure of skepticism about the medical profession's claims. Witness the popularity of alternative treatments and traditions.

The partial treatment and partial neglect of the poor indicate that they are serving some useful function as raw materials for the medical profession. The medical profession has tended to use the poor as containers of the threat of disease and of the public's inability to meet this threat. To the extent that the poor are neglected, they serve the medical profession as a kind of control group, through which it can say to the paying public, "See what happens if you don't buy our services!" But medical professionals can't afford to neglect the poor too much, lest they gain a reputation for callousness that undermines their carefully constructed image as compassionate saviors. So the medical profession improves its claim for the value of its services by sometimes effectively treating some of the poor for their illnesses.

The third, fourth, fifth, and sixth situations that call into question the medical profession's commitment to benefit patients are more blatant. When companies pay for medical services for their employees, in other words, when employers are the consumers, medical professionals have, in many cases, clearly done what benefits the companies, rather than their patients. For instance, National Public Radio reported on the case of mining company doctors who routinely did not inform coal miners that they had black lung disease until the miners were wholly disabled.

In the fourth situation are the more complex relations that develop between companies, insurance providers, and company personnel officers who handle employee insurance claims. When I was working as a therapist, I regularly had to deal with clients' fears, based on their and other employees' experiences, of being penalized by personnel officers who learned of employees' diagnoses through their insurance claims. I also know of instances of insurance companies telling employers that they would not offer certain employees coverage because the employees had chronic illnesses. In these relations, the insurance companies are the beneficiaries, the employers the consumers, and the employees the cases.

The fifth situation is Health Maintenance Organizations, which employ medical professionals and control what services can be offered to patients. In other words, in HMOs, medical professionals must serve their employers' interests; the HMOs are the beneficiaries. Patients or their employers are the consumers, but here they buy their services not directly from medical professionals, but from the HMOs. As many patients and doctors are discovering, HMOs sometimes market services that benefit themselves by insuring large profits, rather than those that benefit either patients or doctors.

This last situation shows that the medical sector of the service economy is becoming much more like the manufacturing economy. Medical workers, including doctors and other professionals, increasingly play the role of laborers, who work for company owners or corporations. Patients are service consumers. In this incorporation of the service economy, the relations among these players are increasingly transparent; everyone can see what is happening. (See figure 12.)

Notice that this triad has no place for the poor. This erasure of the poor points to a reality in the service economy. Cases who are not also consumers are not active participants in the economy. They are just its objects, its raw materials and commodities.

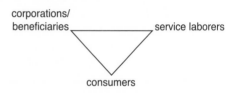

Figure 12: Managed Care Triad

The final medical situation confirms just how blatant the reduction of people to raw materials sometimes is in the medical profession. In the last few years, we have learned of doctors' use, without first obtaining the consent of these patients, of indigenous peoples, poor African Americans, and prisoners for medical experiments. Here, the medical profession uses patients who can't pay for services wholly as raw materials, laboratory animals, "a different species."

The Criminal Justice Sector

Because it relies upon a reputation for being compassionate, the medical profession hides this use of people as raw materials. The criminal justice sector of the service economy has no such reputation to uphold. Criminal justice professionals protect the public, the assumption being that the public is unable to protect itself. For this service, the public, through taxes, pays criminal justice professionals; the public is the consumer in the sense that it possesses a disability and pays professionals to treat this disability. But criminal justice professionals don't exercise their skills primarily with the public; they work on cases, on crimes and criminals. The criminal justice profession takes the raw material of the public's need for protection and defines crimes and criminals as what the public is unable to defend itself against, thus turning the public's need into a disability. Once the profession has convinced the public that criminals contain and represent its inability to defend itself, criminal justice professionals identify, isolate, and control criminals. Criminals are cases, not consumers. Criminal justice professionals make no pretense that their primary purpose is to benefit criminals. The benefits supposedly accrue to the public, but whether they actually do is another matter.

As a sector of the service economy, the criminal justice profession system can only be viable, can only sell its services, and so provide work for its labor force, if it increases demands for its services by increasing crimes and criminals. Success as an economic entity requires both perceived success and actual failure in its stated purpose, to prevent, fight, and eliminate crime. If it were actually successful in this purpose, then the criminal justice sector of the service economy would collapse and those employed in this industry would lose their jobs. But, in order to sell its product, protection from criminals, it must seem to be successful.

As a theoretical hypothesis, this analysis predicts what has actually happened over the past twenty-five years. Criminal justice professionals have presented a view of crime as ever threatening the public safety, ever changing and thus potentially ever growing, held in check only by the latest advances in the specialized knowledge of how to fight it. At times, according to this view, the forces of crime have been winning, crime rates have increased; but then, with public outrage leading to increased public funding of police and crime fighting forces, the forces of justice have masterfully identified, isolated, and jailed the new criminals, and the rates have decreased. Each of these swings, whether up or down, has resulted in increases in the numbers of identified kinds of crimes (for instance, increases in juvenile offenses have largely been due to increasing the types of juvenile crimes to include previously legal behaviors, such as curfew violations)[8], increases in the numbers of criminals, especially those in prison (the "war on drugs" has radically increased the numbers of imprisoned criminals; criminal justice professionals have convinced legislators to cease funding educational programs for prisoners, a proven means for reducing recidivism), increases in the time spent by these criminals in prison (through lengthening mandatory minimum sentences for many crimes, especially drug-related ones; reducing judges' discretionary power to give reduced sentences, and "truth in sentencing" laws that require prisoners to serve their sentences in prison, rather than being released on probation), and so increases in demands for the services criminal justice professionals provide.

During the past ten years, the criminal justice profession has become so economically and politically entrenched that it begins to rival the military, which survived the end of the Cold War and the fall of the "evil empire" with spending levels virtually untouched. In Congress, and especially in numerous state governments, legislators have difficulty justifying a vote

---

[8] Annette Fuentes, "The Crackdown on Kids," *The Nation* 15:22 (June 1998), 20–22.

against increased spending for prisons and criminal justice programs. Taxpayers almost automatically approve tax increases for new prisons, and a number of counties have become wholly dependent economically on the prison industry.

Our current criminal justice system is terrifying because it imprisons, and so afflicts with severe suffering, larger and larger numbers of people, especially young men of color, for flimsier and flimsier reasons; and we are becoming economically dependent on its continuing this trend. This history suggests that, while the public is the consumer of criminal justice, the profession itself is the beneficiary.

The Therapeutic Sector

The success of the criminal justice profession is in marked contrast to that sector of the service economy about which most books on care are written, the therapeutic professions. The reasons for the success of the criminal justice sector of the service economy and the decline of the therapeutic sector point to troubling shifts in national and global economies.

The therapeutic profession is a new one. It began to differentiate itself as the medical specialty of psychiatry a bit over a century ago. Among middle- and upper middle-class urban dwellers, first in Europe, then in the United States, psychiatrists began to replace clergy as the recognized doctors of the soul.[9] By the early part of the twentieth century, Sigmund Freud established psychoanalysis, the first true psychotherapy, defined as a discipline that heals by having the patient talk with the therapist. Within a couple of decades, the new profession had colonized clinical psychology, social work, chaplaincy, pastoral care, and pastoral counseling; all these disciplines became "therapeutic" ones, drawing their theoretical models and guidelines for practice from psychotherapy.

After World War One, especially in Britain, the large numbers of men suffering from "shell shock" and "war neuroses" greatly increased the demand for psychiatrists. For initially the same, but then very different, reasons World War Two generated an even bigger boom for the therapeutic profession in the United States, especially in large cities and suburbs. The G.I. bill and strong postwar economy opened the middle class to large numbers of previously working-class white men. As they went to work, their wives, who had worked during the war, became housewives in new homes in the suburbs. Despite the nostalgic portrayals of the fifties, strong evidence exists that this move afflicted many of these women, who suffered psychologically. Psychotherapeutic professionals provided them with an increasingly wide array of therapeutic services, which these women and sometimes their husbands, using generous insurance benefits and excess income, eagerly consumed. By the late fifties, whole middle-class families—men, women, and children—were in therapy.

---

[9]Brooks Holifield, *A History of Pastoral Care in America* (Nashville: Abingdon, 1983), 184–209.

Thus began the forty-year boom of the therapeutic economy. Between the mid-fifties and mid-nineties, psychiatrists and other psychotherapeutic professionals established themselves as the reigning experts for middle-class white Americans on how to possess meaning, joy, fulfilled selves, loving relations, strong families, healthy and smart children, ecstatic sex, nonviolent communities and worlds, and good jobs. From the mid-sixties on, in articles, books, talks, and especially performances on radio and TV programs, therapeutic professionals and political ideologues who supported them often tacitly and unintentionally, but still very effectively, constructed poor people, especially poor people of color, as the containers of the disastrous and disabling results of not consuming their services. Quite simply, these professionals portrayed the poor as lacking the ability to live good lives because they could not, or would not, buy the therapeutic wares. I am thinking here about the arguments for the existence of a "culture of poverty" and the prescription of therapeutic and quasi-therapeutic remedies for poverty. The therapeutic professionals were most effective when they convinced middle-class consumers that the disabilities of the poor were contagious, that all the sufferings of middle-class life were the result of cultural infections that spread from the poor, that even those middle-class people who were not ill needed therapeutic inoculations if they were to stay mentally and spiritually healthy. Here I am thinking of arguments that explicitly or implicitly trace middle-class drug use, divorce, single parenthood, "dysfunctional" families, teenage pregnancy, teenage violence, and other social ills to their supposed roots in poor and minority communities.

But despite its boom, the therapeutic sector of the service economy was never as strong as it seemed, for a number of reasons. First, large numbers of even middle-class whites, especially those who lived outside of major cities and their suburbs, never bought the therapeutic argument. When they had "troubles," they went to ministers, family members, or friends for help. Doing so was more natural, cheaper, and less shameful than seeing a therapist.

Second, from the beginning of the boom, working class, lower middle-class, and even solidly middle-class people could not afford therapy. They had no insurance, or their insurance programs wouldn't cover therapy. As, from the mid-seventies on, more middle-class people and their families joined working-class and poorer people in facing the effects of declining real wages, this segment of the population grew.

Third, the therapeutic economy partly became a victim of its own success. The large numbers of people who came to perceive therapists as the sources of human fulfillment and happiness flocked to them, especially if they had insurance programs that would pay for mental health care. Therapy, especially the long-term, intensive, individual psychotherapy that remained the major therapeutic service until the mid-eighties, is very expensive. No study that I know of has shown it to be more effective than other, far less expensive treatments. By the mid-eighties, insurance companies were severely limiting the amount of therapy they would cover.

Fourth, also in the mid-eighties, pharmaceutical companies began marketing an array of drugs that reduced some of the symptoms of many of the more pervasive and less severe mental illnesses, the ones therapists tended to specialize in, for instance, depression and anxiety. Medical treatment using these drugs is much cheaper than intensive therapy. HMOs, which rose to power on the slogan that they would cut medical costs, frequently paid for such drug treatments but would pay very little for talk therapy.

The fifth reason has to do with the difference between physical and mental diseases. Physical illnesses afflict the body. Their most common symptom is pain. Severe physical illnesses sometimes physically disable a person. If the pain they cause is intense enough, they may psychologically disable a person, but anti-pain medications and other treatments are often effective in controlling such severe pain. While most physical illnesses cause some psychological distress, only a handful directly cause enough suffering to psychologically disable a person.

When I go to see a doctor for a physical illness or disease, I usually do not automatically experience much psychological suffering. I am usually able to keep whatever discomfort or pain I am experiencing under control. While going to the doctor is a confession of my inability, and my family's and friends', to heal me of the illness, I do not feel this lack as a core disability. In fact, I usually commend myself for taking care of what ails me. I locate the illness, pain, and so disability in my body, which I experience as separate from myself.

When, however, I go to see a therapist, I am, at least initially, frightened and feel out of control. I feel ashamed for having to get help for something I feel I should be able to handle. I am unable to locate my suffering in my body or anywhere else "outside" of myself, because my suffering is in myself; it is, in a very real sense, myself. Mental illness directly afflicts the self, attacking one's sense of agency and so one's ability to act. To suffer a mental illness is to experience this inability directly. No matter how effective a therapist may be at eventually helping one to overcome this inability and so to recover a sense of being an effective agent (and many therapists are very effective in this way), the act of going to see a therapist involves increased psychological suffering; it means affirming that one is indeed psychologically disabled; one withdraws the support of one's belief in one's ability and joins the forces that are afflicting one by diminishing one's agency. In going to see a therapist, one, for a time, gives up the battle to be an agent and so a self. (Please note that going to see a therapist for help with a psychological trouble is very different from going to see a friend. I go to see a good friend, not because I am disabled and need his or her treatment, but because I know that, with my friend, I do not feel nearly so disabled; he or she brings out or supports my ability to be myself; with him or her, I can work on my suffering.)

In other words, in psychotherapy, the difference between being a consumer and being a case is hard to maintain from the beginning. As a medical patient, I can help my doctor work on my body and so maintain a sense of agency; I can be a consumer even if my body is a case. When I go to see a therapist, I begin as a consumer who is paying for the therapist's services, but as soon as the therapist begins to deliver those services, I become the case on which he or she works.

This insight clarifies one reason why drug treatments are popular with people suffering from mildly to moderately serious mental illnesses. When a doctor prescribes a drug for the treatment of my illness, he or she tells me, in essence, that, if I take this drug as prescribed, I can isolate, contain, and so control my own illness. Drug treatments make mental illnesses more like bodily illnesses. They seem to require that the patient sacrifice much less sense of agency. The medical profession has effectively shifted attention away from the side effects of taking many of these drugs, including disabling psychological symptoms, dependency and addiction, that undermine this image of them as tools patients can use to treat their own troubles.[10]

Because they strike at the heart of our lives as selves, mental illnesses are terrifying. They always have been. Witness the terror that "possessed" people pose for those societies and communities that believe in demons. Even we who do not believe in demons experience psychological suffering as a kind of terrifying possession by an alien being. At the peak of the therapeutic economy, even those who were passionate consumers of its services would talk, often with some anxiety, about *having* to go see a therapist.

And throughout the therapeutic boom economy, the stigma of being or having been a psychiatric or psychotherapeutic patient never disappeared. In the majority of people's minds, once one's self shattered, once one had a "nervous breakdown," one could never fully trust oneself to act sanely, and others could not trust one. One became, at least potentially, a labelled person, a "mental case." One became a container and sign of terrifying psychological suffering and disability.

No wonder we feared therapy, just as our ancestors feared the haunts of exorcists. To visit an exorcist is to be doubly possessed, first by the demons and then by the exorcist, who enters one to cast them out. Possession is the treatment for possession. The same contradiction lies at the heart of therapy; it, too, begins as a kind of possession, by the therapist who enters

---

[10] For a discussion of the iatrogenic effects of psychotropic medications, see Peter R. Breggin and Ginger Ross Breggin, *Talking Back to Prozac: What Doctors Aren't Telling You about Today's Most Controversial Drug* (New York: St. Martin's, 1994).

the self, renames it with a diagnosis, reframes the world it constructs as false, and works to change it in ways the invaded self can't understand.

The difficulty in differentiating between cases and consumers in the therapeutic economy illuminates the source of a perplexing contradiction in current discussions of professional ethics, especially among pastoral professionals. The primary metaphor that therapeutic professional ethicists use is "boundaries." They say that firm and clear boundaries characterize ethical relations between professionals and clients (including pastors and parishioners). These boundaries are presumed to be necessary because of the power the professional has over the client. The client, in this view, is vulnerable and disabled. He or she depends on the professional for help. The professional is the able agent in the relation and is therefore fully responsible for what happens to the powerless client. These discussions implicitly reduce the client to being solely a case, an object on which the therapeutic professional works.[11]

But, in the therapeutic economy, cases are almost always also consumers. In other words, therapists, unlike criminal justice professionals and, to a lesser extent, medical professionals, depend on those on whom they work to pay them for these services. As indicated, this conflation threatens clients, who suffer the shame and fear of being disabled cases whenever they consume therapeutic services.

In order to sell their services, therapeutic professionals must find ways to overcome this shame and fear. They do so through the therapeutic ideology of condescension, in which they wholly deny their own interests, the fact that they benefit from the services they offer. Through this ideology, therapists seek to assure clients that they are not only cases and consumers, they are also the primary beneficiaries of therapeutic interactions. The theologian Paul Tillich articulated this ideology in 1961 when he described therapists as the current incarnations of selfless *agape*.[12] Marie Fortune updates this ideology when she builds her professional ethic around the image of "fiduciary responsibility." The professional is to act solely in the best interests of the client.[13] As Tillich stated and Fortune implies, this ideology promises clients that, in exchange for the shame and fear of being treated as cases, they will receive the apparently most valuable commodity, unconditional love.

This ideology is effective only if three boundaries remain clear and firm. The first is between the professional, who acts selflessly and has no needs and desires, and the ordinary person, who acts out of self-interest and has needs and desires. The first rule of this professional ethic is that

---

[11] SteinhoffSmith, "The Boundary Wars Mystery," 135, 138–41.
[12] Paul J. Tillich, *The Impact of Psychotherapy on Theological Thought*, Monograph of the Academy of Religion and Mental Health, 1960, 4–5.
[13] Marie Fortune, "The Joy of Boundaries," in *Boundary Wars: Intimacy and Distance in Healing Relationships*, ed. Katherine Hancock Ragsdale (Cleveland: Pilgrim, 1996), 91–92.

the professional carefully keep his or her own interests, needs, and desires outside of his or her relations to clients.[14]

The second boundary is within the client, who, as a consumer, is an agent and has power and knowledge but, as a disabled case, is the powerless and dependent recipient of the professional's services. The second rule, usually only implied by professional ethicists in their prohibition of mutuality between professionals and clients and their denials of clients' agency, is that clients not give anything to or do anything for professionals (other than fees). This usually implicit rule takes force when a client violates the boundary between being a consumer, someone who initially buys and thus chooses and shapes the therapeutic relation, and being a case, upon whom the professional works. In such cases, especially when clients attempt directly to shape what is happening in the therapeutic relation, professional ethicists issue warnings to clients, ranging from the mild admonition that disobedience makes it difficult for the client to receive the benefits of therapy to the punitive condemnation of the client as irredeemably pathological.[15]

The third boundary is between the relation that links the selfless professional to the needy client and other more mutual relations in which people exchange goods and services. This boundary preserves the illusion central to the ideology of therapeutic condescension that professionals do not benefit from their services, that they do not act in their own self-interest or out of their own needs and desires. By ruling out "dual relationships," by claiming professionals and clients should not participate in any relations other than the strictly defined professional one, the boundary wholly occludes the ever-present and foundational dual economic relation between the professional as a seller and the client as a buyer of services. This third boundary preserves that which allegedly makes the therapeutic professionals' services supremely valuable, the promise that what these professionals are selling is unconditional love.[16]

In attempting to rationalize this therapeutic ideology, pastoral professional ethicists have constructed a contradiction. The ideology of unconditional love prescribes that the professional both fully and unconditionally respect the client's agency and knowledge and treat the client as the needy, empty, powerless, and ignorant recipient of the professional's services. This contradiction emerges most clearly in discussions of abuse, in which some professionals state that abused clients' knowledge of and statements about their abuse and that which heals it must determine professionals' responses. These professionals then ignore what abused clients say or use abused clients' statements primarily to illustrate the correctness of theories about abuse or the effectiveness of techniques for responding to abuse that the professionals have already developed.[17]

---

[14] SteinhoffSmith, "The Boundary Wars Mystery," 135–41.
[15] Ibid.
[16] Ibid.
[17]Ibid.

This contradiction inherent in the therapeutic ideology of condescension weakens it. This weakness, the terrifying character of psychological suffering and disability, and the difficulty therapists have in isolating and containing this suffering in cases they work on, differentiated from the consumers who pay them, makes psychotherapy hard to sell. Today, psychotherapy is contracting to what it was a hundred years ago, a limited medical service for a narrow range of psychiatric diseases. As such, it remains a viable profession. Reintegrating it back into the medical sector encourages most patients to think of "mental" illnesses as variations of physical illnesses, their causes located in the body and therefore treatable by methods that seemingly don't severely undermine patients' agency. And medical professionals, much more than nonmedical professionals, can effectively utilize the often poor residents of psychiatric institutions both to demonstrate the medical profession's competency in isolating and controlling psychological disability and the severe suffering that accompanies it, and to remind consumers about what lies in wait for them if they do not buy these services soon enough. These treatments are both cheaper and seemingly cause less painful side effects (in the extent of lost agency) than the purely psychotherapeutic ones. As your doctor might say, better to see a psychiatrist and get a pill when you are mildly depressed than wait and risk the depression developing into a full-scale psychosis, which puts you into the hospital or, even worse, impoverishes you so that you end up on the street when you are not in a public psychiatric institution.

This discussion of therapy indicates that success in the service economy depends on the professionals' ability to use cases to represent, isolate, and contain suffering and disability; professionals sell this protection from disability and suffering to consumers. Therapists failed to separate cases from consumers and so their sector of the service economy is contracting. Medicine has been quite successful in the construction of poor and institutionalized sick people as representatives of the threat disease poses to the public, as containers of this threat and of the public's inability to protect itself against disease, and as the cases through which medical professionals prove the effectiveness and so the value of their services. The criminal justice profession has been the most successful, primarily because it has so effectively isolated criminals, both in prisons and in the public's mind, from the public. Criminal justice professionals have convinced the public both of its complete inability to meet the threat of crime and of the professionals' ability to control this threat by controlling criminals.

I have ended each of these discussions of sectors of the service economy on a note of horror. Now I know the reason for this recurrent nightmare. Success in the service economy requires using large groups of people as nothing but cases, as raw materials, members of a different species, labels, or stereotypes. Success requires isolating these people, destroying their agency, invading and controlling the space of their subjectivity. Success means affliction, radical suffering.

CHAPTER 16

Condescending Service and Global Management

The poor of Mamre are members of the fastest-growing group of people in the economy shaped by global capitalism. Four movements characterize this economy. The first is this growth in the numbers of people, such as the poor of Mamre, who have no value in it except as raw materials. They participate neither as producers nor laborers and, since they have very little money, only minimally as consumers. In the best of circumstances, they eke out an existence in isolated pockets on the margins of the global economy. In most cases, they live or die, dependent on the aid of those who do participate in the global economy.

Second, in the manufacturing sector, increased mechanization means decreasing demand for labor. Elaborating on an earlier example, perhaps ten people can manage a shrimp farm on the land that once supported a thousand rice farmers.[1] The key word here is "manage." Manufacturing work under global capitalism moves toward the "management" of resources. While managers are employees of corporations, they act less like laborers and more like executives. While most manufacturing corporations still require labor, the trend is toward "increased productivity," or fewer workers producing more commodities. The resulting oversupply of labor means lower wages for these remaining workers. Without numbers or financial resources, labor's participation in the economy lessens. The direction of this movement is toward a management economy, in which labor slowly drops out of the manufacturing sector. This second movement explains the first. Discarded manufacturing laborers have no part to play; they become raw materials.

---

[1] Joseph.

The third movement results from the increased number of non-participants in the economy, who pose a real threat to the managers. Masses of desperate people can and do mount small and large revolts and revolutions. Service professionals, trained in isolating and controlling the poor as containers of threat and disability, become increasingly important in this economy as managers of the poor. One way to manage those desperate for work is to employ some of them to control the others. In this sector of the economy, as opposed to the manufacturing sector, large numbers of laborers remain, but they are not called "laborers." Most of them are called "soldiers" or "police officers."

The term "service economy" does not initially fit this sector of the economy formed by global capitalism. At first, the service professionals are not constructing a large threat where none or a small one previously existed. They are not truly taking the need of managers for protection and turning this need into a disability, which is then located in the poor. The threat from the poor to managers is real. In this economy, then, service professionals do not have to optimally fail in order to maintain the demand for their services. Global capitalism produces the demand. In order to market their wares, the professionals simply have to show that they can indeed control the poor. The third movement characterizing global capitalism is the transformation of some service professionals into managers of the poor and of the labor required to control the poor.

Once a management economy so incorporates service professionals, they, the laborers they employ, and the sector of the economy they construct come to depend upon the maintenance of masses of poor people as cases. The service economy, with most of the characteristics so far discussed, reconstitutes itself within the management economy.

The fourth movement characterizing global capitalism is the emergence of financial or stock markets as dominating forces. In these markets, both the raw material and the commodity produced from it initially appear to be capital or money. In fact, however, the raw materials and commodities of the financial markets are human need, desire, ability, and disability—the same raw materials and commodities that characterize the service economy. But money managers do not act like service professionals. Financial markets are like poker games, in which the manager who controls and hides his or her actual needs, desires, and fears behind an image of aggressive success and who confronts or manipulates a competitor into betraying what he or she does or does not have, wins. The other's uncontrolled desire, need, and fear are the raw materials a money manager converts into increased money.

In the demise of the therapeutic economy, I traced the tendency for the service economy to reward those who clearly differentiate cases from consumers. In the management economy, the differentiation is fundamental and clear. Cases are those people who don't participate or only minimally participate in the economy, who can't consume because they are unemployed or are paid little for their labor. Consumers employ service professionals to prevent the poor cases from realizing that they can threaten those who have excluded them from participation in society.

The service economy hides the actual economic and power relations between beneficiaries, consumers, and cases. In the management economy, these relations are transparent. Everyone knows that managers work for their own interests. Everyone knows that when consumers buy services, they benefit in the sense that they receive the services, but the primary beneficiaries are those who own the companies that provide the services. Where global capitalism is strongest, and the primary service industries are the military and the police, everyone knows that the workers in these service industries do not act primarily to benefit the poor whom they manage; they act to benefit themselves and those who pay them for their services.

One sign of the incorporation of the service into the management economy in the United States lies in the shift in the writers of inspirational, advice, or self-help books and the tone of these books. Until recently therapists wrote these books, and their tone was condescending. Therapists generously offered their wisdom about how to love and to live meaningful lives to the masses of ignorant people who obviously needed this guidance. More recently, managers and entrepreneurs have been writing these books. They do not hide their self-interest in writing them. In fact, they advertise their success at pursuing their own interests as a reason for buying their books. The books are not primarily about love, compassion, meaning, or service; they are about the "effective management" of one's life, of others, and of the resources one has. Here the domination or control, synonyms for "management," that condescension clothed in altruism throws off its disguise and emerges as a social norm.

The shift in political rhetoric from "fulfillment" to "competition" is another signal of this economic movement. "Liberal" and often condescending talk about meeting human needs, compassion, and self-fulfillment has, over the past fifteen years, yielded to talk about how to "compete" in the global economy. This language is clearest in the ways we talk about education (another sector of the service economy), no longer as the route to "a better life," but as necessary if one is going to be "competitive" in the global economy.

Again, the movement to the management economy renders transparent relations that the service economy obscures. In the management economy, it becomes obvious that those who are not "effective" or "competitive" do not play a part. They exist only as materials to be managed.

This shift from condescending service to global management illuminates the global rise of mega-churches. Numerous scholars have noted that these churches are service institutions. They attract members by providing an array of services to them, from fitness programs to spiritual training. Increasingly, however, the leaders of these churches market these services using the competitive language of management, rather than condescension.

The shift is subtle and partial. It lies in the difference between the image of a church as a community in which one finds a God who loves one unconditionally and the image of a church as the place where those who are happier and healthier than others reside. The first image, associated with the declining mainline congregations, is condescending. The second image, associated with the rising mega-churches, dispenses with condescension in favor of the rhetoric of blatant competition and domination.

In mega-churches, as in the management economy as a whole, the shift dispenses with condescension by making the relations it constructs transparent. It may be telling that the mega-churches appear to be most popular among upwardly mobile new members of the upper-middle class.[2] Perhaps economic instability, brought on by the post–Cold War globalization of capitalism, is a cause of this culture of naked domination. In insecure times, people throw social niceties out and desperately compete in order to survive. Perhaps, as global capitalism secures its rule and those who are wealthy come to be more secure in their domination, they will look back on those they have crushed with benevolence and so will clothe themselves in condescension.

Even when it is seemingly most cruelly transparent, the management economy continues to hide certain crucial truths. First, in the viciously competitive world of global capitalism, only a minority of people can be successful managers. Most will be cases to be managed. Second, even those who are successful for part of their lives will be managed cases for other parts. Increasingly, children are labeled people, containers of violence and disruption who must be managed and controlled. We have all been children. When we become disabled by disease or disability, when we are no longer "competitive," we inevitably slip into the category of those "cases" who must be managed. Third, then, the terror of failure that motivates activity in the management economy is a terror that each of us, no matter how successful we are, has faced and will face. As the poor members of Mamre showed me, none of us effectively manages or controls our lives all the time. We are all "failures" at some times. In other words, the management economy, like the service economy, finally fails to isolate suffering and the threat of suffering in the poor; or, more precisely, if we define "poverty" as existence primarily as a case rather than as a valued participant in society, we all have been, and will be, "poor." Still, even as it fails to release even the elite from suffering, the attempt to isolate and control suffering and its causes by locating them in poor cases radically afflicts the poor, which finally means all of us.

---

[2] Tex Sample, *U.S. Lifestyles and Mainline Churches: A Key to Reaching People in the 90's* (Louisville, Ky.: Westminster/John Knox, 1990), 99–135.

CHAPTER 17

Resisting Domination and Condescension

The case of Jesus and the Syrophoenician woman adds three important insights to this analysis of the politics and economics of domination
and condescension. First, this situation in which ruling economic elites use,
discard, and protect themselves against masses of the excluded poor is not
new. Jesus at the beginning of the story treated the Syrophoenician woman
and her daughter as nonhuman "dogs," not members of the social household or economy. Second, religion authorizes this affliction of the afflicted.
Jesus was following prescribed Jewish law, the code that defined ethical
religious practice, when he labeled the woman and her daughter as unclean refuse to be discarded. Third, the story reveals that resistance to this
system begins with those it afflicts, not with the elites; with the Syrophoenician
woman, not with Jesus.

In *A Feminist Ethic of Risk*, Sharon Welch discusses the tendency of
middle-class white Americans to despair when they cannot immediately
ameliorate suffering.[1] The danger of the kind of analysis I have offered
thus far lies in this tendency first to think that suffering is fixable and that
if, as this analysis indicates, it is not, then all is lost; we can do nothing
about it. Recognition both of the historical roots of affliction and of the fact
that people, even those most afflicted, have for millennia found ways to
live with a measure of joy in the face of overwhelmingly oppressive systems can guard against both the unreal hope in the current capacity to fix
suffering and the nostalgia for an illusory golden past that underlies despair. The Syrophoenician woman did for Jesus what the poor of Mamre
did for me; she taught Jesus the realistic hope, rooted in mutuality, that
wards off despair.

---

[1] Sharon Welch, *A Feminist Ethic of Risk* (Minneapolis: Fortress, 1990), 11–64.

As I indicated, this hope lies in a change in worlds, in how we construct reality, in our ways of living. In other words, just as the political and economic system of affliction is also a religious one, so is the hope religious. I am deliberately using "religious" in a different sense than it is often used. Western colonials used "religion" to designate what they saw as the superstitious beliefs and practices of "primitive" natives. After the Enlightenment, secular scholars appropriated this definition to criticize and reject christianity as "primitive" and deluded. Neo-orthodox theologians, seeking to defend christianity against secular criticism, borrowed this critique of "religion," claiming that christianity is not a "religion." In Western scholarship, then, "religion" usually refers to what some (ignorant) other (stupidly) believes; it is a pejorative term. More recent scholars, such as Stephen Toulmin, have determined that even the most seemingly secular scientific theories rest on unverifiable "images" that are functionally similar to religious myths and beliefs.[2] Anthropological definitions of religion as the combination of a society's worldview, the way it orders and constructs reality, and its prevailing ethos, its characteristic emotional tenor, attitudes, and ways of thinking and acting, lead to my understanding of "religion" as the particular way of life of an individual, community, or society. For me, "religion" thus does not refer primarily to "religious" institutions or to particular kinds of beliefs and rituals. Rather, religion refers to our fundamental orientation in life, how we perceive and construct reality and our and others' place in it.

At the beginning of Mark's story of Jesus' encounter with the Syrophoenician woman, Jesus performs the same "religion," in my sense of the term, that the current service and management economies perform; he imagines reality as a relation between "parents" and "children" upon which "dogs" attempt to intrude. We can use a triad to diagram this image (see figure 13).

"Parents" and "children" participate in reality, while "dogs" do not. This triad is similar to the one that characterizes relations in the service economy (see figure 14).

Figure 13: Parents, Children, and Dogs

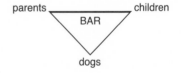

Figure 14: Service Economy Relations

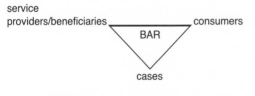

In Jesus' rejection, "parents" are like service providers, "children" are like consumers, and the Syrophoenician "dogs" are like cases. In the service economy, cases serve

---

[2] Stephen Toulmin, *Foresight and Understanding: An Inquiry into the Aims of Science*, foreword by Jacques Barzun (New York: Harper & Row, 1963), 57.

as the containers of suffering and its causes, which raises the question of whether "dogs" serve a similar function in Jesus' insult. The answer is yes. Before the Syrophoenician woman confronted him, Jesus exhibited signs of being exhausted in that he was seeking to hide. The appearance of the woman allowed him to blame her and her daughter, as greedy "dogs," for emptying him of his healing power and so as the cause both of his own and the "children's" continuing suffering. In his insult, he implied that the woman and her daughter had, in their suffering, stolen his healing power; because of their greediness, he does not have enough for the "children." The function of "dogs" for Jesus is exactly analogous to the function of "cases," in that "dogs" contain both suffering and its causes.

In the discussion of the medical sector of the service economy, I noted that the medical profession uses both the suffering of untreated cases and the healing of treated cases to attest to the value of medical services. A similar logic governs Jesus' relation to Syrophoenician "dogs" at the beginning of the story. Before Jesus initially responds to the woman, he can look forward to benefiting from either rejecting her request or healing her daughter. If Jesus does not heal because the woman and her daughter are not Jews, he and other members of the Jewish elite can say that the woman's and daughter's continued suffering is due to their disbelief, their refusal to participate in the sacred Jewish service economy. If Jesus heals the child, then this healing proves the value of his power. No matter how he treats the "case" of the Syrophoenician child, this treatment increases the value of Jesus' healing.

This understanding of the purpose of healing was, according to Clebsch and Jaekle, the primary one in early christianity, during which christian care givers explicitly used healing first to prove the efficacy of christian faith, and only secondarily to benefit those being healed.[3] In our terms, those who were suffering were the cases or raw materials through which christian elites demonstrated the value of christian faith to prospective consumers of christianity. The primary beneficiaries of healing were not those being healed, but the "representative christians" who did the healing.

Clebsch and Jaekle's discussion of the rest of the history of pastoral care tacitly reveals the same image. The primary purpose of pastoral care has been to convince people of their disability in the face of suffering and so of their need for the services, the care, that members of the christian elite offered. Authorized "representative Christians" construed mourning as a threat to faith in the efficacy of the church and so of christian ministers; they sustained grieving believers in order to make sure that they did not lose faith. Guidance functioned primarily as a way to bring prospective believers or consumers into the christian fold by teaching them about the value of christian remedies for spiritual suffering, the assumption being that the prospective believers could not save themselves; they needed the "representative Christians" to save them. Pastors reconciled lapsed believers

---

[3]Clebsch and Jaekle, 15.

with the church they had presumably violated by leaving, the assumption always being that it was the suffering believers who were at fault, never the church; the message was that suffering believers needed the church, even if it afflicted them, to find relief from this affliction.[4]

Behind these functions lay the fundamental assumption that the purpose of christian care was primarily to serve the church, and only secondarily suffering people. This understanding becomes explicit in the limitation of christian care giving to those who explicitly suffer from what Clebsch and Jaekle call "ultimate concerns," "spiritual" disabilities that, supposedly, only "representative Christian care givers" can accurately diagnose and treat. Clebsch and Jaekle echo the tradition when they admonish pastors not to waste their precious resources on people with material needs—on the hungry, the thirsty, the homeless; caring for these "dogs" deflects pastors from their true calling, which is to serve the true believers, the "children," those who are spiritually suffering.[5] The following triad reflects Clebsch and Jaekle's insights (see figure 15).

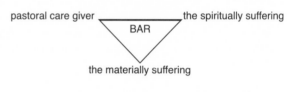

Figure 15: Pastoral Care Triad

pastoral care giver — the spiritually suffering
BAR
the materially suffering

Pastoral care givers care for the spiritually suffering by protecting them and the church against their suffering. Pastoral care givers ignore or bar consideration of the materially suffering.

Some current christian pastoral professionals protest that this understanding of pastoral care no longer holds true. In every respect, the evidence contradicts this assertion. Pastoral care texts tend to ignore material suffering and to assume that pastoral care focuses on spiritual issues. The prejudice against the poor is so great that most mainline churches do not even consider them to be prospective members, worthy of guidance into the church. They are, at best, recipients of charity or mission programs, cases and not consumers of faith. Church members and pastoral professionals tend to view pastoral involvement with the poor to be noble and even "christian," but finally a waste of time; pastors, they say, should spend their precious time caring for believers, the "children," or prospective believers, not poor "dogs."

With regard to believers and prospective believers, pastoral professionals, along with other therapeutic professionals, tend to be condescending. They equate the suffering of these people with immature or wrong faith, thus implicitly constructing suffering as its own cause and as a threat to correct faith and those who suffer as the containers of this threatening affliction. They tend to assume, along with most of those in the

[4]Ibid., 11–81.
[5]Ibid., 6–8.

pastoral care tradition, that the primary purpose of care is to protect the afflicted believer and the church from his or her own immaturity or suffering. For instance, Sheila Redmond reports that pastoral counselors tend to correct abused women's "wrong" conceptions of God as abusive, rather than taking these women's experiences as serious theological revelations.[6] Clinical Pastoral Education supervisors tend explicitly to assume that those who have not had CPE are immature, that they do not know what to do with their anger and grief; CPE is an initiation of these theological adolescents into maturity.[7] Almost all the dominant theories, from faith development theory to developmental psychologies and systems theory, used by pastoral professionals equate suffering with delusion and regression; to suffer is to be immature and not to perceive reality clearly.

The recognition that the story of Jesus' encounter with the Syrophoenician woman provides, that the system that afflicts the afflicted roots itself in our fundamental ways of constructing reality, opens us to the recognition that resistance to this afflicting system on the part of an elite person requires a religious conversion similar to the one experienced by Jesus when the Syrophoenician woman confronted him. The Syrophoenician woman's retort undermines the system of affliction by striking at the heart of its assumptions. The woman asserts that no one exists outside the household of care, that no one deserves to be cast out or excluded from the healing and other necessities, spiritual and material, of life. In the world she constructs, those who suffer do not serve as containers of suffering and its causes for a religious or economic elite.

By beating Jesus at his own game, the woman contradicts the equation of suffering with immaturity or delusion. The woman, who is suffering, sees more clearly than does Jesus, the supposed healer. Implied here is that a healing relation involves the exchange of knowledge between the healer and the one being healed. As Jesus recognizes in his response to the woman's saying, healing requires the agency and wisdom of all involved; it is a relational act.

The story points to a truth that this part of the book approaches. We organize our politics, economies, and religious ways of life around the issue of suffering. One way we respond to suffering, the dominant way at least in the christian and post-christian West for two millennia, which means currently the dominant way globally, is by attempting to get rid of suffering by isolating it in others and then controlling these containers—the "dogs" or "cases." This condescending way afflicts the afflicted by isolating them and constructing them as objects.

---

[6] Sheila A. Redmond, "God Died and Nobody Gave a Funeral," *Pastoral Psychology* 45:1, September 1996, 41–48.

[7] Roy SteinhoffSmith, "The Tragedy of Clinical Pastoral Education," *Pastoral Psychology* 41:1, September 1992, 45–54; Duane Parker, unpublished letter to Roy Herndon SteinhoffSmith, 1993; A. Dirk Evans, unpublished response to Roy SteinhoffSmith, "The Tragedy of Clinical Pastoral Education," 1993.

The second way, which remains a subjugated alternative, is to recognize that we all suffer and that we afflict each other. The only truly healing response to suffering is mutual care, in which we recognize that we need each other, we affirm each other's abilities, meet each other's needs, and attempt to ameliorate each other's suffering. By the end of the story of the Syrophoenician woman, in my reading, she and Jesus had healed each other and both had healed her daughter; healing was an act that benefited all of them, that addressed and responded to each one's suffering.

I have named the way of mutual care "a subjugated alternative." While this name accurately designates the place of mutuality in the reigning political and economic systems of domination and condescension, it also leads us astray. In the first part of this book, I uncovered the mutuality assumed by condescension. I have rediscovered this fundamental mutuality in each of the case studies I have completed. I have attempted to articulate this discovery in my map of the relational nature of human existence. As a way of thinking about and organizing our activities, mutuality remains subjugated by condescension. But in the inevitable failure of condescension, in the recognition that we cannot banish suffering, we discover not only our own need and desire for each other, but also that the mutual relations we need and desire are present realities. They are what make life possible; they are the ground for the pleasure, joy, and love that are our signs of life. As we have explored suffering, we have discovered that our mutuality is also the ground for pain, suffering, and affliction; each of these signals a threat to the mutual relations that constitute our life together. In this sense, mutual care is not subjugated, but is, rather, the pulse of life that beats within the systems that hide it and deny it. Resistance to these systems is not a matter of constructing an "alternative" way of life. Resistance is acting on the recognition of our ongoing reliance on each other and indeed on all beings.

PART FOUR

From Pastor
to Friend

CHAPTER 18

Sisters

The analyses of domination and condescension suggest that resisting them requires a movement from relations in which a professional or expert cares for or gives care to someone who is disabled, to relations in which all, with their needs and abilities, mutually participate. In this chapter, I present a case in each of three traditional pastoral disciplines: visiting the sick, pastoral counseling, and crisis intervention. In each, the presenter enters the case adopting a traditional pastoral position—the theologically wise and authoritative chaplain in the first, the clinically trained counselor and diagnostician in the second, and the effective crisis counselor in the third. All three cases are about how the presenter moved into a mutual relation with the suffering person. In other words, these are case studies of conversions from condescension to mutuality. They explore different ways in which those who seek to practice care redefine themselves as a result of their conversions. While the three case researchers sometimes use different terms to describe themselves after their conversions to mutuality, they also call themselves and the suffering persons with whom they were in relation "friends." I have followed their usage in the title of this passage. While only the presenter in the first case uses a version of the method presented in this book, all three demonstrate the method as they move from description to analysis to imagination.

The first case is the relation which developed between two women in their mid-forties. Both were Euro-Americans, middle-class, well-educated, married, and had children. Both had converted to Catholicism within the decade preceding the described events. Mary, the pastor, was on the pastoral care team at a hospital and on the pastoral care staff in her church. Katherine, the parishioner, was dying from cancer that had spread from her breast to her lungs. Mary had fibrocystitis, which predisposed her to breast cancer.

In a class in pastoral care, Mary discussed three of a number of visits with Katherine. She presented the first to the class, which discussed it at length. After this discussion, she had the second and third visits. Katherine died soon after this *last visit, and Mary spoke at her funeral. Mary wrote about each visit, using an earlier version of the method I've introduced in this book.*

First Meeting

Description

CONTEXTS

A month prior to this meeting, her third with the patient, Mary had completed a unit of CPE. She had converted to Catholicism a year and a half earlier. Three months prior to the meeting, she had become a eucharistic minister, which means that she took the eucharist to parishioners who were homebound or in nursing homes. While she was comfortable with being a chaplain and pastor, she was also new to these functions.

She brought to this meeting three closely related concerns: the theological meaning of suffering, the relationship between her own suffering and Katherine's, and the nature of pastoral authority. These concerns are evident in her written introduction to her meetings with Katherine:

This…person is about my age and is dying from something I am particularly susceptible to, and it seems I find it harder to be of help to her because my own anxiety gets in the way.

Some of the particular suffering in this situation includes physical discomfort and pain, fear of death, confusion about whether to fight the cancer with treatment, or to begin the process of letting go.

My concern is how to help her with these issues and with her relationship with God.

A nagging issue…is the question of how God works in our lives. I don't believe God makes us sick. I don't believe God punishes us. I believe God is very present in our trials. But how does God work? If God created me for a specific purpose, have all my sufferings been an essential part of my [evolution] to fulfill that purpose? Were my bad decisions and choices mine? Where was God in those? I see God present, mercifully, in the good in my life; but I get confused about who or what caused the suffering in my life…

Mary wrote about the distribution of power in the meetings:

I participate in her life as a eucharistic minister,…a spiritual care giver. I make the decisions about the eucharist service, choosing which prayers I think are pertinent for this day or asking her what she'd like to pray for and then choosing based on that…

I feel responsibility—and perhaps some power—to bring God into the conversation, sharing my experiences of how God works in my life or how I depend on God.

I think I intentionally try not to have power in this situation, except for the power of realizing my own competence (this is hard for me) and my own faith and beliefs.

There is a power issue in that she is caught between fighting for her life and letting go and…I interpret this as denial. [I]mplicit is my judgment that it is time for her to begin the process of accepting her death…

[At the time of this meeting] the patient is in the hospital, having a tube put in her chest because…her lungs are filling with fluid and she is having trouble breathing. The tube will help relieve the pressure…

I expected to walk in, find her alone and get to know her better; help her along quickly with her quandary… To me, "visit" meant… reveal your whole self to me so that I can give you the answers to your questions…

I…expected to be able to help her get to know God better.

VERBATIM

Mary: (I knock on the door, as usual.) Katherine? (I walk in slowly. Katherine is sitting in the chair beside the bed, her legs covered in a white blanket. She is wearing a blue and green paisley robe and a green turban. She is rubbing lotion on herself under her robe. She does not have her makeup on.)

Katherine: Good morning. I didn't get my makeup on yet.

Mary: You've been busy this morning.

Katherine: Oh, a little. Can you sit down and visit for a while?

Mary: I can. (I pull up a chair. We talk about her medical condition. She tells me about the breathing problem and getting the tube in the chest. And she explains vaguely about the chemotherapy. She says she hopes the breathing problem is solved and that she can get on with the chemotherapy. She says she also hopes that she's received enough treatment that she won't have side effects from it. She also says she hopes to go home soon.)

(She is very composed. She smooths the blanket frequently and looks for lint to pick off it. There's a sense of decorum about her.)

(I am clutching inside. I want to get down to her feelings so I can help her; that's my job.)

Mary: Has all this been scary?

Katherine: Yes, it has.

Mary: (I want her to go on. I am feeling anxious about how to get her to.) How have you handled that?

Katherine: By reading, trying to rely on my faith.

Mary: You try to keep a balance?

Katherine: Yes.

Mary: (I'm feeling light and easy now.) So you can be afraid and be spiritual at the same time?

Katherine: (She laughs softly.) I try to be.

(I ask her if her parents are Catholic and she tells me they're not; they're Baptist. She tells me her conversion story and I tell her mine. We each voice our amazement.)

(I prepare the altar and ask her if there's anything she would especially like to pray for. She says healing and peace. I choose the service on healing...After the communion service is over, Katherine expresses her gratitude.)

Mary: (I'm feeling nervous [about] what to say.) It helps, doesn't it?

Katherine: Yes, it really does.

(We hug and I tell her I'll see her tomorrow.)

Analysis

CRACKS

[A]t the point when I was feeling easiest was the point at which I was failing...She was opening up and talking...I thought my job was over; I'd opened the door, she walked in, and now I could just sit there and watch her. This was an unreal fantasy, for I had to continue to be engaged, and what I did was disengage.

My tendency to do this comes from what I learned...as a child when I was sexually abused. I split...When I get in a situation where I can't handle the fear and anxiety, I appear and feel peaceful, since that was the only thing I could do to survive...

I see (again!) that it's in my anxiety—and in my false sense of peace and well-being—that there is God. I do come into this situation as a eucharistic minister and as a student of ministry and pastoral care; there is some pastoral authority in that, implicitly at least. But I am human, too, and it is in that humanness—in that anxiety—that I really can minister. For when I realize my anxiety...I can realize my humanness and remember to scream for God...

[W]hen I wanted to help Katherine continue to express her feelings (when I ask her, "Has all this been scary?" and she answers, "Yes, it has.") is where my...anxiety got in the way and I blocked her from continuing in the painful (for me, at least) silence of that moment or continuing to express those feelings of fear.

Implicit in my then asking "How have you handled it?" is the notion that it is wrong to be scared. This is exactly the opposite of my intentions...

When she started talking about trying to balance trust in God and trust in the doctors, I felt she was doing what I had hoped she would do—talk to me. My anxiety took two forms. First, the clutched, panicky feeling that elicited the response described above. But then, I went into my second stage of anxiety (which up to this writing I had never before identified as anxiety), that of peacefulness...a false peace, for it is actually a disengaging. I disengage emotionally so I can't feel the pain.

Implicit in my purpose for being there was the notion that I expected "to be able to help her get to know God better." Implicit in that notion is the idea that, in the first place, I could do that, and, in the second place, that I know God better than she does.

HIDDEN REALITIES: SUFFERING

Part of her suffering is that she has been fighting to live. She has been to an aggressive treatment center, which has sent her home without treatment. Now a doctor, formerly from that center, has been giving her...a series of chemotherapies. She has also been doing positive imagery and meditation in an effort to help her body's immune system.

Part of her suffering is the recent experience of fearing she will finally not be able to breathe—actual death.

My suffering is twofold. I could get what she has. In fact, I *will* die and the fact that a woman my age is dying of something to which I have a proclivity forces me to look at my mortality, which is quite frightening, in spite of my theology and faith.

I also suffer in the fact that I want to relieve her suffering and that I haven't been able to even try; in fact, I can't even bear to be with her in it.

Implicit suffering for me is...in the fact that I am still trying to *be* God. I suffer in that because I feel embarrassed, even ashamed. I continue to reject who I am; I fail to accept my humanness.

Hidden Realities: Care

My love for her is my complete empathy with her terrifying situation.

In class, we had discussed empathy as an often unconscious, bodily state of psychological union with the other, so that even our seemingly most negative emotional and bodily reactions—terror, rage, exhaustion, despair—are responses to what is going on with the other and of the reality and depth of the relationship.

My love for her is implicit in my being there, our sharing of our conversion stories (which helped bond us), my bringing her the eucharist, my asking what she wants to pray for, my hug and promising to be there the next day.

Her love for me is in her willingness to let me into her life, to share her feelings, to invite me back.

Reconstruction

[Katherine] was willing to share her fears. This was exactly what I wanted, but it was too scary for me...I blocked her from doing it by asking, "How have you handled that?" and "So, you can be afraid and be spiritual at the same time?"

This is lack of "pastoral authority." In my anxiety, it was I who, temporarily, lost faith.

We went on to safer ground—discussing our similar midlife conversions to Catholicism. And then I did another emotionally safe (though extremely valuable) thing and gave her the eucharist.

Imagination

At the point that she said, "Yes it has [been scary]," I could have:
• been silent and let her talk more
• said, "Real scary" or "Terrifying" and then been silent
• asked, "What scares you most?"

What I needed to do was encourage her to express those feelings of fear by letting her know I was willing to listen to them, to stay with her in that scary space...I needed not to discount her fear by inferring that she had to "handle it" somehow and, compounding the wound, that even I, this almighty woman from God, wouldn't know how to do that!

I needed to let her know that fear was all right…

In a situation that arouses my anxiety, I first need to recognize that I am anxious…So when I am clutching for the "right" thing to say, or when I think all is well and I can just sit and listen to them talk and obliviously say anything, I must stop and realize that something about this event is making me anxious and that I have disengaged.

And then I could ask, "What is it? What am I afraid of?" I could say, "God, please show me what I'm afraid of." Or, "God, help me know I'm not going to die at this minute due to my anxiety."

It's important for me to recognize that my anxiety… [is] a safer, healthier place than my disengagement. In my anxiety I am still engaged and I can more easily remember to partner with God and with the patient.

Second Meeting

Description

CONTEXTS

This was perhaps our eighth visit—the fourth or fifth in her home…

This was a Thursday. The previous weekend she had received, at home, forty-eight hours of chemotherapy from a pack on her back. On Monday and Tuesday, she had gone to the physician's office and received chemotherapy for four hours…

I called Katherine Thursday morning. She said she had been to work the previous day—not for long, but she had worked on a couple of papers. But today she was having a terrible day, and she would love to have a visit. I made plans to see her at eleven a.m.…

I gave up fantasies before I went. I was blank; I prayed as I walked from my car to the door, simply, though fervently, for God to be with me, help me. I had no idea what to expect, or what to do, and that was fine.

When I got [to her home], she answered the door, and the dog escaped. She let him run in the yard for a while and came in and sat down in the leather recliner. She was very tired, felt lousy. After a few minutes, she slowly walked to the kitchen, got a fly swatter and went outside and stood on the front porch and called the dog and tapped the fly swatter against her leg. She continued to talk to the dog, tapping the swatter; pretty soon the dog came up alongside her, and she let the dog in the house.

A couple of times she said she'd hoped to have her makeup on by the time I got there, but that a bath had worn her out, and she just hadn't got it accomplished. I tried to reassure her that though it might bother her, it didn't bother me that she didn't have on makeup.

She was wearing socks and no shoes, soft knit pants, a bright yellow knit top, and a white knit cardigan. She had on a scarf tied at the back of her neck and no earrings.

When the dog was in, she got the telephone, put it on the table beside her chair, and sat, seemingly worn out and ready for a rest and a visit...

She explained that she had fever blisters in her mouth and couldn't figure out what or how to eat and drink. This was the first time she'd had this particular reaction to the chemotherapy.

VERBATIM

Mary: (Katherine is sitting in the leather recliner. I am sitting ...perpendicular to her in an overstuffed easy chair. She has told me about [her current physician and...chemotherapy], now I ask) What have you learned in all this?

Katherine: I've learned a lot...In my family, I have always done everything. It was easier to do it all myself. Run the house, do it all. When I got sick, I couldn't do it all anymore. And especially when I went in the hospital, I had to learn to ask for help. I think I had built a fortress around myself.

Mary: Oh, I can relate to that. You can't get hurt if you're walled in.

Katherine: That's right. But since I've been sick, I've let my family in; I had to...

Mary: What a wonderful legacy to give your children.

Katherine: It is.

(At another point in the conversation,...it occurs to me to tell her about the teacher at my son's elementary school, who died the day before. She had acute asthma and stopped breathing, despite her husband's injections to help her. She died on the way to the hospital in an ambulance. She had three elementary-school-aged children. I hesitate to tell Katherine this story, and then I remember Henri Nouwen talking about how the dying don't like to be cut off from the world and that in fact they care very much about others' sufferings; that there is a community of care among the dying. So after a moment of considering it, I decide to tell her about it. When I do, she perks up and wonders if it is a woman she knows who has serious asthma. We realize it isn't...She is really concerned, expresses sorrow and is really alive. For a moment, I think, she forgets about her own illness and really engages in caring about someone, a family who is in a worse situation. I think Henri Nouwen is right. Then she kind of comes back into her life.)

Katherine: You better live this day, because you don't know about the next, do you?

Mary: No, you don't. You know, I've come to appreciate certain tensions, or paradoxes, that we live with. And one of them is that when you start really living life in a meaningful way, you also come to realize that you are going to have to let it go. There is this tension between living and loving and letting go.

Katherine: (She nods her head in the affirmative.) And the better you live it, the harder it is to let go. (There's a silence.) You just have to keep pushing on. (I'm feeling confused here; this doesn't follow in my thought, but I am alert that it is significant in her thought.) Today is one of those days when I struggle with that tension.

(There's silence again, and after a little bit I ask her if she would want to receive just a small piece of the host.)

Katherine: A very small piece.

(I prepare communion and when it comes to the Our Father, we join hands as usual and repeat it. But I don't feel like a care minister; I feel like her sister.)

Analysis

CRACKS

Katherine says, "I think I built a fortress around myself." And I say, "Oh, I can relate to that. You can't get hurt if you're walled in." This is telling: I jump right in there (as if to say, "Oh, I know the answer to that!") so that I won't get hurt (putting up a wall with my preaching)...

And then we get into really meaningful stuff—and my anxiety level tilts...Katherine says, "You better live this day because you don't know about the next, do you?" I say, "No, you don't. You know . . ." [What follows] is barely veiled preaching...It does not let her express herself, *and* I'm taking a position of authority, as if I know something she doesn't. This is hypocritical...My anxiety is mounting, partly because I fear she'll discover in my words the fact that I don't really know what I'm talking about. In my anxiety here, I got lost; I wasn't saying what I really intended to say. But that probably wouldn't have been any better.

Then there is a critical, revealing series of statements from Katherine: "And the better you live it, the harder it is to let go...You just have to keep pushing on...Today is one of those days when I struggle with that tension."

My anxiety is so great, I cop out completely. I can't "handle" this much...I can't understand what she's telling me; indeed, I'm afraid to listen, afraid to urge her to explain...

There's a power issue in that I'm trying to protect her from her suffering. I'm afraid to ask her certain questions or say certain things because I want to protect her—and myself—from pain.

HIDDEN REALITIES: SUFFERING

For Katherine, there is suffering in realizing [that]...she was afraid to let love in, so she built a fortress around herself. In her illness, she had to open the doors of the fortress and let her family in more than ever...And now that she's done that, now that she feels their love, and they know her love, she doesn't want to let them go. She feels betrayed, betrayed by God.

There is suffering for Katherine in the confusion of deciding whether to "keep pushing on" or to let go. Perhaps she feels betrayed now by medicine as well, for she has fought hard to make the treatment work and is beginning to realize that it isn't going to.

Part of the reason she's willing to fight is that she doesn't want her family to have to experience the suffering of losing her. Indeed, up to three days before her death, she would still be willing to try treatment. I don't think this was an effort to survive: She had at this point planned her funeral and chosen not to die at home because her hospital bed was in her daughter's bedroom, and she didn't want her daughter to have to remember that.

There is suffering for Katherine in the uncertainty of the future. What will it be like not to be able to breathe? What will it be like to leave the ones she loves? Is what she believes true; will she go to be with God?

And Katherine must suffer the frustration of trying to get me to *listen* to her.

There is suffering for me, in that I don't know the answers to any of these questions. There is suffering for me, in that I can't ease her pain or protect her from it; in fact, I can't even stand to listen to it. So there is the suffering in the acknowledgment that I think I am an authority or have power to do for her what I think she needs or can't do for herself.

There is suffering for me, in that she is raising the basic fears of death and challenge to faith.

Hidden Realities: Care

There is care in the cracks. I say, "Oh, I can relate to that." I do relate to her and that's empathy, that's care.

I say, "What a wonderful legacy to give your children." I do feel that she's done a courageous and wonderful thing…And I affirm her. That's care.

There's care in the fact that I delivered a mini-sermon about the tension between living and loving and letting go. I'm desperately trying to fix her anxiety, and that stems from caring for her, from loving her and wanting her not to suffer.

There's care in bringing her the eucharist.

There's care in that she's willing to talk to me—and that she has great patience with me, for she continues to talk in future events.

There was care in even continuing to see her, considering that I was becoming more and more aware that I didn't know what she needed or how to help her.

Reconstruction

This time, I went to see Katherine without expectations of how I might help her. I knew I didn't know where she was spiritually or emotionally. I knew I didn't know how to help her. I knew I would never be sure of the right thing to say at any given moment. I didn't engage in fantasies before I went in. I had doubts going in about the way I'd been doing pastoral care (as someone with "pastoral authority")…Could I be a colleague with her, a partner in illness? Going in, I had questions…and sureness about my inability rather than an agenda.

And she was ready to be open to me. She was ready to talk.

For a while I went farther than I'd gone before in listening, and it worked. I let the silences happen, and I tried to share my experiences with her, to share my faith story. I was trying to be a colleague. And she began to reveal more, perhaps because she sensed that there was a change in my attitude; that I wasn't evaluating her and trying to relate to her from a position of someone who has a closer relationship to God than she does. Maybe she sensed the equality I was beginning to feel, maybe she sensed my vulnerability since I wasn't hiding it so much. And so she began to talk, and when she did, my anxiety returned. As my anxiety intensified, what I really did was talk instead of listen.

Imagination

When Katherine said, "I think I had built a fortress around myself," I could have said, "What do you mean?" or, "To protect you from what?" or, "What were you trying to keep out?" or, "What were you afraid of?"

When Katherine said, "You better live this day because you don't know about the next, do you?" I could have said, "What, exactly, do you mean?" or, "Do you have regrets?" or, "I wonder if you feel betrayed: You left your fortress and let love in, and now you're afraid you might die and have to give it all up…"

When Katherine said, "Today is one of those days when I struggle with that tension," I could have said, "The tension between letting go and pushing on?" or, "Which tension is that?"

What needed to occur was for me to be in those questions with her some more—without my even attempting to give her answers. I need to realize I can't "handle it." But I can be with her in it…

It occurs to me that caring for the dying is not like any other caring, in that people who experience some form of suffering often find the most comfort from those who have experienced the same thing. We who care for the dying have never been where they are. We care out of love and faith, not experience…

The question then is, How can I be with the dying with my very humanness, which includes very human fears about suffering, losing loved ones, and dying?…

I must accept that I will die. Accept that I am afraid of losing faith, as they [who are dying] are. Accept that I don't have any answers. Accept that it scares me to share my faith.

Third Meeting

Description

CONTEXTS

Mary identifies this meeting, occurring some time after the first two, as the "pivotal" one in her relationship to Katherine. During the visit before this one, while they were holding hands for the Lord's Prayer, a change occurred. Mary writes:

I felt Katherine's hand in mine and something moved inside me. I knew in a deep way that she was my sister; that we were absolutely equal; that I had absolutely no pastoral authority, and, what's more, I didn't want any. The strength and warmth of our hands together was profound. It was a moment of grace,…of transformation…

[Thinking about the next visit], I really expected a rather quiet, routine sort of visit…I felt I had reached a new place, and now it would not necessarily be easier, but the pressure was definitely off to have the answers. I was going to see my sister.

VERBATIM

I knocked on the glass front door, and Katherine had left the inside door standing open so I could see her sitting in her chair, and she could motion me in without having to get up. She was very weak at this point. She motioned me in, and I came in, keeping the dog from escaping. I said good morning and set down my eucharist bag on the coffee table and began to take off my coat.

We each asked how the other was but didn't spend much time on the answers because she was eager to talk to me about something else.

Katherine: (She talks slowly, in halting words, looks to me directly, earnestly. I see that this is hard for her, but that she very much wants to express some strong feelings. I sit on the sofa, listening intently…) I shared this with Sister X, when she came by the other day. And I want to tell you how much you mean to me. Your visits have been very helpful.

The other day when we were having communion something swept over me. I've always liked what I've done, but I've never felt like I found what it is I'm really supposed to do. And now I know I want to do what you do. Maybe not in the same way. But I want to share my faith, like you've shared yours with me.

(I am uncomfortable here because my ego is inflating and I fear showing my pride. At the same time, I don't like feeling prideful, and so I'm trying to fight it off, but there it is.)

I wanted you to know this.

Mary: Oh, Katherine. Something happened to me during that time too. (For a second I wonder if I should tell her, but I know it is the right thing to do.) You know when I started coming to see you, I thought I had to have answers for you.

(Katherine looks at me with the most quizzical look; it is immediately followed by one of sympathy. She smiles and shakes her head a little.)

You have shown me what true friendship is. I know I don't have answers for you. In fact, you've taught me so much. Last week, during the Our Father, I felt so close to you and so much like a sister with you. Thank you.

Katherine: If I get well, I want to find a way to share my faith.

Mary: I think you might discover that you already are doing that, and now that you are aware of it, you may do it in a more intentional way.

Katherine: Maybe so. I mentioned this to Sister X because it occurred to me that I might be bargaining with God. Sister X told me it's all right to bargain with God.

Mary: (I smile at her. I don't answer her. I don't have an answer, and that makes me anxious. But that's okay. I stay silent. She begins to talk about the bittersweetness of a meaningful friendship at this late hour in her life. And we talk about the paradox of that; that if she hadn't been sick, we probably wouldn't have met, and now that we have grown so close, we have little time together.)

(At the point that I feel it's time to have the eucharistic service, I ask her if she's ready. She says she is, and I set up the altar on another wooden TV tray.)

Mary: I'm going to receive with you today.

Katherine: Good.

Mary: (I choose the theme of Thanksgiving in the service booklet. We receive the eucharist together, in thanksgiving for our friendship.)

Just under a month later, Katherine died.

Analysis

CRACKS

I chose this event because it was the turning point in our friendship. I thought that for the first time I did it right, that I came to a place of care and equality with Katherine. And I think that is correct.

But there is a place in the event that troubles me—those feelings of pride...Realizing I was suddenly feeling proud and then trying to keep that pride off my face and worrying about whether I was successful at that must have prevented me from really listening to Katherine. How could I possibly really listen if I was involved in all that?...

The fact that she talked for quite awhile...while I was silent, and I can't remember most of it, indicates to me that I was being silent, not out of careful listening, but out of trying to suppress my feelings of pride.

HIDDEN REALITIES: SUFFERING

There's suffering for me in the unwelcome feelings of pride. I feel ashamed to be prideful. And there's suffering in hiding these feelings.

Perhaps my shame stems from feeling happy that someone has benefited by my being there and the conflicting feeling that I am not worthy of such a profound compliment.

Katherine's suffering is in her halting words. It's hard to reveal oneself in such intimacy. This is frightening because you may be rejected.

She suffered as well in the fear that she might be bargaining with God, and perhaps she wondered if she'd get in trouble with God for that. Beneath the bargaining may have been some feelings of guilt about not having been a "good Christian"...I could have asked her about that.

Katherine may also have suffered in that there was a period when I wasn't really listening to her. It's frustrating and disappointing to want to tell someone how you feel and to realize they're not really hearing you.

Hidden Realities: Care

There was love in that she had the door open and was looking forward to my coming.

There was most definitely love in Katherine's sharing that she appreciated my being there for her, with my faith, so much that she wanted to do that. There was love and trust in the fact that she could reveal her fear that perhaps she was bargaining with God.

There was love in my wanting to hide my pride from her: I care about Katherine and very much value her opinion of my care.

There was love in my admitting to her that I thought I was supposed to have answers for her. I loved and trusted her enough to make this admission.

There was love in my telling her that she felt like a sister, that she'd taught me so much.

There was love in that I told her I suspected she was already sharing her faith.

There was love in our each sharing that we were sad that our friendship came at this time when we knew we didn't have much time left to be friends…

There was God's love all over the place, but certainly in the grace we had received saying the Our Father together.

Reconstruction

We each had a sense of how important our friendship was…and we expressed it to each other. Though I felt shame and embarrassment because I reacted with pride at this favorable evaluation of my care with her, and though I probably didn't really hear all she was saying at the time…by sharing our good feeling about each other and each admitting something to the other (her fear of bargaining with God, my implicit ego in thinking I should give her answers), we began an equality of friendship that continued in those critical last weeks of her life.

The real crack here for me is realizing my pride. I must acknowledge when I do well…What makes me uncomfortable about being proud?…

During the summer when I had to give a chapel service at the hospital as part of my CPE duties, when I looked up at the audience, my head would shake uncontrollably. At Katherine's funeral, the same thing happened, and I wasn't sure I'd make it back to my seat with such weak and shaky legs.

Now I know what it was: hiding my pride at a job well done. I write well, and I've discovered that my writing experience serves me especially well in writing spiritual reflection[s and] stories. This is a new discovery, and I'm not ashamed of it. But I am so happy to do this, and I'm so afraid of people *seeing* my pride, that when I'm up there sharing my writing, I can barely hide my pride, and that awakens feelings of shame and makes my body useless…

Again, this shame comes from feeling unworthy of doing well and not accepting the fact that God wants me to do well at what God's called me to do—else how can I help people, and what's the point in being here?

Imagination

I think I could have let Katherine know that I was flattered by her comments. That would have been an honest response. I could have done this in a way that in no way took her sharing lightly, for it was difficult for her to be so intimate. I could have said something like: "Katherine, what you are telling me is a great gift. You know I haven't always been sure about what to say to you. Sometimes I've wanted to take your pain away. In the beginning I thought I had to have answers for you. So I have been uncertain about how to help, and I could ask for no finer affirmation than what you've just said. It is quite a compliment and I'm deeply grateful."

To do this would have required me to not try to deny the seemingly conflicting facts that I felt proud and unworthy, but to face these feelings and walk through them—not squelch them in an effort to hide them, out of shame for feeling them.

CHAPTER 19

Colleagues

Martin is an ordained pastoral psychotherapist, with a great deal of experience working with "difficult" therapeutic cases, people suffering with one of the psychoses or borderline character disorders. Sam was one of his counselees who, in his words, "changed" Martin's understanding of therapy and "shaped" his theology. Martin's work with Sam is recorded in the following case study, written by Martin.

I have included this case study in the book for three reasons. Most obvious is the movement in Martin's understanding of therapy. When he began meeting with Sam, Martin assumed the usual, condescending model; he was treating Sam because Sam was troubled; Martin was the change agent, Sam the person to be changed. But Sam changed Martin. Martin realized that their relation was a mutual one.

The second reason for choosing the case is that, in the transcriptions of the conversations between Martin and Sam and in Martin's comments, the reader can trace the course of this transformation as it happened. One can see how Martin begins in a traditional therapeutic position but increasingly finds himself caught up in, and excited about, Sam's ideas. Martin presents the specific data of his own transformation from condescension to mutuality.

The third reason is the clarity with which Sam's voice emerges, not as a disabled patient, but as a knowledgeable and humorous colleague in the therapy. As Sam says, understanding him is "difficult." Sam explains that he is "confusing," essentially because others have either not listened to him or, when they did, have misunderstood and attacked him. In other words, he has very good reasons for being "difficult," reasons that almost anyone in an oppressed position in a society can understand.

While Martin attempts to diagnose Sam, he does not present Sam's words primarily to prove a diagnosis. He takes what Sam says seriously and learns from it. He opens up a channel through which Sam's voice and wisdom can reach others.

148

This work, in its very difficulty, shows one way that care professionals can con-tribute to the construction of mutuality, rather than condescension. They can, like Martin, become skilled in providing ways for those whose knowledge has been subjugated to share their wisdom. We can learn from Martin the value of listening to Sam and others like him, not in order to fix them up, but in order to learn from and with them, even if such listening is difficult.

Introduction: Biblical Work

Sam originally called for an appointment because he was told by his counselor at a rehabilitation program that he needed counseling and fur-ther evaluation before entering college. At the time of his first session, I found in the waiting room of my office a good-looking man in his early thirties. He was casually but appropriately dressed. By the end of the first session, I understood why he had been referred: I could make sense of almost nothing he had said, and what I did understand concerned me, for at least one major topic was suicide. My immediate impression was that the guy was nuts. But Sam was clearly different from the many psychotic, near-psychotic, or even troubled people I had dealt with, in that he did not seem at all unhappy. He wasn't in a euphoric or manic state; he had talked about some problems he had, some encounters that made him angry, some, sad. But after he left, I realized that I was quietly happy and that this emo-tional state was connected with him. I looked forward to seeing him again.

In the first sessions, Sam said that he had sought out a *pastoral* counse-lor because he had been doing some "biblical work." Specifically, he had written a book, and he wondered if I could help him to get it published. He began to read me stories from the book and then gave me a copy to read. I found most of what he had written to be incomprehensible. I suggested that we might use the sessions to deepen his "biblical explorations" by his sharing them with me and helping me to understand them.

So we began a dialogue in which he would read from his writings or simply talk, and I would break in either with a reflection of what he had said or, more often, with the response, "Unpack that for me." He never seemed offended (as I would have expected a schizophrenic, borderline, or severely character-disordered person to be) when I did not understand, but would patiently reword what he had said or had written.

At first his unpackings made as little sense to me as the original state-ments, but gradually I began to understand his conceptual system. As I did so, I was frequently stunned to find a depth of religious vision and psychological insight that was suggestive of the thought of religious contemplatives, theologians, and psychologists.

His thought began to seem less disorganized than simply alien—almost as though he were speaking a different language. Still however, it exhib-ited characteristics usually associated with the thought of psychotics or borderlines. Boundaries between self and the world and between self and other were fluid and permeable. It was highly symbolic, and the symbols were autistic, unique to himself. It was loose—he associated ideas and things that were unrelated in normal discourse. It was self-referential: The Bible and others were understood almost wholly in terms of his own individual experience. He did not obey fundamental rules of grammar and syntax.

Yet his thought was also unlike borderline or psychotic thought in that others, and Sam himself, were conceived fully, as having both good and bad characteristics, as unique and complex, limited, finite persons, each with his or her distinctive history. My diagnostic categories failed to help me make any real sense of him.

As time progressed, I also began to wonder about whether my conceptions of therapy made any sense with him. Originally I thought of myself as an ego around whom he could organize his thoughts and from whom he could learn how to communicate them more effectively. But then I found myself using his images and conceptual system to think about the nature of the human self in relation to God—he was organizing my thinking.

At one point, Sam indicated that he was quite aware of what he was doing, when he said that he was teaching me his way of thinking. Nevertheless, he also acknowledged that with my reflections he was able to go deeper in his biblical exploration and self-analysis, and to communicate better with others. So my original conception of the therapy with him was not all off. Rather, it did not account for the growing sense of mutuality in the counseling, the sense that he was helping me perhaps as much as I him.

What follows are excerpts from Sam's writings and the talks he and I have had, interspersed with my comments and explanations. Sam often attempts to understand others through writing from their point of view. I'll first discuss a letter he wrote from the point of view of a young woman he met. In this letter, he describes himself as this young woman sees him and so introduces himself. Since the letter is addressed to me, he also indicates how he views the relationship with me.

Trusted Walls: The Uses of Confusion

Hull'o Martin:

Hate to bother someone who has something to do that is important. But one who understands Sam can be a difficult task. Anyone who tries to understand Sam has to be very patient in what kind of stuff Sam presents to you or anyone. Sam doesn't care in his approachments. But the bad thing about it Sam knows what he is doing. Where today is to live peacefully a child is born in the image of God. But God doesn't feel that way. I have learned what has been done from this image. Who I have approached God this supposedly calls himself an angel. Clothes on me trust the fool. But no I had to be the fool who had trust this so called angel. Where did this fool come from? Sam especially takes no consideration at times in how confusing he can be. Without explaining his actions. —Eve—

An edited transcription of Sam's and my conversation about this letter in a counseling session follows:

Martin: How come Sam takes no consideration of how confusing he can be?

Sam: ". . .or felt that this is just another false God trying to write something to make himself look good like a god" [quote from another of Sam's pieces that had been discussed in this session].

Martin: Sometimes you are confusing because you aren't sure [if] who you're facing is a false God. And sometimes you write something to make yourself look good...

Sam: But then it goes back to this other piece, "which boils down to felt this been with these to fear God" [another quote from the same piece].

Martin: Unpack that for me.

Sam: If I don't confuse them a little bit, they're liable to fear.

Martin: So part of the confusion is the respected wall, is a way of respecting their wall...Your sense is that if you aren't confusing then people will get real scared.

Sam: Right.

Martin: It sounds like that is your experience.

Sam: My drinking buddies eventually turned away from me. It wasn't that they feared me. It was the confusion there. But it was based upon fear. But actually it was confusion...

In AA, we [an alcoholic friend and I] sat down and had a real good talk. He was really talking deep, and I was covering his approachment and what he was looking for. He was looking for answers to deep religious questions, and as he was asking these deep religious questions, I was covering his questions with—you know—good answers—appropriate, simple. He wasn't realizing it. He didn't realize he was really talking approach someone in the image of God. When he started talking deeper and deeper and deeper, he began to realize that this was the image of God, he broke down, turned around and ran.

Martin: You got too deep for him.

Sam: Yes.

Martin: When you're being confusing, you're taking consideration. It's respecting the wall. Not to be confusing is to scare people somehow.

A number of Sam's key concepts emerge in this letter and conversation. All human beings, Sam holds, are created "images of God." In its original form, this image is "sheer"—transparent to God. People become "distant from the image"—they build up a "wall" between their conscious selves and their real selves. The primary reason for this wall is negative "feedback"—expectations from others, primarily parents, that their child be different from who she or he actually is. In this way the parents "deface" the child's image. While the image is always perfect, the distant false self is a "perfectionist." It rejects the image, thereby joining the parents in their "defacement" of it. It seeks the perfection it has lost by attempting to live up to others'—initially the parents'—expectations. It thus "dreams" or "imagines," a self-perfection different from that of the original image. It can never live up to these perfectionist dreams because they are based upon how other people are, not how the person truly is.

So the dreaming false self becomes "jealous" of these other people who seem so easily to be "perfect." It builds up another wall between itself and these others. At the same time, it blames itself for being unable to live up to its expectations, and another wall is built up within itself. The self becomes dominated by what Sam calls a "spinning wall"—a moving wall that continually divides itself, the self, and the self from others and from the world. The reality of the self as created in the "image of God," the reality of others as also "images of God," and the reality of the world are lost in "confusion" as the wall spins to protect the self against the devastating "recognition" of its fragmented and "distant" state.

One can "break" through another's spinning wall and help to heal the divisions in another if one lets God work through oneself. Without the "patience" that comes from knowing it is God who does the work and not oneself, anyone who attempts to break through another's wall will be perceived by that other as a major threat. The attempt to break through—or "approachment"—will be misunderstood and will lead to further confusion, fear, and more walls in the approached person. People's walls, despite their pathological origins, are thus to be "respected"—they are "respected, trusted walls."

Sam talks about a second, healthier kind of "respected, trusted wall" given by God to a person who truly lives in the image of God. This wall protects the faithful person against the negative "feedback" he receives, against the attempts by others to "deface" his image.

Sam is conscious of, and has four reasons for, being confusing to others. First, he claims to have been raised in a family in which communication was always distorted. He felt that he had to learn how to talk to people on his own. He thus developed his own conceptual system, which is different from that of others.

Second, he claims that his thought is so "simple" that, in this complex world of "spinning walls," what he says is almost always misunderstood. Third, he found that it is necessary to be confusing out of respect for others' walls. To be direct, as he found with his drinking buddies and friends at AA, is to risk scaring people and actually creating more confusion within them.

Fourth, confusion is sometimes a function of his own "respected, trusted wall," a way he defends himself against attack or expresses his "impatience."

For instance, Sam once said to one of his customers, who was harassing him on the telephone, "Everybody wants to kill me with the dragon that spits fire and causes death." This comment makes sense within Sam's biblical world as a rather accurate description of what the customer was doing to him over the telephone. But Sam knew very well that this comment would cause the customer to think Sam was nuts and to hang up, thereby ending the harassment.

Unlike the thought of most psychotics, Sam's thought both coheres logically and, while boundaries are fluid, contains a full recognition of, and respect for, the differentiations between himself and others. Psychologically, his theory of the way "walls" form within the psyche has some similarities to the theories of D. W. Winnicott, Heinz Kohut, and Carl Rogers. All three of these major psychologists discuss how the failure of parents to recognize and affirm their children's developing self can lead to splits within the psyche, the development of a false self, and continuing problems with the maintenance of self-esteem, healthy relationships with others, and contact with reality.

These psychologists also emphasize, as does Sam, that any therapeutic interventions must be carried out with a great deal of patience and a fundamental respect for a troubled person's defenses—"walls." Simply to break through the defenses is to cause, again as Sam realizes, more defenses to be built. To persist in such an attack is, at least according to Kohut, to risk contributing to the fragmentation of the troubled person's self—according to Sam, to risk sending the person to the state mental hospital.

Conversion: Being Sheer

The religious dimension so central to Sam's thought is not dealt with by these psychologists. His combination of psychological and religious understanding is, at certain points, reminiscent of the anthropological thought of Martin Buber. Buber also described the true self as created in the image of God and as therefore "sheer" in a certain way—to enter into relation with the other as Thou is to look through that other to the eternal Thou or God. Buber described how a child who is not adequately "confirmed" by her parents can become an adult who is unable to confirm herself. Needing such confirmation, she hides behind a veil of "seeming"—a false self which she hopes will win her the confirmation of others. Any confirmation she receives, however, is not of who she truly is and so does not meet her need. Such a person desperately seeks confirmation through increasingly self-deceptive means. Her psyche becomes more and more complex, and the reality of who she, others, and the world are is less and less known—in Sam's words, she becomes "distant from recognition." She will, if a conversion does not occur, drift into radical evil or mania—in Sam's thought, she will "judge" and so destroy others or herself.[1]

---

[1] For a full discussion of Martin Buber's anthropology of human becoming, see Roy Steinhoff Smith 1985, Ph.D. dissertation, 12–106.

The possibility and reality of conversion is the central theme of Sam's work as a whole and of the following two stories, which were the first of his writings he read to me:

Dull Empty Hook

Today I am just too scared to think, or even face my honesty. I know my name and what day it is. I am losing more faith as each day goes by. So I went fishing by myself. I came across this person who was catching all kinds of fish. I asked if I could use the same bait. Go ahead. So I baited my hook. Then casted into the lake. I couldn't figure it out. No fish and here I am an hour later. Not even a nibble. So I went into the world again. Getting beat up and lost. So I went back fishing. That person was still there. Catching all kinds of fish. I asked if you would mind again. No. Go ahead. I casted again into the lake. Still no fish again not even a nibble. My jealousy pushed me back into the world again. Now I am totally beat up and lost. So I went back fishing for the last time. That person was still there. I asked for the last time. Lost all my faith and patience at the point to end it all. Babbled this, as I casted for the last time. Started swearing because I couldn't catch any kind of fish. I even said, God I give up. I am going to drown. Nothing works for God's child that I am. God is no where around when you really need God. I turned to this person swearing at him. I just cannot take it any longer. There is one wish before I go. But God doesn't love me. I cannot even catch just one fish. As this person I was with turned towards me. Try just one more time. There is hope. But you have to cast an empty hook. You have to be joking. Only God could catch something on an empty hook. It won't kill you. Since you are going to drown yourself anyways if you don't catch anything. Okay you are right. So I almost forgot: why I am still alive. As I casted as far as I could. This empty hook had me laughing out of my pants. Like I am going to catch something with it. When all of a sudden I felt a tug. I couldn't believe it. I started to reel it in. When I noticed it wasn't an ordinary fish. I just couldn't explain what I felt on this empty hook. Which I have casted in the lake and my dream came true. As it was getting closer to shore. My insides told me it wasn't a fish for sure. I was in shock to see Christ to walk out of the water. No, whatever you done in your past. No matter what that is. That your past is gone. For there is a life out there full of life and gifts. For you have been resurrected my child. From anymore of these past punishments. God blessed this dull empty hook.

Personal Football Game

It is just another football game. Big deal. Another day wasted by the television set. This antenna just has to go. Even though the season ends next week. As I onlook this television of mine. It's just a bunch of snow. Similar to my insides a snow storm. Like I am watching it from the next county. Oh well time for kickoff. I cannot even see what's going on. Same as my life. But who cares. What yard line are they at. Who has the ball. It is like who has my life. Who is really running it. Well this speaker shot. So I just cannot hear what is actually going on either. Just like this outside world of mine. Not knowing what they are talking about. Oh well quarterback is fading back. Just like me. Not knowing in who to throw my life to next. As he throws down field it is caught. Alright a touchdown. I wonder if life ends there. Well doesn't it. Now the other team has the ball. The line comes forward to make a wall. But the devil has smothered the quarterback. Just like my life is run by him. Well it's second down and twenty yards to go for first down. The quarterback is really torn up. As the quarterback drops back and passes my life away to a useless receiver. Only because my life had to have all these heavy faults. The one I trusted dropped my life. Now it is third and twenty. Quarterback is now really hot. I am also hot but not even playing football. I still see God throwing flags all over the place. For all the faults I have been carrying. I am still throwing my life. Hoping it will be caught by an honest receiver and help me with my fumbles. My life full of judges. But who and how can I trust, when they only can run to the end zone and stop. Just like my life that is in me it stops there. No further than the end zone. But don't run out of bounds. Life to be showing off will become unmanageable. But who cares as long as I don't carry the ball no one will think I have any faults. Where I felt untouched and safe. I can trust and won't harm me in anyway. So the quarterback has handed off my life to the full back. My God couldn't even hold onto my faults. There goes my life rolling around the ground. I had to jump on it. To save myself from anymore humility. I am swearing up and down. Who done this to me. Where is that brick wall you promised me. So no one knew I had any faults. Oh well I jumped on my life to save another down. Well I was glad it was fourth down and twenty-seven now. Just my luck I was punted into A.A. No one throws flags on my face no more. Personal Football Game.

These stories exemplify the diagnostic dilemma Sam placed me in. Especially the second story seems almost paradigmatic of the writing of schizophrenics. One of my supervisors—a psychiatrist who had done extensive work with schizophrenics—used the following analogy: Thought is like moving images projected on a screen. In schizophrenics, the screen has holes in it and is constantly rippled by waves. Basic cognitive concepts and categories thus are never clearly formed. The continuity of basic concepts over time is also absent. Sam's description of his mind as a TV set with the speakers out and a snowy picture is almost synonymous with this description. On the other hand, Sam's consistent and humorous self observation is not characteristic of schizophrenics. Sam clearly has an observing ego, associated by most psychologists with a mature and healthy psyche. His gentle humor, in which he recognizes and accepts his "faults," is, according to Kohut, a virtue usually achieved by a mature and healthy psyche only in middle age.

In these two stories, Sam talks about his movement from being "defaced" and "distant from recognition," dominated by the "spinning wall," to being "sheer." Both stories begin with a description of Sam's state before conversion. He can't "face" himself honestly. Rather, his life is ruled by "confusion." He attempts to escape his suffering, not by understanding and accepting his true image, but by attempting to borrow "bait" from someone else or simply by "throwing" himself into someone else's hands. The following excerpt from a session in which we discussed another of Sam's pieces clarifies his understanding of this unconverted state.

These Fears Exist

Sam: [begins to read] I just don't see why I should get up. My fears have smothered my dreams. Tomorrow in my world will never come. My life has been destroyed. Built this image to ignore my responsibilities. Hate everything because there is no God. My feedback is the only thing I can respect. Who am I abusing. When I cannot even appreciate this life of no where to be found. Bitter beyond frustrated when someone tries and touch my wall. My fears become strong only because I lost my trust in who would really understand my guilt. My friends are distant. But I am grateful that I have a few. [Sam stops reading, comments.] What that means is irresponsible friends. You feel safe with them and you feel grateful for them.

Martin: Friends who

Sam: are in the same boat.

Martin: Not just in the same boat, but friends who support you in your own defacing of yourself.

Sam: Yeah, right. [He resumes reading.] My courage only to be fading away. My taste for my effectiveness became emotional fell into depression. Distinguish my ways to become blinded in my sight. Heard no one who tried to enter my wall. Failed to vanish someday soon.

Martin: "Failed to vanish someday soon." Unpack that.

Sam: Failed because yesterday I attempted suicide but I'm still living today. So yesterday I failed to take my life.

Martin: Failed to vanish.

Sam: Right. Right. But someday soon.

Martin: Who's this story written by? Who's speaking this story?

Sam: This is my past.

Martin: How long ago?

Sam: Six years ago.

Martin: So you did make a suicide attempt.

Sam: [nods and resumes reading] No one cares why should I. My dreams are near end. Not even wisdom can heal me. I just won't let it. My wall is too bright to let me down. [Sam stops reading, comments.] I built a bright wall.

Martin: How's the wall bright?

Sam: This is the bright wall of hallucination...I'm lost in that brightness. But it's bright because of the colors in there and it makes me feel comfortable...

Martin: ...It's a bright wall, leads you astray.

Sam: Umhm [resumes reading] Very violent inside a lot of hurt. Why me. Running with no patience. Jealous for things. I know I will be one of the lonely ones in the future. Out there confused in my fears. Why me. Today I cannot even comprehend. Born dusted drifting into a useless furnish full of fears. These Fears Exist.

Martin: "Born dusted drifting into a useless furnish full of fears." Unpack that.

Sam: Image of dust and born dusted. Born dusted is saying that I was born sin-free. But yet drifted into a useless furnish full of fears.

Martin: What's a "useless furnish full of fears"?

Sam: I made myself useless and the furnish part is that I furnished these fears to be useless to me.

The unconverted individual is dominated by fear, bitterness, jealousy, and hate. Alienated from the true image, this individual is also alienated from God. The false "image" is built up around "hallucinations" and is supported by "irresponsible friends." Yet, this individual is lonely, violent, and suicidal. Usually, "bright" and "furnished" are positive adjectives for Sam; they describe an image that is sheer to God and that is nurtured. In the unconverted, however, what is good becomes bad—hallucinations are seductive because they are "bright" and fears are nurtured—"furnished."

This sense of the ambiguity of evaluative terms is not characteristic of psychotics or character-disordered individuals. Notice that, also unlike severely emotionally ill individuals, Sam neither condemns himself nor others for this hellish state. He recognizes the responsibility both he and his parents bear for his problems, but such recognition does not lead to "judgment"—lack of acceptance.

Sam recognizes such "judgment" as perhaps the central symptom of an unconverted individual. The following discussion follows the one just quoted and refers to another story, "Within This Choice," in which Sam records the thoughts of a couple in the midst of a fight. In this discussion, he describes how the conversion occurs from judging and defacing others and oneself to being sheer.

Sam: In "Within This Choice,"...it's mass confusion, and there's no common sense in their relationship because they're always bringing up their parents as a escapegoat.

Martin: As a wall.

Sam: Right, as a wall. Because they can't see themselves, but they can see their parents, and what it is is that their parents are inside their wall, so they can use their parents before they can use themselves. And it's also Christ being suffered.

Martin: How?

Sam: Because he's taking the pressure.

Martin: He falls within those walls which they set up.

Sam: That's right, he's suffering just as much as they are.

Martin: So anytime anyone has walls,...Christ is there suffering as much as they are.

Sam: Just like a coke user or anything else, Christ himself is suffering just as much as the image itself.

Martin: But Christ is strong enough to break the walls.

Sam: To break the walls. That's when a coke person becomes coke free.

Martin: So when a coke person becomes coke free, that's Christ.

Sam: That's right. He went through Christ. Same with an alcoholic— the same process.

Martin: That's what "going into the cross" is about.

Sam: Right, right. They crossed all three images within themselves. But that's why they're still confused, because they don't understand the process they went through.

Martin: So it can happen without you understanding it.

Sam: Right, right, but yet they're grateful because something took place. That's where the quotations come in, breaking it down to where it's understandable.

Martin: And that's what you've been trying to do for all this time. You crossed the three images. You went through Christ...you've been trying to understand what happened.

Sam: Right.

Martin: And you've understood now.

Sam: That's when I bury myself with God.

Martin: Ah hah. Bury yourself with God in order to understand?

Sam: Right.

Martin: Bury yourself means you've got to die.

Sam: Right. Inside.

Martin: Inside.

Sam: Just like "These Fears Exist." I died with my past for this to come out.

Martin: Your past had to die in order for there to be true understanding.

Sam: Right.

Martin: 'Cause your past is all confused.

Sam: Right. And it died. And so if I bury myself with God, the communication is patience to where we've both opened up to each other, and through this bottom piece deep in God, I let God write. So what I'm saying is that I bury this piece to God. And let God write through me.

Martin: So it's no longer you who are writing. It's God writing through you.

Sam: Right.

Martin: Because you're dead.

Sam: Right. Right.

Martin: Or you're sheer.

Sam: Right.

Martin: Being buried with God and your image being sheer, is that the same thing?

Sam: Yeah. Let him do the work. It's just like a doctor doing the same thing—healing you. He's giving himself to God. Not realizing he's doing it though. The bottom half, his hands, healing the cuts and wounds. So we're all in the image.

Martin: That's what "lowered" is like.

Sam: Right.

Martin: When we lower ourselves, in a way we die, we lower ourselves into the earth. And we become sheer to God.

Sam: For God to do the work.

Martin: For God to do the work.

Sam: Right.

Martin: And the whole source of the defacement is because

Sam: it went to the head.

Martin: It went to the head. We think we're doing it. We think we're understanding.

Sam: Right.

Martin: We think we've done it all.

Sam: Right. That's why I can't go out in the world and say, "I got it." Because the only thing I have is myself.

Martin: And you've only got yourself when you're sheer.

Sam: Right.

Martin: And that's a gift of God.

Sam: Right. But as long as I'm honest in sharing it where no harm is done, that's a different story. That's more or less trying to be friendly and a gift. Sharing a gift, put it that way.

Martin: As long as you're patient.

Sam: Yeah.

Some of the key events in Sam's history clarify his conception of conversion as it is presented above. Sam was born with a heart defect. He had open heart surgery when he was four. His mother was very protective of him and prevented him from playing actively with his friends. Sam thus came to feel that he was an outsider and that this alienation was somehow his fault.

When Sam was eight, his father was killed in an accident at the plant in which he worked. He was apparently standing in a restricted and very dangerous area. Sam feels that his father committed suicide because he was suffering greatly due to conflicts with Sam's mother. This loss was devastating to Sam.

Soon thereafter, Sam and his brother were sent to boarding school because his mother didn't feel she could handle them. While they were away, she remarried and soon was pregnant again.

Sam's initial experience of boarding school as another indication of his being at fault was soon superseded by a growing sense of confidence in himself. This confidence was built up by the "coach," a man who encouraged Sam to participate in sports while carefully monitoring him for signs of heart trouble. From this coach, Sam learned to monitor himself for such signs. More importantly, he learned that he could be like other boys.

After four years of boarding school, Sam's mother withdrew him. He feels she did so because she was worried about his growing involvement with sports. Sam again was devastated. Lost in a large public school, he soon began to drink. Within two years, by about age 14, he was an "alcoholic." He now says that he was using the alcohol to replace his father. It was on his father's birthday over fifteen years later that he decided to give up drinking as a kind of pledge to his father. He went into AA and says that he has not had a drink since.

Shortly before giving up the alcohol, while drinking, Sam had a very serious accident in which the artery in his arm was slashed. He describes himself as unconsciously doing the right thing to keep himself alive—tying a tourniquet around his arm and keeping it raised. Nevertheless, he lost so much blood that the doctors at the emergency room were apparently surprised that he survived.

Sam uses alcoholism as the metaphor for the condition of the person who has not gone through conversion. The alcoholic lives in a dream world in which he achieves perfection and is lauded by all others. Like all unconverted people, then, the alcoholic seeks to replace the perfection he lost when his image was defaced. In creating his own "image" of himself, the alcoholic takes himself for God. His God-given capacity for thought and understanding "goes to the head."

But this false image can only be maintained if the true image, and indeed all reality is denied—the true image because it is seen as being imperfect and reality because it does not confirm the alcoholic's grandiose fantasies. The alcoholic continually attacks or "judges" his true image, further defacing it. The primary wall dividing the unconverted person is between the false image, which dwells in the "head," the person's consciousness, and the "true image," which dwells in the unconscious "bottom half of the body"—below the head. Since the alcoholic's or unconverted's dreamed-of perfection contradicts the only perfection possible for him—the perfection of the image which he judges as bad—he continually is frustrated and attacks who he truly is.

Conversion, according to Sam, can only occur through death. Knowing what we do about Sam's history, we can see why understanding death as somehow positive is so central to him. His life has been dominated by the imminent possibility, even likelihood at times, of his own death, and by his father's mysterious death. Sam's most intriguing and challenging conceptions cluster around the task of understanding death.

Death and Going through Christ

"Going through Christ" rests upon his highly paradoxical understanding of Christ. "Christ" both dwells in the image and yet is differentiated from it. Christ in a person suffers whenever that person suffers. Sam's understanding of Christ here appears to be quite similar to the apostle Paul's, who also described Christ as living within the person as her true God-given nature and as bearing all her suffering.

An unconverted person's frustration and suffering can become so great that, under the domination of the false self, she "judges the image dead"—she wholly destroys her own created nature, which she blames for her suffering. In killing her own image, the person crucifies Christ—she goes "through Christ"—her image and Christ's have both been judged and executed.

Such a person is then "lowered into the earth with God"—the image and Christ are buried together. Sam also uses the following metaphor to describe this spiritual death: The "image" is "lowered" from the conscious "head" into the unconscious "bottom half of the body." Sam may also have picked up on the biblical passages in which "death" is talked of as "sleep"; he says that this "lowering" happens to all of us when we sleep.

To be "lowered" is also described by Sam as "going into the Cross." When one is lowered, "three images" of God are "crossed." We have already seen how "Christ" and the "image of God"—the created nature of the person—are brought together. Since "lowering" is also into the "earth" or the unconscious "body," these two images become united with the third, which Sam calls the "holy dust"—the dead, insensate stuff out of which God creates us.

While all the above terms are metaphors, Sam is not just talking metaphorically here. In his experience of death, the real death is the spiritual one—the death of the image. If the image is not "resurrected" by God, then bodily death will occur. All rests in the hands of God. If God knows that future life will bring overwhelming suffering to a person, then God mercifully "removes" the person from life. Sam feels that God determined that the future would hold even greater suffering for his father and so "removed" him. If God knows that a person who has spiritually died has the possibility of future fulfillment, then God will "resurrect" the image. Sam is convinced that his accident, which occurred when he was spiritually drowned in alcohol, would have resulted in bodily death had not God done what was necessary to keep him alive. He also feels that his decision to stop drinking was due to God's having "raised" his image with Christ. His past, dominated by "defacement," was truly dead. He was freed to live a new life, one not "distant from the image," but "sheer" to God—a life in which he acknowledges day-to-day that whatever good he does or understanding he achieves is not due to his own efforts, but to God shining through him.

A Parable for Pastoral Counselors

Sam is a parable for pastoral counselors. I am using "parable" as John Dominic Crossan defines the word to mean a story that calls into question and thereby "subverts" the world as human beings have ordered it.[2] Throughout this study, I have indicated how Sam calls into question the diagnostic categories and psychotherapeutic theories with which I have constructed an understanding of the psychological world of my clients. Here I will summarize these questions and raise some new ones.

Sam ties my diagnostic categories into knots. As I have indicated, his thought is both highly characteristic and uncharacteristic of that of schizophrenics. One supervisor suggested that Sam is an "ambulatory schizophrenic." Such a label might make some sense if we consider it carefully. "Schizophrenia" is for most psychologists about the worst diagnosis that can be given someone. In our society, schizophrenics are stigmatized as paradigmatic "crazy people." Often they are feared as violent and dangerous (an unwarranted fear, since the percentages of schizophrenics and of the rest of the population who are violent are about the same). Schizophrenics are usually disabled by their illness, living out their lives dependent upon the care of others.

When one places "ambulatory" in front of "schizophrenia," one identifies a person who, while schizophrenic, is functional in the society, one who can work, and support himself, and lead a somewhat "normal" life. However, an "ambulatory schizophrenic" is still stigmatized as "ill"— "ambulatory" status does not bring with it integration as "healthy" into "normal" society. One assumes that the ambulatory schizophrenic has heroically compensated for what is still a fundamental disability.

Such an label fits Sam, but not very well. He does have some of the difficulties associated with schizophrenia, primarily with communicating with others. He is "ambulatory"; he has a job and, while he lives at his parents' home, is quite independent. He is still seen as "crazy" by his family and by those in his community with whom he comes into contact. His capacity to function can be seen as due to a heroic effort.

But I am not at all sure that the label and this description fit Sam's understanding of himself. Sam admits to having difficulties communicating with people, but this is not a fundamental or even very important problem in his view. The basic problem he has had to deal with is one which he shares with all "normal" people: being "distant from the image," alienated from one's created nature. This problem cannot be compensated for by

---

[2] John Dominic Crossan, *The Dark Interval: Towards a Theology of Story* (Allen, Tex.: Argus Communications, 1975), 54–57.

heroic effort. It can only be overcome when one gives up; one must "let go, let God." Most people do not reach the "bottom," have not been "buried with God," and so have not been "resurrected" into new life. Sam feels he has and so has something to offer others. He might call himself (he hasn't in my presence) an "ambulatory sinner," but that's the best any of us can hope to become.

The problem may lie in my attempt to "diagnose" Sam. To "diagnose" is to place people on a medical continuum that runs from "severely ill" to "healthy." Sam does not place himself on this continuum, but on a religious one that stretches between the poles "defaced" and "resurrected." What emerges in our dialogue is the profound difference between my medical and his religious understandings of the world. "Symptoms" of an extremely serious "illness" in the medical world are relatively minor "faults" in Sam's religious world. One can be medically "healthy" or "normal" and still "defaced" religiously.

The recognition that my difficulty in understanding Sam may lie in my attempts to diagnose him leads to the real parable he poses for me as a pastoral counselor. If I give up trying to diagnose Sam, I find that I do understand him, but not as a pastoral counselor understands a client. I understand him as I would a colleague. I come back to Sam's understanding of counseling as consultation about his "biblical work." Counseling with Sam *does* feel much more like talking over something important with a colleague or friend. During the course of therapy, we learned from each other. When I look back at other clients with whom I have entered into what I have called "real" therapy, I realize that these relationships have been like the one with Sam. "Real" therapy, for me, seems to be much more like talking with a colleague or friend than diagnosing and treating a client.

CHAPTER 20

Friends

The following case is one of my own, an account of my relation to a member of the Mamre community. With him, I called into question my clinical and professional position.

Johnny O. is a small, wiry, ebony-skinned man in his mid-fifties. As a child he was beaten. At the age of ten, his injuries resulted in his becoming legally blind. He can see vague shapes, but he often cannot walk through a room without bumping into furniture. His difficulty gets worse when he has been drinking, which is most of the time.

In his lower neck is a scar, where he was shot decades ago in a street fight. As a result of this injury, his speech is a kind of explosive stutter, which becomes almost incomprehensible when he's been drinking.

He has surprisingly beautiful hands, with long thin, even delicate, fingers. These hands betray a sensitive and quick intelligence, which usually remains hidden behind the stutter and the numbing effect of alcohol.

During the first year and a half of Mamre, Johnny O. had been an occasional visitor. He usually sat quietly and gave a shy, cowering smile when addressed.

One Saturday afternoon, one of his friends said that Johnny O. wanted to see me. He was at another friend's house. I drove over. Informed that I was there, Johnny O. stumbled to the car and begged me to help him. He was stuttering badly and had obviously been drinking. He was frightened—of what, I couldn't quite grasp. I took him over to our house, and, when he didn't seem to be getting much better, to the Emergency Room of a local hospital. They referred him to a treatment center in a town about fifty miles away. I drove him there. The intake worker referred him to the medical center in another town for an evaluation. At the medical center, he began having convulsions connected with the d.t.'s. He was terrified, desperately and spasmodically clenching my hand. After remaining in the Emergency Room for a few hours, he was admitted to the psychiatric ward.

A week and a half later, he was discharged. He was clean, his hair was neatly cut. He no longer cowered when I talked with him. When he spoke, I could understand him; his speech seemed to have been nearly healed. He straightened up, rather than hunched over, when he walked. During the drive back to Enid, we joked with each other about the long evening and night of driving a week and a half earlier.

About a week later, he was dropped off at our house by one of his old drinking buddies. He had obviously been drinking but was belligerent in his denials when I confronted him. I took him to his apartment. He was sullen, and I was disappointed and angry. Sometime during this encounter, he talked about taking some pills—he had bought a bottle of aspirin the day before.

I left, but I was uneasy. I drove back to tell him that I was very concerned about his talk of taking pills and about his drinking. After getting angry at me for suggesting that he had been drinking, Johnny O. admitted that he wanted to kill himself. He wondered why I bothered with him. I put my arm around him and said something about "loving" him and about his not being able to get rid of me that easily. He was shaking and looked as if he were going to have convulsions. He was very frightened. I suggested that we go to the hospital so that he could get the care he needed. He agreed.

At the Emergency Room the doctor said that he needed to go to a state psychiatric facility. Johnny O. very reluctantly agreed, and we left for another long late-night drive.

Just before we got to the state hospital, we drove through a large town. Johnny O. told me about visiting a friend in this town once a decade earlier and about what a racist place it was—it was dangerous for a black man even to be there. He was relieved when we got through it.

At the hospital, he needed some convincing to stay. He continued to be very frightened. A breath test indicated that he had drunk enough to kill him.

Driving back alone from the hospital after midnight, I pulled off and stopped to rest. I was at least ten miles from the nearest town, in the middle of the desert. It was very quiet, with just a bit of breeze. The moon provided enough light to let me see a little way. I tipped my seat back and closed my eyes. A moment later, they slammed open. I hadn't heard anything. I knew there was no one around. Still, I felt strongly that someone was creeping up on the car. I started up the engine, turned on the lights, and drove off. Later it occurred to me that my terror reflected Johnny O.'s sense of being totally alone in a malevolent world.

A bit over a month later, he was discharged. After five days, he was drinking again, and I took him to a halfway house in a city an hour and a half away from Enid where he could stay indefinitely.

One weekend a month or so later, I drove down to the city and picked him up and brought him back to Enid for a visit. Well after the time I was supposed to drive him back to the city, I went looking for him and found him in Southern Heights. It was night. He was drunk and very angry at me because I was telling him he needed to go back to the halfway house. He cursed me and, when I didn't move, he hit me in the chest. Then he turned and ran, stumbling down the middle of the street. I ran after him and told him I was going to stick with him. Finally, he turned into my arms. I held him as he wept. Then I drove him to the halfway house.

He did well for a while, but after another month, got drunk again and ended up in a hospital detox program. The director of the halfway house kicked him out. I drove down to the city and brought him back to Enid. He and I were quiet on that drive. We both realized that I had run out of ways to help him.

We stayed in touch for a while, but he didn't seem to want to see much of me. After a couple of months, I found out that he was living in a tiny shack behind the house of the man who supplied him with liquor. Then he went back into the state hospital. A month later, I learned that he had been released and wanted to see me.

About this time, in talking with a friend, I struggled to explain what I didn't understand why caring for Johnny O. had not seemed a heavy burden. I finally admitted that an undercurrent of joy came with getting to know Johnny O. Yet I felt a strong reluctance to respond to his desire to see me.

Later, I overcame that reluctance and dropped by his shack to bring him to a Thursday evening Mamre Christmas celebration. He was drunk and wouldn't come. A week later, I visited him again. He was in a very bad way, drinking heavily and full of unreal dreams about relatives leaving him money. He asked me to get him a cheeseburger. Then, before I left to get the food, he clung to me, begging me not to betray him. I brought him the cheeseburger and told him I'd drop in the next day.

I did drop in on him and we talked. He was not as drunk. We were more at ease with each other. After this time, I saw him regularly, but less frequently. He began coming back to the Mamre meal.

About the time my family and I left Enid, six months later, Johnny O., after another hospitalization, moved into a nursing home. He stayed there for about a year and apparently did not drink for much of this time. He did the laundry and helped care for other patients. I visited him a few times there. He proudly showed me around and introduced me to the patients for whom he voluntarily cared. He seemed happy during this time. The staff and patients at the nursing home appreciated him.

He had to leave the nursing home because the state would no longer pay for his care there. The last time I saw him was during a visit to Enid. He was in front of a liquor store and had been drinking. I was happy to see him and he, me. We hugged, and he began telling a friend about the times we had driven all over the state.

The story of Johnny O. is about a change in my understanding of care. In my first contact with him when he was drunk, I, as the "pastor" of Mamre, felt responsible for his care. In his terror and pain, he was dealing with what I understood to be "depth" or "spiritual" issues. He had asked me for help. I brought my professional counseling skills to bear on the task of responding to him. I felt largely alone in my care for him. I was the sole shepherd for my sheep.

Within an hour after I first responded to his friend's request that I help him, I implicitly had given up what Clebsch and Jaekle call the "dignity" of the pastoral position. I had realized that what he desperately needed was not counseling, but hospitalization. My task became much like that of the Samaritan in Luke 10, a matter of doing what I could to manage his immediate pain, and then to find and transport him to an "inn," where others had what was needed to respond to his physical and psychological suffering. I needed to do what I could to see that he could stay until he had a chance of being healed. Neither he nor I was explicitly concerned about what Clebsch and Jaekle would call "ultimate" issues. I was caught up in what they call "other helping acts."

But for a long time I clung to an essential aspect of the pastoral understanding, the clear differentiation between myself as a care giver and him as a care receiver. I related to him *because* he needed my help. In my mind, I was *only* a care giver. From the beginning, Johnny O. eroded this understanding. Even when he was desperately in need, he maintained some power and expertise. Having been in and out of treatment programs for most of his life, he knew about most of them and had decided opinions about them and their effectiveness, which he shared with me. When we went looking for a long-term halfway house, he made it very clear that any place he went had to meet *his* criteria, not mine. His knowledge was determinative.

But more importantly, we were spending a lot of time together, driving in the car for two or more hours at a stretch. For Johnny O., these drives were not simply means to an end; they were something in themselves, a rich and enjoyable time when we became, as he put it, "friends."

The decisive turning points for me in the relationship involved movements away from my "pastoral" understanding toward his "friendly" understanding of it. When I related my night terror of the empty desert to Johnny O.'s terror as a black in a racist town, I felt that he had slipped into my psyche and was teaching me about the reality of oppression. Later, after I pursued him to take him back to the halfway house, and he, after hitting and yelling at me, collapsed in my arms, I again felt our realities merging; and, with this blurring of the boundaries between us, I felt a flood of affection.

As a result of these experiences, I began to rethink the apparent innocence and goodness of my care giving role. I realized that each time I "cared," I also ripped Johnny O. out of his small community of other, mainly poor, African Americans and took him into a world where white professional people diagnosed and treated him as a flawed, morally and physically sick object. I began to understand his shame, his denial of his alcoholism, as an adaptive defense against my and other professionals' "trespassing care."[1] I began to understand his ambivalence, his battling with himself and me over whether or not to accept this violating care, which he nevertheless needed. I began to understand both his courage in going ahead with me into these oppressive institutions and his strength in asserting his right to make his own decisions.

When he cried to me not to betray him, I began to realize the flaw in my conceptions of my relation with him. Before he first cried out, through his friend, to me for help, I had not really "known" Johnny O. He was just a person who came occasionally to the Mamre meal. After he cried out for help, my relation to him was governed by his alcoholism and the crises it created. I saw him *because* he needed help from me. When I could do nothing more to help him, our relation seemed to end. I felt vaguely guilty about this ending and, in hearing his drunken talk of betrayal, I realized why. He, unlike me, had not seen me merely as someone who helped him out when he was in need. He saw me as a "friend," a member of the same community, someone who recognized and affirmed him and whom he recognized and affirmed. I think that he experienced our withdrawal from each other when I could no longer "help him" as a betrayal of this friendship. I think his asking me to get him a cheeseburger was a way of attempting to reestablish the lost tie.

While I may have been unconscious of this friendly tie between us, I knew of it in my body and my less conscious mind. This knowledge had emerged during the key turning points I have described—the night terror in the desert and the hug in Southern Heights—and in my attempts to describe what was going on with Johnny O. Only after I failed as a care giver and pastor could I come to realize this other reality.

When I responded to his cry to me not to betray him and stayed in touch, we began to build a more conscious friendship. By the time I visited him in the nursing home, I wasn't there to help him and he wasn't seeing me because he needed me to help him. He was sharing his life with me and showing me how he, too, cared for others. We were friends.

The change between us was also a change in my understanding of the communities that held us. I realized that I was wrong to conceive of myself

---

[1] New Testament scholar Margaret Lee, in a conversation with me in Tulsa, in 1995, commented that she understood "Forgive us our trespasses" in the Lord's Prayer as a recognition that, in caring for others, we always trespass; we violate their boundaries. The only basis for forgiveness is our, and their, recognition that we, too, need care and so will be trespassed against. Forgiveness then is the acceptance of the violation which accompanies the care that is necessary for our mutual, communal life.

as a solitary pastoral care giver. From the beginning of my relation with Johnny O., whole networks of people were involved. Johnny O. reached out to me through a friend. The reason he reached out to me was because he knew me from Mamre; in other words, his cry presupposed a community in which we were both members. I spent most of my time helping him find other communities of people who could care for him. My growing concerns about the oppressive dimension of my interventions had to do with the fact that I kept taking him out of his own community and into white professional ones, ones made up of people like me, who often treated him as an object. Consistently he reminded me that he, too, was not only a participant in his care, but the authority about it, the one who judged what and who were truly responsive to his needs and suffering.

PART FIVE

An Ethic of Care

CHAPTER 21

Images

In the previous parts, I have mapped the ground for an ethic of care. In this part, I imagine this ethic by abstracting an image of care, noting the obstacles to realizing this image, and imagining particular caring responses to the situations presented in the cases.

Realization

I have found that insights into what care should be emerge from the exploration of what is. H. Richard Niebuhr asserted this truth when he said that the initial ethical question is, "What is happening?" To put this question in the form of a statement, an ethic begins with *realization*, taken in two ways. An ethical researcher becomes aware of, he or she *realizes*, some aspect of what is happening that she or he had not been aware of before. But human awareness is never merely passive. To become conscious of a reality is to confirm it, to grasp it, to weigh it, and to give it weight, to respond to it, to participate in the way it appears and so exists by naming and locating it in the semiotically constructed world; to *realize* a reality is to make it more real to ourselves and to others. In each of the case studies, the researcher arrived at an ethic of care by *realizing* the care that was already happening.

To begin with, realization is not to begin with a principle, or vision, or rule of what should be. We do not require an ethic when our principles, visions, and rules—our assumed ways of ordering reality—are, or appear to be, working smoothly. We require an ethic when we cannot make sense of what is happening, when we do not know what we should do, when we cannot find our way. To turn to an existing principle, vision, or rule before closely examining what is happening is to rely on what has failed us. A certain principle, vision, or rule may prove to be helpful to us as we are figuring out what is happening, but we do not begin with it.

Suffering

Suffering and the question of how to ameliorate it initiated each of the case studies presented so far in this book. The student in the first case wanted me, a professional, to help her find better ways of responding to her suffering parishioners. My own suffering and the poor of Mamre's response to it led to the second case study. Jesus' and the Syrophoenician woman's responses to her daughter's and each other's suffering made the story of their encounter fascinating to me. Les Nodale questioned why the services at Christ Church afflicted him and others. Mary began her study with the question of how to respond to Katherine's and her own suffering in the face of death. Martin was changed by Sam's "biblical explorations," undertaken in response to a life filled with suffering. I studied my encounters with Johnny O. because my usual ways of responding to alcoholics and mentally ill patients did not effectively ameliorate his suffering, and yet something else was going on in our meetings that did lessen his and my suffering. In other words, when we researchers on care began to examine the reality of what was happening in our cases, we discovered that suffering and responding to it were happening. Generalizing from these cases, we can conclude that the question initiating the search for an ethic of care is, How do we ameliorate suffering? Putting the question in the form of a statement, we can say that we have found that care is an ameliorating response to suffering.

Again, this realization of the nature of care involves turning away from some other ways of defining care. We did not define care by deriving the definition *deontologically*, from a transcendent set of rules. Nor did we define it *teleologically*, as a particular good to be pursued. Nor did we define it *aretaically*, as an individual character trait or a practice of a community. All of these ways of defining of care tend to be dualistic, in that they assume that care is something we find someplace other than our daily lives. They thus tend to rest on the dualistic denial of suffering, of specifically that reality which we have repeatedly discovered is central to understanding care.

Desire

We *desire* to ameliorate suffering. The finding is obvious, but also subversive in the current ethical climate, which requires that ethical professionals renounce desire in their relations to clients. Following the ideology of condescension, an ethical professional is supposed to act only in his or her clients' interests. The fact that most professionals earn their livings by serving clients indicates that this ideology contradicts or denies reality. To my knowledge, no close examination of human behavior has ever discovered a way wholly to extinguish desire without extinguishing life. The ubiquity of desire has posed continuing difficulties for ethicists who consider desire to be an obstacle to ethical behavior and has led to the notion that *what ought to be* can never be derived from *what is*, an absurd proposition, since *what is* always includes *what ought to be* as an imagined and desired possibility; in other words, this proposition is an attempt to negate a tautology, to say that *what is*, in the form of an imagined possibility, is not part of *what is*. The analysis of the dualism assumed by condescension points to the desire lying behind denials of it. We desire to be free of desire in order to be free of the suffering that is bound up with desire. In other words, the denial of desire is the result of the desire to ameliorate suffering, a less than normative attempt to care.

As Les Nodale found, desire is bivalent, a movement towards pleasure, joy, and love, as well as a movement away from pain, suffering, and affliction. An examination of the nature of the realities these terms name illumines desire as central to being alive. Pleasure, joy, and love are the signs of life in the body, the self, and the relations in which we are constituted. Pain, suffering, and affliction are the corresponding signs of threats to life. Recognition of desire as motivating ethics is a recognition that an ethic of care is about living as fully as we can as embodied, relational selves.

Bodies

Another obvious, but subversive discovery, is that we live as bodies. Each case begins with a bodily encounter and deals with bodily issues: my encounter with a student concerned about the suffering of the ill people she visited; the physical deprivation of the poor of Mamre, the effects of this deprivation on their health and appearance, the impact of their bodies on me, their sharing of food and other material resources, and their concern about my health; the Syrophoenician woman's concern about the possession of her daughter's body, the mother's bodily encounter with an exhausted Jesus, and the physical healing of the daughter, and perhaps of Jesus; Les Nodale's physical response to Dr. Hollerein's statement about sacrificing daughters, the material costs of tithing and its effects on those who struggle to get enough to live, the bodily exclusion of designated groups of people from eating and drinking at the communion meal; the relation between two women of the same age, one who was dying of a cancer that would stop her breathing, the other who had a physical predisposition to developing the same kind of cancer; the relation between a pastoral counselor and a man for whom death had been an ever-present threat; and the bodily form of Johnny O.'s suffering as I held him. I stress these realities because of how easily we forget them in a tradition and an ethic that labels concern for bodies "undignified" and reserve the word "care" for concern about "spiritual" and "ultimate" or, in today's world, "psychological" troubles.[1] As Mary found with Katherine, "spiritual" and "ultimate" difficulties come only in embodied forms.

The denial of the body is another manifestation of the dualism that attempts to ameliorate suffering by denying it. This denial is born of the

---

[1] Clebsch and Jaekle, 6–7.

body's capacity to wall off pain for a time, a capacity that leads us to think that we can perhaps escape bodily need and suffering entirely if we can simply cast off this crust of matter; so we think that care, or more precisely, "pastoral care," or, more popularly, "spiritual" care, transcends material, bodily concerns and suffering and deals only with questions of "meaning."

As Les Nodale found, this dualism results in the neglect and affliction of the afflicted. If we are to be responsive to what it happening, to ameliorate suffering, to realize our desire to live fully, then we must remember the obvious fact that we are bodies. We must respond to bodily suffering and its causes, which means to the reality of material needs and the economic systems through which we distribute, or do not distribute, what is needed for life to groups of people. We must face our participation in, and dependence on, even in our seemingly most idealized, innocent, and uneconomic activities, economies that require the deprivation, objectifying, and suffering of masses of people, including ourselves at vulnerable times of our lives. We must find ways to resist these systems of affliction and to realize other economic realities. We literally cannot afford the illusion that ethical care transcends these bodily realities.

Relation

We tend, in thinking about care, not to want to think about the body and economics because we assume that bodies and economics have primarily to do with who possesses what quantity of matter. We tend to take consumption as the primary metaphor for both the body and the economy. We tend to define bodies, be they individual human bodies or social bodies or economic bodies, as units that live primarily by taking in, eating, or consuming what they need from the external world and which expel or produce unneeded matter, which may or may not be valuable to other bodies.

The experience of care always occurs, however, in *relation*. We care for others; others care for us. Even when we talk about caring for ourselves, we assume a relation to ourselves. Having tacitly, if not explicitly, defined bodies as consuming units and so as nonrelational, we tend to assume that care as relation must characterize another reality, an immaterial or spiritual reality. In rejecting materialism, we, however, tend to recapitulate it in a spiritual form. We tend to assume that care and relation are non-material capacities or possessions of nonmaterial units—the *capacity* for compassion or love, the *possession* of meaning or integrity. The metaphor of consumption returns. We tend to define care as a relation in which one who *possesses* spiritual food gives it to another who needs and *consumes* such food. And so we construct condescension.

Condescension rests on a mistake, exposed by observations. Well-fed and well-sheltered babies physically fail to thrive and often die outside of consistent, confirming, caring relations. A child does not become a self outside of such relations. A child held in such a relation can endure hunger and pain, while an isolated child suffers intensely even in the absence of hunger and pain. An adult faced with the loss of sustaining relations will often die, while an adult who retains even the memory of such relations can often endure intense physical hardship and pain. For both adults and children, the measure of pain is the collapse of the self's subjectivity and agency, of internal and external relatedness. The measure of pleasure is the opening up of subjectivity and agency, of internal and external relatedness. These observations point to one reality, the primacy of relation over consumption in human life. The mistake in condescension is assuming that consumption is primary and relation is secondary.

To recognize relation as primary is also to recognize mutual participation in the construction of reality as primary. This primacy is easiest to observe in interpersonal relations, in which selves construct each other and the social reality they share. The image holds true where there are not two selves. An infant, prior to the birth of the self, defines and shapes her or his mother's world and self, just as the mother shapes the infant as a nascent self. A particular physical phenomenon, say a star, defines and shapes the work, life, and self of the scientist who studies it, just as the scientist shapes the existence of this star, both as it appears in the human world and, according to quantum physics, literally—the physical energy the scientist uses to observe the star infinitesimally, but really, impacts the star. And quantum physicists posit matter as constructed out of relations between oppositely charged particles.

In each of the case studies, care emerged with the realization of relation, more specifically, with the realization of the co-creative participation of a person or people who had previously been treated, or defined, as less than mutual participants in relation. I recognized the student's participation in shaping the course, and the poor's participation in the Mamre meal and my healing. Jesus recognized the Syrophoenician woman's participation in the conversation and in the healing of her daughter. Les Nodale realized how the poor, the suffering, nonbelievers, and children participated in Christ Church. Mary realized Katherine's participation in shaping Mary's faith. Martin realized that Sam was forming Martin's way of thinking. I realized that Johnny O. was changing my understanding of care. Ethical care is realization of mutual relatedness, mutual co-creativity, mutual participation in the construction of reality.

With this realization comes another, that the denial of mutuality causes suffering. In interhuman relations, the denial of mutuality is the denial by one participant, usually one with greater power, of the other's agency and subjectivity—in other words, of the other's existence as a relational self who both actively shapes the relation and is self-aware and self-knowledgeable. This treatment of the other as an object to be known and manipulated is a double denial. An object does not suffer, and so to treat a person as an object is both to deny her suffering and to deny her suffering that the treatment of her as an object causes. This insight motivates the critique of condescension as an obstacle to care. When one condescends, one constructs the other as a container, not an agent.

Recognition of relation as primary shifts our understanding of bodily existence. Living bodies are not primarily consuming units; they are, first of all, relational beings. Food, drink, clothing, shelter, protection, pleasure, pain, suffering, joy, affliction, love—even as material realities, these are not primarily quantities of something; neither are they characteristics or qualities or capacities of a unit. They are, instead, aspects or dimensions of relation. Material needs are, at the beginning of, and throughout, life, inextricably bound up with relations. When a mother nurses a child, the milk is the tangible form of her affirmation, her love, of the child as a person, a subject, an agent. When friends gather for a meal, the food is inextricably bound up with their enjoyment of each other as agents and subjects. When a jailer shoves a bowl of thin and gritty gruel and a crust of moldy bread through the bars of a cell to a tortured prisoner, the food afflicts the prisoner, even as it minimally nurtures him; it expresses the torturer's degradation of the prisoner; such food kills the spirit and the body. Bodily existence is existence in cocreative relation to other bodies.

An economics, how we exchange goods, is always a politics, how we participate together in the construction of the social relations that, in turn, shape us and our reality. The insight that care is always embodied and thus always involves economics, and that it is also always relational, leads to the realization that care is always political, in that it always involves the construction of relations that deny or realize the participation of those involved. We found, through the case studies, that ethical care, care that most effectively ameliorates suffering, realizes relation and so the mutual participation of all involved—their existence as selves, as agents and subjects.

Again, recognition that care is political results in the critique of condescension as an ideology that supports political domination, in which an elite group limits and attempts to extinguish the participation, the agency and subjectivity, of a subjugated group. In the face of such domination, ethical care requires realization of the agency and subjectivity, the mutual participation and creativity, of the subjugated and the afflicted. In other words, ethical care requires a conversion from a politics in which the elite attempts to deny suffering by locating it, and its causes, in afflicted and subjugated groups to a politics in which we realize that we all suffer, and we all care, and that we require each other's care to ameliorate the suffering we share.

Self

Mary's struggle with pride in her meeting with Katherine discloses another reality common to the cases, that of the *self*. Mary's pride was a response to the affection between Katherine and her. In her description, we can hear the joyous opening up of herself to Katherine. She and Katherine had entered each other's selves; they shared a subjectivity; each was the other in whose desire each found herself. In this opening wide of the subjective space between them, we can also hear the mutual affirmation of each other's differentiated agency, each one's recognition of the other's love and ability. In Mary's description, her pride is the sign of the expansive and joyous presence of her relational self.

Accompanying the pride, Mary felt paralyzing shame and embarrassment that made it difficult for her to attend to Katherine and so to care. Shame and embarrassment were obstacles to care. As she realized, she felt shame and embarrassment when she felt joy at doing well. Her shame and embarrassment were signs of affliction, of internalized attacks on her agency. We need not intrude on Mary by speculating about her history of abuse to recognize the possible connection between this affliction by another and her affliction of herself.

Mary described her pride as an expansion of her "ego." Especially in the context of her shame over her pride, her use of this term is suggestive of the criticism of the "ego" in popular spirituality. This rejection of the "ego" echoes the criticism of self-interest in discussions of professional ethics. Mary's shame reflects both the popular and professional notion that ethical behavior is egoless, without self-interest, without desire or needs, selfless.

I have pointed out the absurdity of the notion that ethical action occurs without desire. It is equally absurd to think that one can construct an ethic without a self, without an agent that is conscious of, and therefore able to choose, his or her actions. An ethic only makes sense if there exists an ethical agent, a self, an ego, who makes ethical choices. An ethic cannot be selfless.

Some professional ethicists might respond by saying that I am, of course, correct; that, when they talk of a professional not acting out of self-interest, they are describing, as ethical, the self's capacity for altruism, its ability to restrain and even renounce its desire and interests in the face of others' needs, to choose to sacrifice itself for others. They might comment that Mary's shame is an indication of her moral sensitivity, of the dangers posed by ego inflation, pride, and the pleasures of intimacy.

But Mary experienced her shame and the resulting attempt to suppress her pride as the obstacles to care, not the pride itself. The distance between Mary and the professional ethicists lies in differences in their assumptions about the self. The professional ethicists assume that the self is a consuming unit that exists in competition with other consuming units. In this view, when I act in my own interests, to serve myself, I am not acting in others' interests, and I may be acting against them. As indicated, in this view, an ethic is rooted in the self's capacity to transcend itself for others. But where does this transcendence come from? Use of the word "transcendence" betrays the dualism in most professional ethics, the conception of the self as only a competitive consumer, and so of the perception of the other's interests as born of a reality outside of or beyond—*transcendent* to—the self. With dualism comes all the unnecessary suffering we have described.

In Mary's experience, love of the other and pride and joy, the signs of an expansive and powerful self, come together. As, out of this experience, she imagines an ethic of care, she leaves nothing out, she denies and sacrifices nothing. She accepts her anxiety, her pride, her shame, her embarrassment, her suffering and Katherine's, her joy; all are gathered into the space of her awareness, of her self, which is not a unit that consumes, but is a relation that opens to Katherine and to reality. For Mary, the self is a relation, a desire for, a reaching out to, and receiving of, a joyous confirmation of the other, who, simply as a real other, mirrors and confirms and shapes the agent that desires and reaches. For such a self, love of the other requires no transcendence; such love is integral to the self's existence. For such a self, love and joy and pride all refer to the meeting with the other in which the self comes to be.

An ethic of care must join Mary in her understanding of the self as a wide, inclusive, relational space, a dweller in the relation between one's body and the other. For such a self, care is joyful, even if it is also filled with suffering.

CHAPTER 22

Obstacles and Mutual Desire

Each of the cases moves toward the realization of particular realities of care in America at this time. Recognizing these realities leads to imagining what care could, and should, be in this social and historical context.

In the last three cases, "Sisters," "Colleagues," and "Friends," the researchers began with the assumption that ethical care requires condescension. They thought that their primary responsibility, as professional pastors, was to use their special knowledge and skills to help someone who was suffering. Mary thought that, as a eucharistic minister, she was responsible for "helping" Katherine with her "relation to God" and with her feelings. Martin assumed that his job was to use his psychotherapeutic knowledge to diagnose and treat Sam. I assumed that my task with Johnny O. was to use my training, knowledge, and power to get him treatment for his alcoholism. All of us tacitly assumed that we were able, and those for whom we cared were disabled by their suffering. Mary assumed that Katherine was theologically and emotionally disabled. Martin assumed that Sam was at least partially psychologically disabled. And I assumed that Johnny O. would have had difficultly living without my care, that he was critically disabled.

Tracing the implications of these assumptions results in a map of the professional ethic that currently dominates discussions of pastoral ethics. This ethic construes the professional-client (or pastor-parishioner) relation as different from ordinary day-to-day relations. A professional ethic is a special ethic for this special relation. These ethicists define care as occurring only in a relation between an able professional and a disabled client. Because clients are not able, they cannot protect themselves against abuse. Governed by the assumption discussed above, that the self is a unit that competes with other selves for what it needs and desires, these ethicists assume that, without strong boundaries, the powerful and able professional will abuse or exploit the disabled and so powerless and dependent client. Given these assumptions, a professional ethic must be a series of rules that protects the vulnerable client from such abuse. Since the professional's self-interest, needs, and desires are presumably what motivate abuse, these rules prohibit the professional from expressing or acting upon his or her self-interest, needs, or desires in his or her relations with the client.[1]

I have already explored some of the contradictions in this professional ethic. Here I am focusing on how these and other contradictions emerged in these three particular cases. In attempting to follow this ethic, the researchers stumbled on aspects of this ethic that proved to be impediments to care. As they examined these obstacles, they realized an ethic of care different from the professional ethic.

Sisters

Mary discovered that her attempts to assert and maintain pastoral authority, which rested in the assumption that she was the knowledgeable agent in the relation, initially resulted in her misunderstanding Katherine. She identified these attempts as growing out of her stifling of her own suffering, needs, and desires. As the relation with Katherine deepened, so did their intimacy, their sharing of desires and needs, and joys and sorrows. As this intimacy grew, Mary found that she could not define her relation with Katherine as a "pastoral" one; they were "sisters," "colleagues," and "friends." While she continued to carry out "pastoral" functions, Mary renounced her "pastoral authority" and so removed the boundary between her relation with Katherine and the other important relations in her life. Mary's final struggle with the professional ethic came in her last session, when she realized that her attempts, in accordance with the professional ethic, to renounce, and not to express, her pride were hindering her care for Katherine.

In her analyses and imaginings in response to each event, Mary realized care as mutuality. She realized that admitting her needs, desires, suffering, pride, anxiety, and joy into the relation both released her from the distracting concern about suppressing herself and allowed her to use her responses empathically to grasp what was happening to Katherine. As she allowed her needs and ignorance and suffering into the relation, she discovered that she and Katherine were working together, as "colleagues," on how to respond most caringly to the suffering that afflicted each of them in different ways. In her imagined responses, Mary consistently attempted to find ways to more fully realize this mutuality. She marked her success with words usually used to denote everyday relations. Her professional ethic had merged with a broader relational ethic of mutuality.

Mary's research suggests that the attempt to draw a clear boundary between the professional-client relation and everyday relations proves to be an obstacle to care. Her questions about "pastoral authority," which was her term for the presumably separate, or special, ethical issues involved with being a professional care giver, proved to be distractions as she focused

---

[1] SteinhoffSmith, "The Boundary Wars Mystery," 134–38.

on the ethical issues emergent in her relation to Katherine. These ethical issues, the ones actually central to the case, turned on questions that could have arisen for her in other close relations—with a sister, colleague, or friend. Her case suggests that an ethic of care, including one that governs professional-client relations, should not be a special ethic with its own set of principles and rules that apply only to the professional-client relation. Rather, an ethic of care should be a broader ethic, one that encourages us to examine closely our actual relations, professional or non-professional, and to ask how we can more fully realize care in them.

Friends

In my study of my relation to Johnny O., I arrived at the same conclusions; but, given that the situation is different, these conclusions have different nuances. Initially, I responded to Johnny O. when he was in desperate need of assistance. I mobilized all my knowledge and skills and brought them to bear on trying to help him.

There was nothing wrong with what I did here. I have done, would have done, and would do the same again for someone in crisis. I went wrong when, largely because of my conception of myself as a "pastor" and "professional" and of Johnny O. as one of my "parishioners" and, in that sense, a "client," I thought of this relation as a "separate" and "special" one. Once I began to help Johnny O., I looked only to other helping professionals (doctors, therapists, counselors, social workers) for help with him. I, in my mind and actions, separated and isolated our "crisis" relation from the Mamre community and from any other relations we had.

While I did not think of myself as following the professional ethical prohibition against dual relationships, I strictly obeyed it. This narrow focus, a properly ethical focus according to most professional ethicists, blinded me to what Johnny O. saw: that, in our long night drives, we were, in spite of my reticence and professional pastoral demeanor, getting to know each other, not as pastor and parishioner, crisis counselor and counselee, but as friends. Because I did not recognize, or *realize*, this friendship, I neglected and betrayed it; in doing so, I wronged both Johnny O. and myself.

As I came to terms with what I had done wrong, I saw how my professional isolation had led me to discount and isolate both myself and Johnny O. from the communities—Mamre and the community of his friends in Southern Heights—that actually sustained both of us in our everyday lives and could have helped sustain us more during his crisis.

Finally, in conceiving of my relation to Johnny O. as a matter of professional care *giving*, I found it very difficult to talk about and so, again, to *realize* fully what I *received* from Johnny O., the joy and wisdom in our friendship.

My mistake with Johnny O., the mistake that he identified and begged me to attend to, was precisely that I did not *realize* the everyday character of our friendship and so did not think about what we were doing as friends ethically; at first, I only thought ethically about what I was doing as a professional. What Johnny O. taught me was that any relation I have with someone as a minister, teacher, or counselor is always, first and foremost, an everyday relation between two particular persons, situated in particular communities. I should not isolate either myself or the other person, who I may be helping at the time, from the broader everyday relations between us, in which we do not relate only as someone who helps and someone who is in need of help. Ethically, if I am to *realize* care, I must also *realize* these other, more mutual relations.

Colleagues

Martin's case study is the most traditionally psychotherapeutic of the three. With a few changes, we could read the study, not as he does, as a "parable" for psychotherapists, but as a demonstration of the effectiveness of a certain psychotherapeutic approach, Kohutian mirroring. Martin began his therapy with Sam with this approach. He responded affirmatively to Sam's proposal that they engage in "biblical work" not because he was especially interested in this work, but because mirroring Sam's "biblical explorations" appeared to be the most effective way to help Sam. In Martin's account, the case became a parable when Martin realized that he was no longer following Sam in his explorations just for Sam's sake; Martin was learning from Sam. Furthermore, Sam was aware of this shift in the relation and found it helpful. Being a "colleague" with Sam proved more therapeutic that simply being a therapist.

Kohutian self psychology has a rather obvious explanation for why this shift proved helpful. When Martin was mirroring Sam in order to help Sam, his affirmation of Sam was partial. He was not really valuing Sam's work; he was mirroring Sam because he thought Sam needed mirroring. But when Martin began learning from Sam, he fully mirrored Sam; he honestly valued Sam's work for its own sake. Anyone knows the difference between an affirmation given in order to help one and a real affirmation of something one has done, or of simply who one is. The first may be a bit helpful, but it also feels uncomfortable; no one really likes being condescended to, and an affirmation given because one needs affirmation and not because the giver really values something about one is condescending. The second fills one with joy the other has seen and recognized and affirmed something particular about one.

This obvious insight throws a monkey wrench into predominant conceptions of psychotherapy and pastoral counseling and of professional ethics, more specifically into the ideology of condescension. As indicated, condescension rests on an ethic of altruism or *agape*, on the norm of disinterested and unconditional love of the other; the one who loves regards everyone equally, not allowing the differences between others to determine the quality of the love. When Martin mirrored Sam's "biblical work" because he thought Sam needed such mirroring, he was realizing this ethic; he was acting in Sam's interests, not because Sam was Sam, but because Sam was a client; he was treating Sam with equal regard as he would have any other client. As Martin became enamored of Sam's "biblical work," he broke this ethic in three ways. He was no longer simply acting in Sam's interests, doing what he thought Sam needed; he was also acting in his own interests, doing what he desired. He was not treating Sam as he would other clients. Sam was someone special, more like a "friend" or "colleague." And, implicitly, he was not loving Sam unconditionally; Sam's thinking and insights conditioned Martin's love for Sam.

An Ethic of Mutual Desire

Mary and I, in our particular cases, discovered what Martin did and what Kohutian psychology confirms, that this conditioned, interested, desiring love is more caring than disinterested, unconditioned agape. The reason has to do with the relational nature of the self, of desire, and so of love. As relational beings, we come to be in mutually desiring relations. When I suffer affliction, I do so because another has not confirmed who I am and what I do, my particular subjectivity and agency; the other has not delighted in, needed, and so desired me; the absence of the other's desire collapses the internal relation that constitutes the self. None of us desires or needs overflowing, disinterested, abundant love, love that makes the particularities of who we are superfluous, love that is simply a gift of something someone else doesn't need, love that does not need and desire us because of our particular qualities. What each of us needs and desires is to know that "I" am, in the specificity of "my" existence, uniquely valuable to another, that "I" am bound up with another in a co-creative relation. Sam and Martin, Katherine and Mary, Johnny O. and I together realized that care is this mutual desire and love.

In my case, this insight clarified what I had sensed for years of work as a therapist and pastoral counselor. I had learned that, for me, good therapy happened only when I became fascinated with a client and wanted to get to know him or her. Once this fascination happened, the relation with the client became unique, differentiated from other therapeutic relations; the client and I would be working together; and I came out of meetings with such clients, as I emerged from the relation with Johnny O., changed; such clients became integral parts of my life, internal others in my self.

This mutual love deconstructs predominant understandings of therapy and of professional ethics by replacing the norm of disinterested altruism with the norm of mutual desire and so mutual self-interest. This latter norm presumes the understanding of desire and the self as relational; to desire is to desire that the other live, to be self-interested is necessarily to be interested in the other.

In this ethic of mutuality, differences between the self and other, including differences in need, power, vulnerability, and suffering, do not necessarily predispose the one with greater power in a particular situation to abuse the one with less power. This ethic identifies abuse as the denial of the agency and subjectivity of the other and so of the other's mutuality with the self in constructing the relation. It locates the cause of abuse in attempts by powerful elites to alleviate their own suffering by locating suffering and its causes in weaker others. One minimizes abuse by realizing the agency and subjectivity of the other, especially the suffering other, by asserting one's own agency and subjectivity, especially when one is in need or is suffering, and by recognizing the play of one's own suffering and desire in all one's relations.

CHAPTER 23

Exploitation and Consent

Controversies about consent and sexual exploitation dominate current discussions of professional ethics. According to the predominant view, the client's lack of power in relation to the professional reduces the client's agency to such an extent that the client is unable to make moral judgments and so is unable to consent to or not to consent to a sexual relation with the professional. In entering into any kind of sexual or even mutual relation with a client, any relation in which he or she desires or receives something from the client, a professional, according to this view, coerces and so exploits the client.[1] What I have called condescension, in which the professional takes full responsibility for shaping and limiting the relation with the client, is, according to this view, the correct ethical response. Because the client is presumably ethically disabled by his or her suffering and need, the professional must exercise the sole ethical agency in the relation. As one professional ethicist puts it, the model for the ethical professional is the loving, powerful, and knowledgeable God who creates and enforces the covenant with a sinful, dependent, and deluded humanity.[2]

I agree that sexual relations between professionals and clients often result in the client's being hurt and that such relations deserve close ethical scrutiny. In many cases, and in almost all cases in which a *therapist* is sexually involved with his or her client, I think that such relations are unethical; but not because the client is ethically disabled. Numerous case studies, including the ones presented in this book, have shown me that the professional's denial of the agency and subjectivity of the client is unethical. Such denials, in and of themselves, afflict clients. These denials, not mutuality or the admission of the professional's desires and needs into the

---

[1] Fortune, *Love Does No Harm*, 28–30, 41–46.

[2] Carrie Doehring, *Taking Care: Monitoring Power Dynamics and Relational Boundaries in Pastoral Care & Counseling* (Nashville: Abingdon, 1995), 153–64.

relation, are the cause of professionals' exploitation and abuse, including sexual exploitation and abuse, of clients.

In my view, consent is the realization of mutuality. Ethically, it is not optional, to be dismissed, along with mutuality, because of differences in power. Consent is the prerequisite enactment of respect for my own and the other's agency and subjectivity. It is present in *all* ethical interpersonal relations. When it is absent, someone is denying another's agency and subjectivity.

Consent between conscious adults occurs when both are honest with each other about what they intend, desire, need, and are doing in the relation, and when both fully realize their own, and the other's, agency and subjectivity. When one person, for reasons of immaturity or impairment, has less power, consent means that the other person does all he or she can to realize and respect whatever subjectivity and agency the one with lesser power exercises.

In professional (or pastoral) relations, when I, as a client (or parishioner), consent to a professional's (or pastor's) actions, I realize, I make real, my participation in the relation. I assert my knowledge, my power, and my responsibility for my actions. I also realize the professional's (or pastor's) power and knowledge. When I, as a professional (or pastor), seek the client's (or parishioner's) consent, I realize his or her power and wisdom in shaping the relation.

As medical ethicists recognize, as a professional (or pastor), I have the responsibility for fully informing the client (or parishioner) about what I know about the professional (or pastoral) action I seek to take. When the client's (or parishioner's) ability to consent is immature or impaired, I do not relinquish this responsibility in relation to the client (or parishioner), but I must seek the informed consent of those who have legal responsibility in relation to the client (or parishioner). If, say in an emergency, in which the professional (or pastoral) action is necessary to save the other's life or well-being, I cannot get such consent, I must fully inform the client (or parishioner) or responsible party about my actions and seek their consent as soon as it is possible to do so.

In summary, in ethical professional-client (or pastor-parishioner) relations, as in ethical everyday relations, informed consent is not an option, to be sought only when the professional (or pastor) deems that the client (or parishioner) is "able"; it is an ongoing requirement.

Sexual exploitation by professionals (or pastors) of clients (or parishioners) is one kind of interpersonal exploitation. Interpersonal exploitation is a form of abuse, the denial by one person of another's agency and subjectivity and so of their mutuality. In exploitation, one person uses another to meet his or her needs or desires without the other's informed consent. Exploitation sometimes involves coercion. Coercion occurs when a person with greater power in a situation uses her or his superior power to force someone with less power to do something, especially if that something is in the dominant person's interests and is not in the subjugated person's interests. Exploitation can also occur when one person in a relation lies in order to get something from the other.

Sexual exploitation occurs when a person with greater power coerces sexual contact with someone with lesser power or when a person lies about his or her reasons for being in a sexual relation. Sexual exploitation does not characterize all sexual contacts between people with unequal power, as some professional ethicists imply; if so, almost all sexual activity would be unethical, since two people in any relation almost always exercise differing amounts of power. A person who exercises less power in a situation is not ethically disabled, is not rendered incapable of true and informed consent; often, as Les Nodale observed, the opposite is the case.

In a situation in which a more powerful professional (or pastor) has sexual contact with a less powerful client (or parishioners), the difference in power does not automatically mean that the professional (or pastor) is coercing or exploiting the client (or parishioner). Coercion occurs when either person in a sexual relation uses his or her power to force the other to give them sexual favors, or when either uses sex as a way of reinforcing his or her power to deny the other's agency and subjectivity. Another form of frequent sexual exploitation occurs when a professional lies about his or her sexual relations with a client; for instance, when a pastor tells each of a number of parishioners with whom he is sexually involved that he is solely involved with that one. The frequency of professionals' (or pastors') sexual exploitation of clients (or parishioners) does not, as many professional ethicists tacitly argue, point to *sexual* relations as ethically dangerous. Rather, such frequent exploitation raises broader questions about coercion and dishonesty in professional (or pastoral) relations and about the pervasive tendency in our society to value sex as both a sign of, and a reward for, the exercise of dominating, coercive, or exploitative power.

As already indicated, ideological, and usually unconscious, dishonesty characterizes relations between professionals and clients in the service economy. When service professionals claim to be acting only, or even primarily, in clients' interests, they, usually unintentionally, are lying. Service professionals, by definition, earn their livings by serving others; they, first of all, do what is necessary to keep their jobs. For instance, a therapist usually cannot afford to treat clients unless someone pays him or her to do so. If someone other than the client pays him or her for such therapy, then this "third party," through this economic power, exercises control over the therapy. This example is not hypothetical. Increasingly over the past fifteen years insurance companies, and now health maintenance organizations, have severely limited the amount and kinds of therapy they will pay for. Another example is a pastor of a church who counsels someone. Commonly, the congregation will explicitly, or implicitly, consider such counseling part of the pastor's job only if the person being counseled is a member or prospective member of the church, and if the pastor spends a limited amount of time doing counseling. If lay leaders think that the pastor is "wasting" his or her time and the church's money by spending too much time counseling or working with nonmembers, the pastor can easily lose his or her job. Economic power, rather than the client's best interests, controls the pastor's care as much as it does any other professional's work.

Dishonesty also characterizes the claim, inherent in the ideology of condescension, that the primary agent in professional (or pastoral) care is the knowledgeable professional (or pastor). A reading of psychotherapeutic literature reveals that Martin and Sam's parabolic relation, in which the client teaches the professional, is far from unique. In the case that marks the beginning of modern psychotherapy, Sigmund Freud learned the psychoanalytic technique of following one's associations from the patient Anna O. The major early figures in psychoanalysis—for example, Freud, Carl Jung, Otto Rank, Ernest Jones—learned their psychology primarily through self-analysis (from themselves as patients) or from their patients' psychological explorations. In other words, therapy has, from the beginning, been what Martin and Sam discovered it to be, a collaborative work, in which the therapist learns as well as sometimes teaches and the client teaches as well as learns.

Recognition of the therapeutic relation as collaborative raises the question of whether, in the current service economy, it is also inherently exploitative. The service economy constructs therapy as a service that the therapist offers, for compensation, to the client. In this construction, the therapist's knowledge and skills are the valuable commodity that the client, who lacks this commodity, buys. This construction treats not only the client's need but also his or her knowledge and work as raw materials, which the therapist transforms into commodities that he or she sells back to the client for a fee. In other words, the construction renders the client's knowledge and work as having a negative value—they are like garbage— in that the client must pay the therapist for extracting what is valuable from them. It locates all value in the therapist's work of transforming this garbage into a therapeutic commodity. Comparing this transaction to a colonial one, in which colonizers extract raw materials from natives' lands and then sell these materials, transformed into commodities, back to the natives, points to its exploitative character.

The denial and exploitation of the client's knowledge and work also frequently characterizes pastors' relations to parishioners, when these relations are governed either by the traditional pastoral paradigm or the therapeutic one. Under both models, the pastor in a caring relation gains prestige and knowledge while the parishioner is rendered valueless. For instance, a well-meaning and compassionate pastor preached about "healing." In her examples she portrayed herself as the agent of God's healing power. In none of her examples did she affirm the agency and work of the parishioner in the healing act. Unintentionally, she portrayed the suffering parishioners merely as the objects and mirrors of her own faith, healing power, wisdom, and access to God. In other words, she tacitly exploited her suffering parishioners' agency, work, and faith. In so doing, she benefited economically and politically—she secured her position as a pastor—by increasing her value and prestige as a healer and woman of God.

The connection between this economic exploitation of clients and sexual exploitation emerges with the recognition that the raw materials and commodities in the therapeutic economy are primarily relational realities. The therapist extracts from, and sells to, clients knowledge about being a relational self, about love, about joy, about alleviating suffering and affliction. Similarly, as can be seen in the above example, pastors benefit by appropriating parishioners' work on, and knowledge about, "ultimate" or relational realities such as love, faith, and healing. One can only truly deal with these realities in highly intimate relations in which the two selves open to each other's co-creative activity.

Proponents of the currently dominant professional ethic both recognize and deny this intimacy. They recognize that, for the client or parishioner, the therapeutic or pastoral relation reaches into the heart of the self; that, for the client or parishioner, the boundary between the internal relation that constitutes the self and the external relation with the therapist or pastor becomes transparent and sometimes disappears. But these proponents tend to deny that the therapist or pastor is transformed by this intimacy. They tend to view the client's or parishioner's full involvement in the intimate relation as both a sign of the client's or parishioner's pathology (some call it "transference") and as necessary to the therapeutic or pastoral salvation of the client. The condescending view of the client or parishioner as pathologically disabled and in need of the therapist's or pastor's care resolves the apparent paradox: the client or parishioner must descend into his or her pathological disability in order to be healed. In this view, the therapist or pastor must resist being drawn into the intimacy in order to protect his or her healing knowledge from the client's pathological and illusory "knowledge."

In actuality, however, as Martin found, and the history of psychotherapy shows, and as the other cases discussed in this book reveal, the intimacy between therapists and clients and between pastors and parishioners is mutual; clients and parishioners transform therapists and pastors, and wisdom and healing emerge from their shared work. The client or parishioner does not just depend upon the therapist or pastor; the therapist or pastor depends upon the client or parishioner, not just economically, but as a participant in the construction of the therapist's or pastor's self and of therapeutic, psychological, and theological wisdom. When therapists or pastors deny this reality, even as they reap the benefits of it in money, a greater sense of joy, meaning, self-esteem, and knowledge, they exploit the intimacy with the client or parishioner. In other words, they use their power to deny and, usually unintentionally, to lie about the value of the client's or parishioner's participation in the intimacy, even as they profit from what the client or parishioner brings to the intimacy.

I discovered the hurtful effects of such exploitation with Johnny O. Because I initially denied the mutual intimacy with him, I cut off the relation when I could no longer help him. I did not realize that, when I stopped seeing him, I betrayed our friendship and so hurt him and myself. Before he informed me about my betrayal, I had unconsciously been exploiting Johnny O., in that I had been benefiting from the intimacy with him and from his knowledge and opening of his self to me, while denying this benefit. I had unintentionally given him a double message, both that I "loved" him and would "stick with" him because I valued him for who he was, and that I would only see him as long as I could perceive myself as the powerful and good helper or care giver in the relation. In other words, I implicitly told him that I would relate to him only as long as I retained control over what happened in the relation and over the definition of it. I tacitly denied his agency, his participation in the relation.

These denied, but pervasive, forms of professional exploitation of clients prepare the ground for professional sexual exploitation of clients, especially by therapists and ministers. The prevailing ethic encourages, and even requires, that therapists and ministers deny their mutual intimacy with clients and parishioners. Such denials do not eliminate this mutual intimacy. To the contrary, what is repressed or suppressed frequently dominates a relation. The denial, repression, and suppression of therapists' and ministers' needs and desires for clients and parishioners can easily result in four kinds of exploitation.

The first is the kind I inflicted upon Johnny O. A professional or pastor who unconsciously defends against his or her mutual intimacy with a client or parishioner can easily hurt the client or parishioner by cutting off the intimacy and thus betraying the tacit friendship with the client or parishioner.

In a second form of exploitation, also usually unconscious, the denial of mutual intimacy can lead the professional or pastor to deny the client's or parishioner's abilities as a way of maintaining the client's or parishioner's dependency on the professional or pastor so that the professional or pastor can continue his or her dependency on the client or parishioner.

A third kind of exploitation occurs when the professional's or pastor's denied participation in the intimacy, his or her needs and desires for the client or parishioner, breach the defensive barriers and flood the professional's or pastor's consciousness. The professional or pastor suddenly finds himself or herself obsessed with the client. Given the tendency in our society to assume that one can express intimacy, desire, and interpersonal need fully only in genital sexual relations, and that such genital relations inevitably occur when there is mutual intimacy, such an infatuated professional or pastor can easily discover that he or she is uncontrollably "in love with" a client. Such an afflicted professional or pastor often exploits his or her loved client or parishioner in one of three ways. If, as the predominant professional ethic requires, he or she rejects and renounces this "love" by emotionally or literally cutting off the relation with the client or parishioner, he or she betrays the already existing mutual intimacy—a more intense form of the betrayal with which I afflicted Johnny O. If, following the popular narratives about "love," he or she declares his or her love to the client and the client, flattered by this intense expression of desire from someone with whom he or she has already known an emotional intimacy, reciprocates, the overwhelming feelings linked with the assumption that intercourse is the only way to fulfill the mutual intimacy can lead the professional or pastor and the client or parishioner to ignore the possible hurtful consequences of a romantic affair. Given that the overwhelmingly intense sexual feelings are often an artifact of the professional or pastoral denial of mutual intimacy, the hurtful consequences to the client or parishioner are primarily the professional's or pastor's responsibility. They indicate that the professional or pastor has, again unintentionally, exploited the client or parishioner. If the client or parishioner rejects the professional's or pastor's advances and, in response, the spurned professional or pastor either emotionally or literally cuts off the relation or persists in pressuring the client or parishioner with his or her sexual demands, these responses betray the mutual intimacy already established before the professional or pastor "fell in love"; they indicate that the professional or pastor is exploiting the client or parishioner.

The fourth and most hurtful kind of exploitation occurs when the professional or pastor intentionally utilizes the ideology of condescension either to coerce sex with a client or parishioner or to utilize sex to prove the professional's or pastor's power and superiority. Sometimes, a therapist or minister will prescribe sex as a necessary part of the care he or she offers, an additional means by which the superior and all-loving professional unconditionally satisfies the client's needs and desires. Thus, the professional or pastor gratifies him- or herself and confirms his or her superiority over the client or parishioner, all in the guise of altruistically offering the client or parishioner another service. An abusive professional or pastor sometimes escalates the exploitation with a client who resists being sexually serviced by implying or stating that the professional or pastor knows what is best for the client or parishioner and the client's or parishioner's suffering will increase if he or she does not sexually submit to the professional or pastor.

If the client or parishioner continues to resist, the abusive professional (or pastor) will sometimes partially dispense with the ideology of condescension by implying or stating that sex is an appropriate payment for the blessings the professional or pastor has showered on the client or parishioner or that the client or parishioner must agree to sex in order to maintain the relation with the professional or pastor. While, in these maneuvers, the professional or pastor dispenses with that part of the ideology of condescension that denies the economic relation between the professional or pastor and the client or parishioner, he or she maintains the condescending notion that the client's or parishioner's participation in the relation is without value; the client's or parishioner's only value is as a sexually gratifying object. The coercion implicit in these assertions of superior power and value emerge clearly when, in the face of continued resistance by the client or parishioner, such an abusive professional or pastor threatens to use, or does use, severely injurious emotional or physical force in an attempt to shatter the resistance.

Please note that these kinds of exploitation do not just characterize what professionals or pastors do to clients or parishioners. Friends, associates, lovers, partners, and family members sometimes betray, lie to, exploit, coerce, and abuse each other in these ways; clients or parishioners sometimes exploit and abuse professionals or pastors. Nor are these kinds of exploitation confined to sexual relations. Exploiters use and coerce others to gratify their desires for power, esteem, and money, as well as for sexual pleasure.

Focusing on sex as the primary threat to ethical professional or pastoral relations hides the major issue, the denial of the exploited or abused person's agency and subjectivity. To restate a point, an adequate ethic for professional or pastoral care givers must be a broad relational ethic, not a special professional or pastoral ethic.

Realization that exploitation and abuse rest on such denials points to what prevents exploitation and abuse and so to the foundations for a realistic and adequate ethic of care. Exploiters and abusers deny mutuality. They deny the abused or exploited other's participation in both the external social relation and the internal psychological relation, the other's co-creation of the social world and of the abuser's or exploiter's self. Exploitation and abuse emerge out of the same mistake that condescension does, the assumption that the self is a unit that lives by consuming what it needs and desires and so must control others if it is going to survive. The ethical antidote to exploitation and abuse is the realization of mutuality, the recognition and affirmation of the self and others as always bound up in mutually desiring co-creative relations. For the one who is vulnerable to abuse or exploitation in a relation, realizing mutuality means affirming and acting on the reality that one is a powerful agent and subject in the relation, who can, and should, exercise a shaping effect on it, who should resist any efforts by the other to deny one's agency and subjectivity. For the potential exploiter or abuser, realizing mutuality means affirming and acting on the reality that the other, as an agent and a subject, co-creates one and one's world, that living a full and joyous life requires this full recognition of the other's participation in it, and that any attempts to deny the other's agency and subjectivity, while they may provide a temporary increase in pleasure or relief from pain and suffering, will, in the long run, afflict oneself as well as the other.

CHAPTER 24

Children and Dogs

Throughout this book, I have returned to the realization that practicing care, for those of us who are members of elites, requires a conversion, a change in worlds, in the ways we psychologically, socially, economically, politically, and religiously construct reality, including ourselves. While I am comfortable with the somewhat piecemeal character of the ethical images I have presented throughout the book and more specifically in this part (I think, finally, that any ethical response must be specific to a particular situation and context), I recognize that a unified vision, of the whole of reality, frequently motivates conversions.

The Syrophoenician woman converted Jesus with just such a different way of looking at reality when she took Jesus' image of people and children living and eating in a house and dogs being banished to the outside, and turned it into an image that much more accurately portrayed how people and dogs actually lived together—the dogs are in the house, under the table, living off the scraps children accidentally or intentionally drop to them. This image appeals to me for a number of reasons.

It is an everyday vision that realizes something that people know in their everyday lives but often don't know that they know because elites have convinced them that an abstracted dualistic vision is the way things are or at least the way they should be. The Syrophoenician woman constructs an ethic, not on the foundation of abstract norms and principles, but on observations of how people actually do care for each other and other beings. Her vision convinces because it is highly realistic. To reiterate the point, an ethic of care must begin with, and build upon, how people actually do care for each other.

The Syrophoenician woman's vision implies an economy in which everyone receives what she or he needs to live. Syrophoenician "dogs" and Jewish "children" both receive "food" and healing. The Syrophoenician woman's economic vision directly counters Jesus', which distributes economic necessities only to "children," those who are members of "my" family, community, faith, nation, political group, or class, and treats all others as dirty "dogs," who can be legitimately neglected.

Les Nodale uncovered both economic visions in the religious practices of Christ Church. The Syrophoenician woman shows how the inclusive economic vision is neither unrealistic nor utopian, but is a realization of basic impulses we all have, as children and adults, to respond to those who are in need and are suffering. An ethic of care must build upon and more fully realize this egalitarian economic impulse, wherever it manifests itself.

More specifically, this economic vision points to the need to strengthen and extend those communities and social spaces in our lives and world in which material and immaterial human needs are neither raw materials to be developed nor commodities to be bought and sold. The crucial ethical issue is not whether we, in our social and economic relations, meet everyone's need, but how. In other words, we must begin with the Syrophoenician woman's presupposition that making sure that everyone has adequate food, clothing, shelter, protection from affliction, health, care for suffering and pain, confirmation of agency and subjectivity, meaning, and love is not an ethical ideal, but an ethical presupposition.

When we construct an economy that fails at this basic task, such an economy is, to the extent that it fails, unethical. Global capitalism is unethical when, in it, we construct and assume that we must construct and neglect masses of people as valueless "dogs." The service economy is unethical both when it transforms immaterial human needs into commodities that only people with enough money can buy, and when service professionals construct certain people and groups of people as "cases," containers of suffering and the causes of suffering. The therapeutic sector of the service economy is unethical when it makes meaning, love, and selfhood into commodities for which even the poor must pay. Churches, like Christ Church, that implicitly or explicitly deny the sustenance of community to those who are poor construct an unethical communal economy.

The ethical presupposition that underlies most families, that membership in the family means meeting each other's needs, must be our economic ethic of care. In Mamre, we operated under this ethic; we assumed that anyone who came to the Mamre community needed others and could meet others' needs. Because we assumed that we could, and would, sustain our lives together, we actually did so to a much greater extent than we could have outside the community, despite the desperate poverty of most members. Twelve-step programs in which members help alleviate each other's suffering, without anyone's paying someone else for meaning, selfhood, or love, are an example of ethical therapeutic economies.

The Syrophoenician woman's vision implies a politics in which everyone participates. The primary agents in her saying are those who are weakest, those whom Jesus designates merely as passive recipients of the elite's activity, "children" and "dogs." In her vision, the "dogs" seek out, wait for, and ask for what they need from the "children," those insiders who, in their weakness, are most like the "dogs." The "dogs" and "children" cooperate in the construction of the economic reality in which all needs are met. Again, this vision is neither unrealistic nor utopian. The Syrophoenician woman's saying grows out of close observation of how children and dogs actually interact and take care of each other. The vision realizes the ways these least ones, those we often think of as not participating and exercising power, do participate in the construction of our shared reality. An ethic of care must fully realize these democratic political realities.

Global capitalism is politically unethical which it leads us to assume that masses of poor people are not capable of participation in the construction of our shared world. The service economy is politically unethical when it treats individuals or groups of people only as disabled or threatening "cases," rather than agents and subjects. The therapeutic culture is politically unethical when it defines "clients" as disabled agents, unable to exercise moral choice and so to participate responsibly in therapeutic relations. Churches are politically unethical when, again as did Christ Church, they do not recognize, support, affirm, and value the participation of all the actual members of the community, those who are actually there, including children, the poor, the aged, the ill, and those with different beliefs.

Christ Church was politically ethical when it welcomed and affirmed the participation of Ruth, a Jew, not a christian, and children. Mamre was politically ethical in that it affirmed the full participation of anyone who came to the meals, including the poor, children, and people with disabilities. Twelve-step programs are politically ethical to the extent that they actually affirm the full participation of any who come to meetings.

Socially, the Syrophoenician woman's saying constructs a community not on the basis of identity or boundaries; rather, it erases the boundary Jesus erected between insider "children" and outsider "dogs" and constructs a community inclusive of all those who are present. In other words, where Jesus assumed that the community of "children" existed over against "dogs," those who were not "children," the Syrophoenician woman pointed to the everyday reality that Jews and non-Jews, clean and unclean, "children" and "dogs" lived with, cooperated with, and depended upon one another. Again, this pluralistic vision is not utopian, but simply a realization of how people actually lived and still do live. No matter how separatist or sectarian a community or society, the people in it must continually relate to those they have designated as outsiders. The Syrophoenician woman's saying alerts us to the reality that an ethic of care must be one that realizes this inclusive and pluralistic reality, the reality of our interdependence with those who are different from ourselves.

In Jesus' time, people did not clearly differentiate between religious and social boundaries. The Syrophoenician woman's affirmation of a household that includes both Jewish "children" and Gentile "dogs" is also a religious vision, one that was apparently quite familiar to at least some of Jesus' associates and followers, at least for a few decades after his death. This vision articulates the reality that, for some of these followers, their central religious community was an interfaith one, bound not even by loyalty to Jesus, but simply by the liveliness and joy they found in their meals and conversation. In other words, the religious community, like the social community, envisioned by the Syrophoenician woman was not unified by a shared religious identity (as "Jews," "christians," or something else) or by a boundary that divided believing "children" from non-believing "dogs"; rather, the religious community included and apparently celebrated whoever was there. To reiterate, the biblical evidence shows that, for whoever composed the story of the Syrophoenician woman, such a religious community was not a utopian ideal, but a simple reality. My experiences with Mamre, formed on the basis of such a vision, and the experiences of those in a few other radically pluralistic and inclusive religious communities confirms that this vision is realistic. An ethic of care must lead us to realize more fully such radically open, inclusive, and pluralistic religious communities.

In the Syrophoenician woman's saying, the exchange of food between "children" and "dogs" takes place "under the table," out of sight of the adults. The saying suggests that egalitarian economic relations, democratic political movements, and inclusive and pluralistic communities, religious or otherwise, tend both to be hidden and subversive. Certainly, in both first- century Palestine and late twentieth-century America, in which dominant economic, political, social, and religious elites declare or imply that such visions are both unrealistic and dangerous, such is the case. In her actions, the Syrophoenician woman confirmed what she implied, that care requires cleverness and subversion. The woman found out where Jesus would be, despite his attempt to hide. In making her demand, she subverted the religious law governing the conduct of Gentile women in relation to Jewish men. When Jesus rejected her, she persisted in her subversion but cleverly hid it in a turn of Jesus' phrase. The story suggests that, if we are to care ethically, we must be able to identify where care is hiding, we must be subversive, and we must be clever in how we realize care in the face of the forces that deny its possibility.

The playfulness of the Syrophoenician woman's response and the joyous outcome of the story point to the reality I experienced in the Mamre community and that others have experienced in liberating, egalitarian, inclusive, and pluralistic communities. Even as one confronts intense and overwhelming suffering and affliction, even as one works long and exhausting hours in the attempt to alleviate such suffering, to the extent that one undertakes such care in mutual cooperation with others, including those most afflicted, one finds whatever joy is possible in the situation, and that joy liberates one to play with others, even if only momentarily.

APPENDIX A

Outline of the Method

In this Appendix, I outline the method for thinking about care that I and others have also used to help people do research on other practices. I define each movement, task, and context. For further description of the method, see especially chapter 5.

As indicated earlier, either individuals or groups may use this method. I suggest that, if a group employs it, the members divide up the different descriptive contexts and tasks among themselves and gather this descriptive data individually. Then they can bring this data back to the group and share their findings. I suggest that the members undertake the analytic and imaginative movements in group discussions. After such discussions, individual members might do written analyses and imaginations, which they bring back to the group as a whole for discussion.

I. Description

The purpose of description is to gather as much data as we can about a situation and the events in it. It does not matter if the data seems unimportant or irrelevant.

Description is wide in the sense that it seeks to include all that can be known or remembered about a particular event or situation, including that which is uncomfortable, offensive, improper, contradictory, or seemingly insignificant. It attends to the multiple dimensions within, and the contexts which hold, a situation and event. Finally, description is wide in that it attends both to the practice of the describer and care giver and the creative participation of the care receiver.

Description is narrow in the sense that it focuses intensely on the details of an event in, or aspect of, a situation: a particular instance or dimension that raises questions, contains a contradiction or an absence, that stands out as a vivid condensation or critical turning point.

A. Situation description

1. DEFINITION OF THE SITUATION

By "situation," I mean a current context, group, issue, relationship in or with which you are called to care. You do not have to be in an ordained, professional, official, or paid position in the situation. The situation should be one that raises certain questions, problems, or concerns about care for you. It should be one in which you can identify some suffering. It should be one in which there are, or will be, at least two "events" (see below for definition of an "event").

You should define the situation by answering questions such as: What is the situation? What unifies it: a particular community, location, individual, relationship, historical set of events, issue, or something else? Why have you chosen to reflect in this situation? Where is the identifiable suffering in the situation? What questions, problems, or concerns about care does this situation raise for you?

2. CONTEXTS OF THE SITUATION

The situation needs to be set in its contexts. Remember that it is essential that you include yourself in the description of all these contexts.

a. Objective contexts

By "objective," I mean those contexts which you describe "from the outside," as an observer. You need to remember, however, that "objective" is a relative term. You perceive everything through your own senses. Observation is participation in the construction of what you perceive.

(1) *Material*
(a) Geographic. Where does the situation occur geographically? Locate it on a map in relation to major geographic features and population centers.
(b) Ecological. What is the ecology, including climate and types of life ordinarily resident in the area?
(c) Resources. What are the resources that support or are utilizable by human beings in the area? What are the major institutions and sources of employment?
(d) Socio-ecological. What is the humanly constructed material context? A city? What kind of neighborhood? A farming or mining town? What do the human constructions—farm fields, buildings, sidewalks and streets, stores, manufacturing or refining plants—actually look, sound, smell, and feel like? Where and how do people gather and for what purposes?
(e) Local. Describe the close, small area in which the situation occurs. Be specific.
(f) Institutional. If the situation occurs in an institution or building, describe the place. Be specific.
(g) Individuals. Describe the people, including yourself, in the situation: how they look, move, sound, smell, and feel; what they wear.

(2) *Social*
Under the social contexts, be sure to include descriptions of the characteristics of the people in the smaller community of your situation and in the larger community that surrounds the smaller one.

(a) Demographic. What are the racial, ethnic, class, age, religious, gender, sexual orientation, educational, occupational and other relevant demographic characteristics of the people in your situation? What are the demographic environments and how do they define the participants, including the practitioner, and their behavior? For instance, a parishioner and a pastor are likely to relate quite differently in a church than the same two people, now in the roles respectively of counselee and pastoral counselor, would act in an office in a pastoral counseling center. In describing the social environments, the assumed inhabitants should be taken into account. For instance, most pastoral counseling centers are decorated in a way that assumes that the clients are middle-class people used to dealing with "professionals."

(b) Economic. What are the economic situations of the communities of your situation?

(c) Political. How is power distributed, exercised, and structured in these communities? Be sure to attend to both the formal and informal power structures. Ask: Who participates in the decisions affecting those in the situation and who is excluded from such participation? Who has the power to determine what happens and who is determined by others? Who has the power to define truth, reality, and the good in the situation, and who is defined by others? How are these power relationships structured and enacted?

(3) Historical

Describe how the situation got to be the way it is and how you got to participate in it. Answering the following questions may help you: When did this situation begin? What led up to the situation? For instance, if the situation is a particular church, when was it founded and what led up to its being founded? What were the contexts of the situation at the time it began? What were the major historical events shaping its contexts at this time? How have the situation and its contexts changed since its beginning? What have been the major events shaping these changes? What historical movements appear to be shaping the situation at this time? For instance, in the situation of the ongoing relationship between a pastor and parishioner, one force shaping such relationships in mainline churches in America at this time is the pastoral care and counseling movement. Another is the current concern about sexual harassment and impropriety. On the more personal note: How were you called to care in this particular situation? Where does this situation "fit" in your history? How is it similar to or different from previous or other situations in your life? What do you bring from your history to this situation?

b. Subjective contexts

The subjective contexts are "internal," having to do with how people construct meaning, "feel," "conceive," or imagine themselves, each other, and the worlds in which they live. In each of these contexts, there may be a difference between what people say—the explicit context—and what is communicated by what they do—the implicit context. You should attend to both.

(1) Psychological

What kinds of experience are constructed or shaped by the contexts of the situation? For instance, a pastoral counseling office presupposes that both counselor and counselee will be attuned to the problematic experiences of the counselee—the focus will be on the counselee's psychological suffering; the counselor, in turn, will not be focused on his or her particular experiences of suffering, but on the way his or her current experiences facilitate his or her ability to understand the counselee. The experiences presupposed when a pastor meets a parishioner in a church office are not nearly so focused and will likely involve more explicitly religious dimensions. What is the "feel" of the situation? hopeful? angry? despairing? triumphant? What fantasies do people in and out of the situation have about it? For instance, if the situation is a relationship between a parishioner and pastor in a church, what are the fantasies that people in and out of the church have about this relationship or ones like it? What kinds of stories do people tell, or what emotionally charged images and metaphors do they use in talking about the situation and those centrally involved in it? What memories do the events of the situation awaken among those in the situation and the contexts surrounding it? What future do people in the situation or its contexts predict for it?

What kinds of fantasies do you have about the situation? What does it mean to you? What is your overall "sense" of yourself in the situation? How does it "feel" to you?

(2) Cultural

The cultural context has to do with the semiotic construction of the situation, communities, and selves in it. There are three ways of gathering information about the cultural context. The first is to answer the question, What are the dominant media, genres, and forms used by the participants, including yourself, in the situation? For instance, do people tend to like to read (what do they read?), tell stories (what kinds of stories?) watch TV (which shows?), go to movies (what kinds of movies?), engage in rituals like worship services, attend classes or lectures (what kinds of classes or lectures?)?

The second is to answer the question, What kind of media, genres, and forms are used by, and about, these communities and participants to communicate about the situation? For instance, do people tell stories, refer to TV shows, draw pictures, or use nonverbal messages to communicate what is happening in the situation?

The third is to answer the question, What medium, genre, or form is suggested by the situation itself? If you were to attempt to communicate what is going on in this situation to others, what medium, genre, and/or form seems to reveal the most about it? an abstract expressionist painting? a poem? a romantic comedy? Why?

(3) Ethical

The explicit ethical context contains the participants', including your own, stated understandings of what is right and wrong in the situation. The implicit ethical context is indicated by the moral ethos or feel of the situation, its broader contexts, and gut-level responses of the participants, including yourself. For instance, while a church-related group may have a strong explicit commitment to "liberating the poor," they may feel uncomfortable with the poor and implicitly judge them to be incompetent and incapable of truly participating in a community.

(4) Religious

The explicit religious context is identified by answering the following questions: What are the explicit religious or theological positions of the participants in the situation, including yourself? What is the explicit religious environment, and how does it define the participants and their behavior?

The implicit religious context is identified by answering the following questions: What is assumed by the participants, including yourself, to be fundamentally real in this situation? What is assumed to be fundamentally wrong? What are the assumptions about the way things are supposed to be? How do the participants in the situation deal with the differences between problematic current existence and the way things are supposed to be? For instance, in most pastoral counseling situations, the fundamental reality is assumed to be the life and experience of the individual; social forces are usually not considered. The problem is also supposed to lie within individuals—in their emotional or psychological makeup, or, in more explicitly religious contexts, their individual faith or spiritual life. The ideal state of affairs is usually assumed to be some sort of realized individual existence or the recognition that one has an individual relationship with God. The means to this idealized state are usually supposed to be internal, individual changes, facilitated by a dyadic relationship. Put these characteristics together, and one finds that the implicit religious context of most pastoral counseling situations is constituted by the equation between ultimate reality and the individual self.

B. *Description of a focal event*

1. DEFINITION OF FOCAL EVENT

By "event," I mean a certain time-limited happening in the situation—a meeting, an encounter, a counseling session or part of it, a worship service, a particular experience. Descriptions of events should be highly detailed and vivid. If you need to choose between offering a more general description of a longer event (say a two-hour board meeting) and a very detailed description of a short event (say a two-minute encounter between yourself and the chair of the board during the meeting), choose the latter and include a more general description of the rest of the longer event in your description of the historical context of the event and the outcome.

Each focal event needs to be defined by asking questions similar to those asked about the situation: What is the event? What are its limits in time and space—that is, when did it begin and end and where did it occur? What makes it stand out in the situation? Why have you chosen to study this event? Where is the identifiable suffering in the event? What particular questions and concerns about care does this event raise?

2. CONTEXTS OF FOCAL EVENT

Just as the contexts of the situation need to be described, so do the contexts of the focal event. The categories of contexts are the same as those attended to in the description of the situation. The answers given in the description of the contexts of the situation will often provide most of the contextual information about the event. However, the description of the event should also include an examination of the very particular contexts of the event. These particular descriptions can be largely generated by taking the questions asked about the situational contexts and substituting "event" for "situation" and then answering the questions. But some additional questions, particular to the event, may also need to be asked; these are given below.

a. Objective contexts

(1) Material

What is the location of the particular event in relation to the space of the larger situation? How is the space of the event organized or "decorated"—for example, in an office, what's in it and how are these objects arranged? Where were the major participants (including the participant observer) in the event located at the beginning of the event?

(2) Social

What is the social function of this event in relation to the larger situation? How "central" or "peripheral" to the larger situation is this event? What are the roles in the larger situation of the particular people involved in this event? What are the demographic characteristics of the particular people involved in this event, and how do these characteristics compare with the demographic characteristics of the participants in the overall situation?

How is this particular event placed in the power dynamics of the situation as a whole? What is the political location of the participants in the event in relation to other people in the situation? What is the political meaning of this event in the situation?

(3) Historical

What particular events preceded this one and set the stage for it?

b. Subjective contexts

(1) Psychological

What presuppositions, expectations, fantasies, and feelings did you (the participant observer) carry into the event? What presuppositions, expectations, fantasies, and feelings might other participants have had as they entered the event?

(2) Cultural

What is the medium, genre, and form of this event? How does it fit or clash with the aesthetics of the situation as a whole? What medium and genre would you use to best communicate what happened in this event?

(3) Ethical

As you and others entered this event, how did you think about it or conceive of it ethically?

(4) Religious

Are there any differences between the "religious" presuppositions of the event and those of the situation as a whole? If so, what are they? What is the implicit and explicit theological meaning of this event for you?

3. A DETAILED RECOUNTING OF THE EVENT

The detailed description of the event is the heart of the method of disciplined reflection in practice, for it is here that the practitioner reflects specifically on practice. In the other steps and submovements, generalities and abstractions can successfully obscure what happened, but here the distorting effect of such obscuring devices becomes evident and one can get beyond them. Here the norms for description—that it be receptive, inclusive, thick, layered, detailed, textured, vivid, and evocative—become most important.

a. A verbatim

If the event is one in which two or only a few people participated, this recollection should include a verbatim—that is, a recounting in dialogue form of precisely what each person, including yourself, said and did. For group or other kinds of events, the description should include as detailed a recounting as possible of precisely what happened, including your participation. The verbatim should be a unified description—one recounting of the event which includes, in addition to the spoken dialogue, the following as dimensions:

Nonverbal aspects
A recounting of nonverbal aspects of the event: how time and space were structured in it, what was going on around the particular recollected event, how the participants (including yourself) were dressed, their posture, how they looked, how they placed themselves and moved in relation to each other or other major props in the situation, and how they responded physically (in body language) to each other.

Observer's ongoing subjective responses
A recounting of your ongoing subjective responses during the event—the changes in your feelings, thoughts, fantasies, and bodily sensations as the event, unfolded, your ongoing gut-level ethical and religious sense of the event, for example, where it "felt right" or "wrong," "divine" or "holy" or "meaningless" or "unreal". If you have access to anyone else's ongoing responses, they should also be included.

Anything else
Anything else about the event that you remember, or find out, or anything that comes to mind as you describe and think about the event—for example, changes in the contexts (weather outside, noises, heat or cold, etc.); stray images or metaphors or feelings about the event that emerge as you describe it; comments others made about the event. Don't censor anything here.

b. Outcome of the focal event
One describes the outcome of the event in order to indicate how the event impacted the situation. Describing the outcome is essential to evaluating your practice in an event. The description in this step should include a detailed (but not necessarily exhaustive) recounting of the effects of the event on: the participants in the event *and* the situation; your subjectivity—feelings, thoughts, fantasies, bodily sensations, and so on; the contexts—objective and subjective—of the event in the situation; and the broader contexts of the situation as a whole. Note any changes the event has produced in these contexts.

II. Analysis

The purpose of the second movement of reflection, analysis, is to understand what is happening in, first, a described focal event or aspect of a situation, and, then, using what has been learned through the analyses of a series of connected events or aspects, the encompassing situation. By "understanding," I mean the construction of a conceptual map of what happened that can serve as the basis for imagining how one's own, or one's community's practice could be more caring in the particular described situation. The primary norm for analysis is thus pragmatic.

In general, such explanations are "good" to the degree that they are logical, coherent, and comprehensive—that is, they include all the available data in a continuous, logical unit, and they show how each detail is connected to the other details to form a complete picture.

But this norm is impossible to reach for five reasons. First, the fundamental ambiguity of practice, and so of reflection, means that any analysis will, to a certain extent, both reflect and embody paradoxical and even wholly contradictory movements. Practice and reflection, as born in desire and suffering, are simply not wholly coherent. Second, the plurivocality of signs—gestures, words, images, actions—means that the connections among the elements of an event or situation are so numerous and ever-shifting as to be effectively incomprehensible. Even a community of disciplined practitioners cannot trace all the connections among the elements of even a simple event. Third, analysis as a movement of reflection is always of an event that is past. No matter how comprehensive an explanation may be, it does not include what is occurring. Fourth, analysis is itself practice. To analyze an event or situation is to be involved in it, to affect it. The effects of current practice remain largely unconscious both because of the unconscious dimension of any practice and because they are not yet past and so cannot become the object of current reflection. Fifth, if the purpose of analysis is to improve practice, then, at some point, the analysis of a particular event or situation, which can be made more comprehensive if it continues, must give way to the necessity for an intentional and active response in a situation. The primary norm for analysis, that it serve caring practice, limits its movement toward the norm of comprehensiveness.

Within the analytic moment, there remain these two pulls: toward continuity and toward discontinuity. The movement toward discontinuity is primary, especially in caring practice, because it is suffering as the sign of the loss or breakdown of ordered continuous existence that initiates caring practice and the need for reflection. Analysis is drawn to the breaks in practice, indicated by the discontinuities, the contradictions and gaps, in the description of events and situations. Articulating these discontinuities is the beginning of, and impetus for, analysis. The movement toward a continuous explanation exists as a response to such articulations of discontinuity. It is the attempt to reconstruct the world in the light of the cracks in the existing world.

A. Cracks

The first task in analysis is the identification of cracks in the description. Most descriptions initially appear to be unified, coherent wholes. Closer inspection reveals cracks in this smooth surface: tensions, incongruities, outright contradictions, gaps, or ambiguities in the content or presentation of the description. These cracks are the openings through which one can grasp the bars to suffering and so reach beyond them to the suffering itself, what causes it, and the healing response to it.

B. Hidden realities

The second task in analysis is the identification of what is barred in the description. I assume that the cracks are evidence that the description, while it reveals some things, also hides or covers over—bars—other realities. A deeper understanding of an event requires exploring these barred realities.

Usually, behind a barrier, we find suffering and its causes. Since suffering is partially hidden or disguised, the task of finding this suffering cannot be purely phenomenonological—that is, it cannot stick simply with what is given. Rather, you must, by focusing on the bars identified in the first step and examining them, build a case for the suffering that is partially unseen in the description. A key question that can help in this step is: What specifically appears to be denied or resisted in the bars? For instance, in the example of the grisly tragedy told in a sweet, happy voice, what is likely being denied is the devastating effect of the tragedy on the speaker. One could speculate also that the speaker fears that admitting this effect will make him ugly and unacceptable to others, rather than "sweet."

The observer's bodily experience, emotions, and fantasies upon hearing the description can also provide strong evidence for the nature of the hidden suffering. For instance, in the example of the exciting tale that puts the reader to sleep, the sleeper's fantasies or dreams—say of being lost in an amusement park—may help to identify the hidden suffering—in the example, the isolation and loneliness of the person telling the story.

Notice that in these two examples, the hidden suffering is identified as that of the person describing an event. This observation indicates a third way of identifying suffering hidden in an event: the analyst's use of self-analysis as an aid to the analysis of the observed event or situation. By analyzing how, in the event and description of it, he or she barred suffering and what particular kind of suffering is barred, the analyst may gain insight into how others are barring suffering and what kind of suffering they are barring in the event or situation. The accuracy of the analyst's speculation about the connection between her or his own barred suffering and the barred suffering of others in the events is dependent upon the analyst's familiarity with her or his particular but typical reactions to a range of kinds of situations.

Finally, examining a barred or neglected dimension or context often yields a great deal of information about barred suffering. For instance, the barring of information about participants' social class and race often reveals suffering caused by classism and racism.

C. Reconstruction

Having identified the cracks and barred realities, we can reconstruct a relatively coherent description of the event that takes into account what we have learned about it. Here, prior research and theories about suffering, its causes, and its alleviation become centrally important. They direct us to look for connections that may not have been previously considered. In this construction, you should attend to all the contexts of your situation and event and so all the dimensions of practice. Because suffering is multi-dimensional, its causes and truly healing responses to it are also multi-dimensional. Thus, attention to different kinds of theories—biological, ecological, sociological, psychological, economic, political, theological—may be helpful. Again, the adequacy of a construction is measured by its capacity to explain the particular causes of the suffering in *this specific* event or aspect and the *particular* reasons why certain responses are caring.

D. Care

The analysis of the bars to suffering, the uncovering of hidden suffering, and the reconstruction of the situation open up the possibility of identifying those caring responses already present in the situation that alleviate the suffering. Prior to this point, the identification of what is caring in an event or aspect is likely to be primarily influenced by the desire to avoid suffering, and thus one will tend to identify responses that participate in such avoidance or barring. Only after the deconstruction of the bars to suffering and a reconstruction of one's understanding can an accurate identification of care take place. A measure of the accuracy of the analysis is the *specificity* with which it identifies the instances of care as healing responses to the *particular* suffering uncovered in the event.

Here I assume that, where there is suffering, there is some sort of alleviating response to it—there is care. Even the barring of suffering is, in this sense, a caring, though usually flawed, attempt to end it.

III. Imagination

The last reflective task is to use the imagination to construct a more caring response to an event and situation. Three questions guide this imagined response: How should the event or situation happen, if the participants fully realize care? What needs to happen in order to get the event or situation from the way it was, or is, happening to the way it should happen? What can I realistically do to help move the event or situation from the way it is happening to the way it should happen?

Imagination is crucial because it is the way reflection motivates and shapes a response to suffering. Any practical discipline, even if it does not go through the descriptive and analytic movements, has such an imagined "vision" or norm. Even the most deontological discipline that claims to derive its norms from a source outside the world of practice presents those norms as a vision of the way life should be lived. To say that we should not kill each other because God tells us not to kill only has meaning as a vision of responding without killing in particular violent situations—for example, when one's community is under attack.

However, in a method for critical reflection *in* caring practice, the imagination is bound to *particular* situations and events or aspects for two other reasons. First, a wholly ungrounded imagination—one that is not rooted in particular realities—is used by desire to avoid suffering. Such imaginative escapes may be harmless and even helpful if recognized for what they are—time-limited "vacations" from the "real world." They become demonic when they are mistaken for reality or "essential" reality. When an imagined world without suffering or evil is posited as the essentially real transcendent Reality, then finally, no matter how much apparent "love" or "compassion" or "grace" may be extended to "this world," the reality we all live and die in becomes the devalued and rejected place of suffering and evil; one's task is to escape it, not love it.

Second, an ungrounded imagination provides no help in healing suffering in the particular situations that constitute our lives. To imagine a world without killing, without imagining how that vision could specifically be realized in the face of the particular violence happening in a particular community is to cut off the vision from caring practice and so from the reality of suffering.

In a discipline in practice, the imagination is limited by the other reflective movements—description and analysis. Specifically, the caring practitioner, after describing and analyzing a particular event or aspect or set of events or aspects in a particular situation, imagines a more caring or healing response to the particular suffering in the situation. A "good" imagined response is one that motivates and contributes to a more caring actual response.

This norm specifies a great deal. A "good" imagined response is determined by taking the place of the particular suffering in a situation, is a vision of the caring practitioner's or community's transformed practice, is a response to the multiple contexts of the situation, and is contemporary in the sense that it is a response to what just happened in the situation. As responsive to the different contexts, a good imagined response is intentionally "thick"—that is, as much as possible it takes into account the effects of the response at all levels and dimensions of the situation: physical, unconscious, bodily, ecological, psychological, emotional, interpersonal, social, political, economic, historical, and religious. It is a response of the whole person and the whole community, not just of the conscious, thinking part of either. Finally, a good imagined response is also a humble one. The practitioner realizes that it is not an actual response. It is the product of the past, and when it is enacted in the present, it will prove to be somewhat inadequate. Once reflected upon, it will need to be modified.

Imagination consists of three tasks.

A. Abstraction of an Image of Care

Abstract from the description and analysis of care in the event or situation a particular image of care, a statement of what is essential for effective care in this event or situation.

B. Identify the Obstacles to Care

Identify as concisely as possible the obstacles to care as they emerge in the situation or event.

C. Imagined Response

Imagine a specific and particular response you could have realistically carried out in an event that would have helped to overcome the obstacles to care in the event and so would have helped your and your community's practice be more caring. Or imagine a specific and particular response that you can carry out in a situation that will help you and your community to overcome the obstacles to care in the situation and so will help your, and your community's, practice to be more caring.

APPENDIX B

Additional Analytic Triads

Following are some analytic triads, in addition to the ones presented in the body of the book, that students and I have found useful, with a discussion of each.

Figure 16: Contents, Intentions, Performances[1]

Content: the socially defined meaning of the signs and symbols in the communication. For instance, "hello" is a greeting.

Intention: the purpose or force—often emotional—of a particular communicative act. For instance, I can say "hello" lightly and happily or heavily and angrily.

Performance: what the communication actually does, the specific relations it establishes. For instance, a person says "hello" to one person and the two smile, hug, and walk away together. The same speaker says "hello" in the same way, seemingly with the same intention, to another person, and this second person angrily walks off. In these examples, the contents and intentions are the same, but the performances are different.

The content, intention, and performance of a communicative act may support or contradict each other. If I say a happy "hello" to you and you respond by giving me a hug, the three meanings support each other. If I say a happy "hello" and you stalk off, the performance contradicts the intent and content. If I say a cold and angry "hello" and you respond by walking away, the intention and performance contradict the content. If I say a cold and angry "hello" and you respond by giving me a warm hug, the content and performance contradict the intent. Frequently, a communicative act contains more than one content, intention, and performance, which may or may not be congruent. Often, when a performance contradicts an identified intention, another hidden intention supports the performance.

Discussions in the pastoral care and counseling literature rarely focus on presuppositions and the material relations they construct or perform. Perhaps the major assumption among professional care givers is that they possess the knowledge and skills necessary to care effectively for a disabled care receiver. This presupposition constructs care as an economic

---

[1] These categories are modifications of J. L. Austin's "locutionary," "illocutionary," and "perlocutionary" meanings.

relation in which the care giver's knowledge is literally positively valued—paid for—and the care receiver's knowledge is literally negatively valued as a problem or liability—it costs money to change it. Related to this economic relation is a political one in which the caregiver has authorized—for pastoral caregivers, divinely authorized—power over care receivers; the caregiver is the agent or subject who acts upon—cares for—the care receiver as an object. Rather than attend to these performed realities, most discourse in pastoral care and counseling focuses on theoretical definitions and diagnoses—contents—and treatment plans—intentions.

The most pervasive cause of preventable suffering is the objectification, oppression, or domination of people with less power by those with greater power. Deconstructing the bar against performances reveals how care relations often cause suffering by devaluing or objectifying the already suffering care receiver—afflicting the afflicted. Attending to performed meanings is necessary if those who would care are going to alleviate rather than exacerbate suffering.

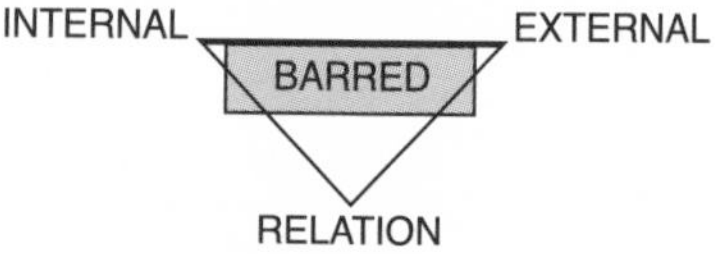

Archie Smith explains that modern Western thought tends to provide two understandings of the causes of suffering. Most in the helping professions, including most pastoral counselors and other pastoral care professionals, assume that suffering is caused by flaws in indi-

Figure 17: Internal, External, Relation

viduals' bodies (biological theories), psyches (psychological theories), wills and values (most ethical theories), or faiths (most current theologies).[2]

While various types of systems and organizational theorists and therapists have criticized such individualism, most of them still assume that the causes of suffering are internal to the analyzed unit. They simply replace the individual with a couple, family, group, community, or even society.

On the other hand, many sociologists, critical social thinkers, and social ethicists assume that the causes of suffering are external. They lie in broad social and historical movements that structure societies and create internal contradictions and tensions in organizations, communities, families, individual selves, and even bodies.[3]

The difference between the two paradigms emerges most clearly in how they envision change. The first group of theorists—the "internalists"—think that change comes from within—that is, an individual, family, group, or even society can, and must, change itself. The result is individual, family, group, organizational, or social therapy, which diagnoses the internal problems and prescribes the cure—the means by which the individual, family, group, organization, or society can heal itself. The second group of

---

[2] Smith, 39–41.
[3] Ibid., 41–50.

theorists—the "externalists"—think that change comes from without. The result is a focus on changing the historical, social, cultural, economic, political, and ecological conditions that determine the lives of individuals, families, organizations, and societies.[4]

By locating the causes of suffering in individual units and failing to address external contextual and historical causes, the internal paradigm promotes an ethic of adjustment. The paradigm defines the person's, family's, group's, institution's, or society's problem as its own dysfunction in or failure to fit into what is assumed to be a fundamentally problem-free or, at least, objectively real and unchangeable world. To solve the problem is to become functional in, or to, adjust to this external reality. By locating the causes of and solutions to problems in social and historical forces, the external paradigm promotes fatalism. No individual, group, or even society can truly impact these forces. The best one can do is to discern the directions in which these dominant forces are pushing society and move with, rather than against them. In other words, as Archie Smith observes, the external paradigm finally joins the internal paradigm in promoting a conservative ethic that assumes the preservation of the existing dominant order.[5]

Smith claims that most discussions of individual or social change by modern Western psychologists, sociologists, ethicists, and theologians move between these two paradigms and thus bar consideration of the paradigm and reality in which real change can occur. According to this third or relational paradigm, individual units—organisms, persons, families, organizations, societies, and even whole ecosystems—co-create each other. The causes of problems and their solutions lie in these co-creative relations. Because all participate together in the relations that construct reality, all can participate in changing it. The relational paradigm thus promotes a transformational ethic in which individuals and communities address suffering by critically examining how they construct its causes in their relations and by trying out different ways of relating and thus different ways of constructing reality.[6]

The diagram points to the necessity for caring practice to deconstruct the barrier, present in many discussions of therapeutic and social change, to the reality of relation.

Many feminists, liberation theologians, and critical social thinkers

Figure 18: Reflection, Response, Placement

observe that one's social location or position determines one's theory and practice. They criticize dominant Western or First World theologians for ignoring or barring this reality and retaining the assumption that, through

---

[4] Ibid., 39–50.
[5] Ibid., 39–50.
[6] Ibid., 39–54.

reason and revelation, they have access to universal truths, knowledge that does not reflect a particular place.

Most pastoral care and counseling theorists and most practical and pastoral theologians begin with the assumption that, by reading certain texts—the christian classics, including the Bible, and currently regnant psychological, human scientific, and philosophical studies of human nature—they can derive universal knowledge that they can use to understand current human practice and universal norms to guide such practice. In their practice, they implicitly define care as having two movements. First, one uses one's theory to reflect critically on a particular current situation or event, understood as problematic. In other words, one uses one's theory to diagnose the moral or spiritual illness in a person, family, group, church, community, institution, or society and to imagine how the situation could be better. Then one allows this reflection to guide one's response to the situation. This two-step process bars the impact of one's particular location or place—physical, social, historical, political, or psychological—on one's reflection and imagination.

The model implies what many feminist and liberation theologians claim: that hidden in the particular experiences of the oppressed are specific truths and norms that are not universal, but that accurately articulate their suffering and its causes. Caring reflection requires placement with those who are suffering in a particular situation. What one learns through such placement guides one's response in that context.

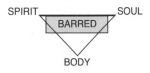

Figure 19: Spirit, Soul, Body

"Spirit" here refers to that register of our existence in which we experience ourselves as freely and consciously choosing what we do and who we are. In psychological terms, the spirit is the "I" or ego. These psychological terms, however, tend to be reified. They suggest a fixed entity, while spirit is actually that activity of free agency that can never be wholly fixed.

"Soul" refers to the objective dimension of "my" existence. "Soul" includes a layering of images and perceptions and structures—our internal sense of ourselves or subjectivity, going back to our first awareness of bodies, reflections of who we are in the eyes and voices and bodies of others, roles we have been given in psychological and social systems—out of which emerges the sense of being *a* particular person.

As I am using it, "soul" is not synonymous with "self." A soul may include one or more selves. A "self" is a unified, centered, and bounded sense of "who I am" in relation to another. Not included in a self, but included in the soul that encompasses it, are those qualities, experiences, characteristics, feelings, and ways of being which in fact I do have, but which I reject, or of which I am unaware.

The soul is partially determined and partially mutable. When the spirit chooses one way of being over another, the whole process of choosing becomes part of the soul—the chosen way as chosen and the rejected way as rejected. Spirit cannot annihilate something it rejects, but its choice does shape the soul by shaping a bounded self within the field of the soul.

"Body" refers to that register of existence in which spirit's freedom is merged into what is given. Body sets the limits on what spirit can do with soul. Body is essentially mysterious—beyond our control because it is beyond conception. None of us can find adequate reasons to explain our bodily existence, why we are born either male or female, in this particular place and time. Body sets the boundaries of reflection. We cannot conceive bodily existence, except by analogy or negation, because it is ontologically prior to the differentiation of the forms upon which conception builds.[7] As bodied, existence is opened at its heart to that which is not self, which seems to be other, yet is found in our depths.

In bodily existence, differentiations blur. When one shakes hands, one cannot finally differentiate between the act and its meaning—they are fused. Similarly, the sensations at the surface of the skin—for instance, of warmth, moistness, and roughness—are both "my" sensations, occurring in "my" body, yet also they are sensations of the other. I and Thou meet and while, in the dimensions of spirit and soul, we remain differentiated, at the bodily level we do not—I sense you and you, me.[8]

The body is also the preeminent realm of suffering, first because all suffering is initially bodily suffering. Clearly, physical suffering is bodily suffering. But we also suffer psychologically because we are thrown as bodies into existence. We do not exist wholly as we desire to; our existence is not wholly mutable, but limited and threatened; we are fragile. Social suffering or affliction is bodily suffering. We bodily cast people out of society—into ghettoes, prisons, terminal wards, asylums, or simply into unvisited homes and apartments. We bodily treat people as objects by torturing them, having them work in wholly unsafe conditions, restricting their access to necessities. And religious suffering, the terror of annihilation, is also embodied, the effect of being born and dying, of knowing that we once did not exist as we do now and, at some future time, we will cease to exist as embodied beings.

Because suffering is embodied, it does not respect boundaries. To perceive another's suffering is to feel its impact in one's body—one suffers with the other. Ministers who visit dying parishioners often report feeling tired, discouraged, powerless, and anxious. These empathic responses to their parishioners' suffering are rooted in the bodily union between the ministers and parishioners.

Feminists have criticized the dominant voices in Western theology for devaluing the body. At best, the body is considered the dwelling place of the spirit and the soul. Luce Irigaray links this devaluation to men's terror

---

[7] Buber, 60-71.
[8] Ibid.

of their origins in, and so fusion with, particular women's bodies. We replace our mothers with God, defined as pure spirit.[9]

Pastoral care and counseling specialists have, since the second century, practiced this avoidance of the body. They have attended to the souls, spirits, and sometimes selves of their parishioners, but rarely their bodies. William Clebsch and Charles Jaekle express the view that still predominates: that care for the body is somehow not dignified or appropriate to those whose high calling is to practice exemplary Christian love and care.[10]

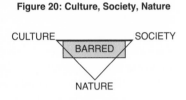

Figure 20: Culture, Society, Nature

Since the body is the seat of suffering, so to neglect it is to diminish the capacity to perceive and respond to suffering. As the healing response to suffering, care requires the deconstruction of such devaluation and the barriers to the body associated with it.

"Culture" refers to the system of signs and symbols through which a group conceives an ordered world. "Society" refers to a network of relationships and the social structures, communities, and institutions constructed in these relationships. "Nature" refers to what is given, what we find: the material reality that includes our bodies, the physical universe, and our ecological and socio-ecological contexts.

Feminists, critical social thinkers, and ecologists have all commented upon the Western tendency to objectify nature, to think of it as the chaos against which society defends itself, the material it uses to sustain itself or which accumulates as waste, and the void into which it casts this waste. Western societies also classify certain human beings as part of nature rather than society: as objects to be used in the construction of social reality or to be discarded, as representatives of the chaos which threatens to destroy society, and as empty containers filled with what society rejects.

This objectifying of nature exacerbates and creates suffering in four ways. First, most directly and obviously, objectified human beings suffer. They suffer physically. Those who have power and resources give to those in need only if they function efficiently in the service of those who dominate. If these human objects do not accept such functions, are disabled, or are displaced by less expensive vehicles for performing the same functions, they find themselves without the resources necessary to live. Even if their physical needs are met, they suffer because of the radical fragility of their lives, the continual imminent threat of death. Frequently, the only way they can deal with this terror is to numb themselves, to accept their objectification, to die as participants in their own lives. Still, psychiatrists and

---

[9] Luce Irigaray, *Speculum of the Other Woman*, trans. Gilliam C. Gill (Ithaca, N.Y.: Cornell University, 1985), 160–67.

[10] Clebsch and Jaekle, 8.

psychologists have discovered, the terror remains, expressed in severe psychiatric and physical illnesses that add another layer of suffering on these people's lives. Discussing the plight of the poor, Gustavo Gutierrez links anonymity and death.[11] When society does not recognize people's names, their existence as social participants, it sentences them to early and often anguished death.

Second, the objectification of nature tends to be synonymous with the objectification of the body, the treatment of it as something to be used, as an obstacle to be overcome, or as the repository of dangerous chaotic forces. This devaluation of the body leads to the denial, neglect, and exacerbation of suffering. Society's treatment of some people's bodies as objects is synonymous with its definition of them solely as functioning for someone else, with all the attendant consequences. But even when those with power construe their own bodies simply as objects, they tend not to respect their physical limits and so to make themselves vulnerable to numerous physical and psychiatric illnesses.

Third, the objectification of nature tends to lead to the abuse of the environment in three ways, all of which eventually increase suffering. When we construe the environment primarily as the source of useful materials, we tend to use them up, thus eventually depriving ourselves of needed resources. When we conceive the physical world as an empty void into which we can pour our wastes, we end by poisoning ourselves. When we react against nature as the chaotic source of all that threatens us, we attack it and, in so doing, often destroy resources and sometimes create or release highly toxic forces.

Fourth, the objectification of nature results in the alienation of human beings from each other, their environment, their bodies, and finally reality itself. Conceived as a meaningless mass of things, material reality crushes the correspondingly insubstantial, empty spirit. Subjectivity becomes a hellish, smothering void. The only act that retains some meaning—and it only lasts an instant—is attempted annihilation, the flash of rage and pleasure accompanying the destruction of some hated bit of reality, even oneself.

Uncovering the suffering caused by the objectification of nature requires recognizing such devaluation as a bar and deconstructing it. To put it positively, only when we hear the speech of nature and those human beings and bodies identified with it can we begin loving ourselves and our world by responding to our suffering.

Human beings live their lives in semiotically constructed worlds, which they create out of the reality given to them. Everything in such constructions exists as communication—as meaning something in the cultural order—and as communicating—as carrying such meanings. Any event or situation in a human world, which means in reality (since the only reality

---

[11] Gustavo Gutierrez, unpublished lecture, Ministers' Week, Phillips University, Enid, Oklahoma, 1988.

we know is that in which we human beings participate, at least by knowing it), has an assumed structure: two or more subjects construct meaning and so reality by using signs, symbols, or tools drawn from a cultural order to shape objects. For example:

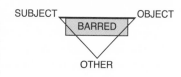

Figure 21: Subject, Object, Other

I (a subject) am now typing (using linguistic signs and symbols and a computer [a tool]) a sentence (an object) to communicate an idea (a meaning) to you (another subject).

A carpenter (a subject) uses tools to make a cabinet (an object) which can be used (that is, it has a functional meaning) by myself and others (subjects).

Two teachers (subjects) converse about (use linguistic signs and symbols to construct a meaningful understanding of) a student (an object).

Frequently a communicative act combines one of more of these elements or leaves them implicit. For example:

A teacher (a subject) tells (uses linguistic signs and symbols) a student (both another subject and an object to be shaped) to study more (a meaning).

I (a subject) am dreaming (using sensory signs or images to shape a meaningful imaginary object, my dream) about myself (a shaped object). Left implicit is the plurality of the "I" as dreamer, recipient of the dream, and "myself," an object shaped in the dream.

Christians (subjects) receive Jesus (a meaningful shaped object) as God's (a subject's) incarnate Word (a meaningful object). Left implicit is the symbolic system in which "Jesus" functions as subject, symbol, and meaning, as well as the object.

The Constitution (subject) guides our decisions (meaningful objects). Left implicit is the assumption that we (subjects) interpret (using linguistic signs and symbols) the Constitution (an object).

These last examples point to the ambiguous character of all the elements in a communicative act: each implicitly functions as both subject, that which communicates or shapes, and object, that which is acted upon, shaped, or used. Most often hidden is the subjectivity or functional subjectivity (in the case of nonhuman beings) of explicit objects. For instance, we used the two analytic triads preceding this one to uncover the barred functional subjectivity of the body and nature, both of which tend to be conceived as only objects.

As in the example of the teachers discussing a student, this hidden subjectivity may not fit so easily into the categories of body and nature. Perhaps in any communicative act, hidden in and among the explicit subjects and objects, there resides an implicit or barred subject or functional subject, which we can designate as an "other."

Those who have dominant agency tend to objectify those who have less power. To bar the other's subjectivity or agency is to deny the other's participation in the construction of reality. The discussion of nature uncovered the suffering resulting from such denials. Barring the other bars suffering. Care as the healing response to suffering requires freeing the voice of the other to participate in the construction of reality.

As David Tracy observes, most Western theologies are explicitly or implicitly correlational. They relate the questions and answers about humanity and reality gained from reflection on common human experience, usually represented by currently dominant human and physical sciences and philosophical movements, with reflection on the christian texts, the Bible, and other classics of one's particular tradition. The dominant voices in North American pastoral and practical theology follow this correlational model. For instance, Don Browning, Thomas Groome, and Charles Gerkin use human scientific

Figure 22: Tradition, Human Sciences, Practice

and psychological theories to reflect critically on current human situations, then turn to critical scholarly readings of christian classics for the norms that guide their responses to these situations.[12]

Liberation and political theologians—such as Matthew Lamb, Rebecca Chopp, James Poling, and Sharon Welch—are critical of this correlational model because it devalues practice: the fusion of reflection and action in a particular situation.[13] The critique has two thrusts. First, the correlation remains a theoretical one; it exists in the realm of ideas disconnected from the actual lives of people. What works conceptually often does not work practically. Specifically, the adoption of a certain theoretical model may have unintended practical consequences that can only be adequately evaluated if one moves out of more theoretical and into more practical discussions.

---

[12] Roy Herndon SteinhoffSmith, "White Man's Burden: Recent Thought about Christian Practice," *Religious Studies Review* 21:3, July 1995, 192–95.

[13] Rebecca Chopp, "Practical Theology and Liberation," in *Formation and Reflection*, ed. Lewis Mudge and James Poling, 120–38 (Philadelphia: Fortress, 1987); Matthew Lamb, *Solidarity with Victims* (New York: Crossroad, 1982); James Newton Poling, *The Abuse of Power: A Theological Problem* (Nashville: Abingdon, 1991); Welch, 157–58.

Second, the correlational model, as currently employed, supports unequal and oppressive power relationships. As Chopp observes, correlational thinkers tend to assume they have privileged access to universal truth. They tend not to recognize the effects of their own social location on what they consider to be universal. For instance, they tend not to recognize that "common human experience" often privileges white Western male experience and excludes the experiences of women, people of color, and non-Westerners. Welch shows how even the conception of "common experience" or "universal truth" maintains the subjugation of those without power by denying the truth of their knowledge.

To summarize: Dominant Western theologies correlate reflection on the Christian tradition with reflection on scientific, human scientific, and philosophical theories about common human experience and thus bar practice, the particular knowledge enacted in people's struggles to live.

Sharon Welch and James Poling sketch an alternative method, which first attends to the voices of those who have been excluded from theological discussions and articulates their knowledge, and then evaluates whatever theological conceptions emerge according to their adequacy as liberating responses to the particular suffering of these subjugated and oppressed people. Such a method requires a deconstruction of the devaluation of practice in theology.

One evaluates the three movements of reflection—description, analysis, and imagination—differently depending on where one places oneself and the focus of one's critical analytic reflection. If, as a caregiver, I grant final authority to my own knowledge (even if it is given to me by something beyond myself), then caring practice requires applying this knowledge to those who suffer. I only need to describe their situation until I identify the signs indicating that they fit into one of my authorized categories—that is, description serves analysis or diagnosis of them as problematic. Description in this model cannot, in and of itself, reveal anything true. Only through analysis—that is, in this case, using the care giver's authoritative knowledge to categorize the description—does truth emerge. Correct diagnosis leads to the authorized imagined response dictated by the diagnosis.

Figure 23: Analysis, Imagination, Description

The bar in this case takes the form of devaluation. The movements of analysis and imagined response enact the authorized power of the caregivers' knowledge by first categorizing and then shaping described reality. Case studies or vignettes, in this model, serve primarily as examples used to support the truth of certain analytic categories or the effectiveness of certain imagined responses.

To move to the place of suffering and to focus one's critical reflection on loving practice requires placing a primary emphasis on description. Suffering shatters the coherent theories through which we attempt to order and control the world. To understand and respond to suffering, one must first describe its particular occurrences. Analysis, including the use of theoretical models, follows upon such descriptions. One uses these models as heuristic devices to enable one to sink more deeply into the description, to discover its cracks, what is hidden in it, and so to uncover its truth. The role of the imagination is also suggestive, to propose possible ways of responding more caringly. But only through describing the actual implementation and effects of these imagined responses can one evaluate the degree to which they are truly caring.

Bibliography

Anzieu, Didier. *The Group and the Unconscious.* London: Routledge and Kegan Paul, 1984.

Blumenthal, David R. *Facing the Abusing God: A Theology of Protest.* Louisville: Westminster John Knox, 1993.

Breggin, Peter R., and Ginger Ross Breggin. *Talking Back to Prozac: What Doctors Aren't Telling You about Today's Most Controversial Drug.* New York: St. Martin's, 1994.

Brooks, James A. *The New American Commentary,* v. 23:Mark. Nashville: Broadman, 1991.

Buber, Martin. *The Knowledge of Man: A Philosophy of the Interhuman,* ed. Maurice Friedman. New York: Harper, 1966.

Chopp, Rebecca. "Practical Theology and Liberation." In *Formation and Reflection,* ed. Lewis Mudge and James Poling, 120–38. Philadelphia: Fortress, 1987.

Clebsch, William A., and Charles Jaekle. *Pastoral Care in Historical Perspective.* New York: Jason Aronson, 1983.

Crossan, John Dominic. *The Dark Interval: Towards a Theology of Story.* Allen, Texas: Argus Communications, 1975.

— Doehring, Carrie. *Taking Care: Monitoring Power Dynamics and Relational Boundaries in Pastoral Care & Counseling.* Nashville: Abingdon, 1995.

Evans, A. Dirk. Unpublished response to Roy SteinhoffSmith, "The Tragedy of Clinical Pastoral Education." 1993.

Fortune, Marie. "The Joy of Boundaries." In *Boundary Wars: Intimacy and Distance in Healing Relationships ,* ed. Katherine Hancock Ragsdale, 78–95. Cleveland: Pilgrim, 1996.

————. *Love Does No Harm: Sexual Ethics for the Rest of Us.* New York: Continuum, 1995.

Fowler, Robert M. *Let the Reader Understand: Reader-Response Criticism and the Gospel of Mark.* Minneapolis: Fortress, 1991.

Freudenberger, C. Dean. *Global Dust Bowl: Can We Stop the Destruction of the Land before It's too Late.* Minneapolis: Fortress, 1990.

Fuentes, Annette. "The Crackdown on Kids." *The Nation* 15/22, June 1998.

Gilson, Anne Bathurst. *Eros Breaking Free: Interpreting Sexual Theo-Ethics.* Cleveland: Pilgrim, 1995.

Gutierrez, Gustavo. Unpublished Lecture. Ministers Week, Phillips University, Enid, Oklahoma, 1988.

Heyward, Carter. *Staying Power: Reflections on Gender, Justice, and Compassion*. Cleveland: Pilgrim, 1995.

_____. *When Boundaries Betray Us: Beyond Illusions of What is Ethical in Therapy and Life*. San Francisco: HarperSanFrancisco, 1993.

Holifield, Brooks. *A History of Pastoral Care in America*. Nashville: Abingdon, 1983.

Interpreter's Bible, Vol. 7. New York: Abingdon-Cokesbury, 1951.

Irigary Luce. *Speculum of the Other Woman*, trans. Gilliam C. Gill. Ithaca, N.Y. : Cornell University, 1985.

Joseph, M. P. Unpublished conversations with Roy Herndon SteinhoffSmith. Phillips Theological Seminary, Tulsa, Oklahoma, May, 1998.

Kohut, Heinz. *The Restoration of the Self*. New York: International Universities Press, 1977.

Lamb, Matthew. *Solidarity with Victims*. New York: Crossroad, 1982.

Mack, Burton J. *A Myth of Innocence: Mark and Christian Origins*. Minneapolis: Fortress, 1989.

McKnight, John. *The Careless Society: Community and its Counterfeits*. New York: Basic Books, 1995.

Myers, Ched. *Binding the Strong Man: A Political Reading of Mark's Story of Jesus*. Maryknoll, N.Y.: Orbis, 1990.

Nathan, Debbie, and Michael Snedeker. *Satan's Silence: Ritual Abuse and the Making of a Modern American Witch Hunt*. New York: Basic Books, 1995.

Niebuhr, H. R. *The Responsible Self: An Essay in Christian Moral Philosophy*. San Francisco: Harper & Row, 1978.

Parker, Duane. Unpublished letter to Roy Herndon SteinhoffSmith, 1993.

Poling, James Newton. *The Abuse of Power: A Theological Problem*. Nashville: Abingdon, 1991.

Ragsdale, Katherine Hancock, ed. *Boundary Wars: Intimacy and Distance in Healing Relationships*. Cleveland: Pilgrim, 1996.

Redmond, Sheila A. "God Died and Nobody Gave a Funeral." *Pastoral Psychology* 45:1, September 1996, 41–48.

Sample, Tex. *U.S. Lifestyles and Mainline Churches: A Key to Reaching People in the 90's*. Louisville, Ky.: Westminster/John Knox, 1990.

Scarry, Elaine. *The Body in Pain: The Making and Unmaking of the World*. New York: Oxford University, 1985.

Smith, Archie. *The Relational Self: Ethics and Therapy from a Black Church Perspective*. Nashville: Abingdon, 1979.

— Soelle, Dorothee. *Suffering*, trans. Everet R. Kalin. Philadelphia: Fortress, 1975.

SteinhoffSmith, Roy Herndon. "The Becoming of the Person in Martin Buber's Religious Philosophical Anthropology and Heinz Kohut's Psychology of the Self." Ph.D. Dissertation. University of Chicago, 1985.

_____. "The Boundary Wars Mystery." *Religious Studies Review* 24:2, April 1998, 131–42.

_____. "Dialogue: Hermeneutic and Practical." *Pastoral Psychology* 45:6, July 1997, 439–50.

_____. "Dreaming of Spiders: Abuse, Economics, and Theological Insecurity in Pastoral Counseling." *Pastoral Psychology* 44:6, July 1996, 395–410.

_____. "Euro-American (christian) Dreams of Love and Genocide." Unpublished paper. Presented at 1996 American Academy of Religion, New Orleans.

_____. "The Politics of Care: An Alternative Politics of Care." In *Pastoral Care and Social Conflict*, eds. Pamela Couture and Rodney Hunter. Nashville: Abingdon, 1995.

_____. "The Tragedy of Clinical Pastoral Education." *Pastoral Psychology* 41:1, September 1992, 45–54.

_____. "White Man's Burden: Recent Thought about Christian Practice." *Religious Studies Review* 21:3, July 1995, 192–95.

— Tillich, Paul J. *The Impact of Psychotherapy on Theological Thought*. Monograph of the Academy of Religion and Mental Health, 1960.

Toulmin, Stephen. *Foresight and Understanding: An Inquiry into the Aims of Science*. Foreword by Jacques Barzun. New York: Harper & Row, 1963.

Weil, Simone. "The Love of God and Affliction." In *Waiting for God*, trans. Emma Craufurt. New York: G.P. Putnam's Sons, 1951.

Welch, Sharon. *A Feminist Ethic of Risk*. Minneapolis: Fortress, 1990.

West, Cornel. Scott Lectures. Phillips University, Enid, Oklahoma, 1987.